The Spokane Valley
A History of the Early Years

Best wishes,
Florence Boutwell

This was the scene on the southwest corner of Sprague and Pines in 1906 when John Janosky (white shirt and black tie, just left of utility pole) and John Allen (just left of the barber pole) opened the Opportunity Store on the southwest corner of Sprague and Pines. Janosky and Allen later sold the store to Myers and Farr. Alice, the widow of Janosky's brother, Gus, is seated in front of Allen. *Courtesy, Bea Goffinet and Patricia Smith Goetter.*

The Spokane Valley
A History of the Early Years

compiled by
Florence Boutwell

THE ARTHUR H. CLARK COMPANY
Spokane, Washington
2003

————

LIBRARY OF CONGRESS CATALOG CARD NUMBER 94-79244
ISBN 0-87062-234-x (cloth)
ISBN 0-87062-235-9 (paper)

Second Printing, 1995
Third Printing, 2003

————

The Arthur H. Clark Company
P.O. Box 14707
Spokane, WA 99214

Dedication

"The past, present and future are inseparable. The present is the fruit of the past and the seed of the future...

"Among our most sacred duties is the endeavor to present in historical form the daring deeds, mighty struggles, heroic efforts and untold sacrifices of the pioneers of our country. We all owe a debt of gratitude to the noble pioneers of Spokane County. They came with hearts prepared for perils and privations. They saw the country in its virgin state, and the stupendous works of nature as they came from the hands of God...

"The study of the records of the past prompts us to say, 'There were giants in those days.'"

[Excerpts from the Preface of *An Illustrated History of Spokane County* by Jonathon Edwards, published by W.H. Lever, 1900.]

Believing the words quoted above, I dedicate this book to the giants of the Spokane Valley who, from all accounts, loved the Valley as I do.

FLORENCE BOUTWELL

Contents

Illustrations

Acknowledgments

Nancy Campau and her Northwest Room at the
Spokane Public Library

Virginia Straughan and the Spokane Valley Museum

Bob Pederson and the Reference Department at Valley Library

The Spokesman-Review

The Spokane Valley Herald

Modern Electric Water Company, Vera Power and Light,
Washington Water Power

Inland Empire Paper Company

Central Valley, East Valley, and West Valley School Districts

My parents, my husband, and my children

The many people, groups and businesses that went "the extra
mile" to provide photos and information and memories —
whom I have tried to recognize in the pages of the book.

Overview
The Spokane Valley

From *An Illustrated History of Spokane County* by Reverend Jonathon Edwards, p.45; W.H. Lever, publisher, 1900

Nature has been lavish in its endowment of splendor in the Spokane Valley. It is nearly thirty miles in length and from five to ten miles in width. The surface is undulating just enough to afford fine drainage. There are seasons of the year when a view of the valley from an elevation is indescribably resplendent; when it is ablaze with green grass and a variety of flowers. In parts the grain can be seen waving gracefully in the breeze, and orchards with trees laden with fruit. The Spokane River winds its way through, rushing as if in haste to reach the series of falls and make the last plunge under the Monroe Street bridge to the charm below, and from thence winds its way between hills and canyons to join the great Columbia on its way to the sea. The Spokane Valley is encircled with pine-clad hills picturesquely broken up with cliffs of rugged granite and basalt rocks, with towering Mt. Carleton, familiarly known as "Old Baldy," away in the distance.

Note: Mt. Carleton is now called Mt. Spokane.

Preface
How This History Came to Be and What it Tries to Do

During World War II, after a brief period of basic training in Massachusetts as a Navy WAVE, I was ordered from my home in New Jersey to the recently constructed Naval Supply Depot, Velox, Washington.

In response to, "Where is Velox?," my commanding officer offered: "Velox is a new inland Naval installation that I know nothing about except that it is supposed to be near *Spo-cane.*"

That did not tell me a lot about my soon-to-be new home. Nor could I find anyone who knew any more about the Spo-cane area—so remote was the West to Easterners in those days.

After a three-day and three-night trip across this vast country on a train crowded with service personnel, I arrived at dusk on June 21, 1943, at the Northern Pacific Depot, Spokane, Washington. I spent my first night in Spokane at the world-famous Davenport Hotel.

The next day the mail orderly from NSD, Velox (about seventeen miles from Spokane in the Spokane Valley), chauffeured me to the Depot—then located at the present site of Spokane Industrial Park on Sullivan Road.

Captain Joseph E. McDonald, Supply Officer-in-Command, had recently received a memo ordering that a history of the Depot be forwarded month-by-month to Washington, D.C., for the Navy archives.

There were thirty-two male officers aboard, all either awaiting overseas orders or having returned recently for R & R after active duty in the South Pacific. I was the only woman officer aboard and the only one on more or less permanent duty.

The assignment of Depot historian immediately became mine.

My first job was to write a catch-up history of the construction and commissioning of the Depot. By talking to oldtimers, I learned that the then-bustling Naval Supply Depot site only a year before had been wheat fields at Velox, a railroad whistle stop.

The breath-taking change at Velox, from wheat fields to concrete and steel, was just a preview of what would take place Valley-wide during the remaining war years. Orchards fell, truck farms were plowed under, roads and houses were built to provide for the influx of people being brought into the Valley by nearby military installations—the huge Naval training station at Farragut, Idaho; Geiger Field, Baxter Hospital, Galena Airfield, all in Spokane; and, of course, the Naval Supply Depot at Velox.

My fascination with Valley history began.

During my tour of duty at NSD, Velox, I met and married Lt. Cmdr. Larry Boutwell. We both loved the Valley; and so, after the war we settled in the Valley where we raised three daughters.

In 1979 Gerald D.(Bud) Green began publication of *Spokane Valley Today*, a feature magazine that included many articles dealing with Valley history. In one issue he asked readers to write their early experiences. Having dabbled in free-lance writing, I sent him an article about NSD Velox-days and thereafter contributed historical articles regularly.

My love for the Valley and Valley history became full blown. As I researched the articles for *Spokane Valley Today*, I accumulated a wealth of material about the Valley—some, although written down, usually only duplicated or printed in early newspapers. Some of my material was the result of interviews and had not been formally written down at all until it appeared in *Spokane Valley Today*.

There was no single book on Valley history, although several had been written about Spokane city. City history is not Valley history. There were no falls in the Valley to invite industry, no Glover to build a sawmill, no mining money to erect mansions.

The history of the Spokane Valley is the history of the Native American, of families and acreages and bridges across a river, the history of women and men and children struggling as one to clear the land and farm the land, caught up in the freedom of forests, mountains, lakes, and the total beauty of the place we call the Spokane Valley.

The story of the Native American in the Valley is one that only a native American should tell. Therefore, I will begin my story, Volume I of the History of the Spokane Valley, with the coming of the white man. I shall divide it into chapters, each prefaced by a chronological outline, followed by in-depth articles meant to explain, flesh out and bring to life the outline. The chronological outline provides a quick look at Valley history. Names and Valley places are in bold type. Dates are isolated. Thus important elements of Valley history are easily recognized.

The in-depth articles are complete in themselves, can be enjoyed in one sitting, and need not be read in chronological order. Each can stand alone.

Much use is made of excerpts from early writings, newspaper accounts, and the personal reminiscences of old-timers. I believe the words of those who lived during the early days (when available) are more valuable than my own retelling would be. Therefore there are many direct quotations. All of the material credited to *Spokane Valley Today* and any that does not have a credit line was written by me unless otherwise identified. Due to space limitations, much of the source material had to be condensed and edited.

Some information is incomplete because details have vanished with the passing years. Sometimes sources did not agree on dates or the spelling of names*. In such cases, I chose to use the source that seemed to fit most logically into the total picture. Also for brevity's sake, choices had to be made. I whittled down the wealth of material available by focusing on "firsts"- the first person who arrived at a place, the first settlements, businesses, churches, schools, newspaper, banks, and farms.

This volume of the Valley history deals primarily with pioneers, places, and dates that had their Valley beginnings before and during the formation of the Chamber of Commerce in 1921. The "early days" ended with that event. A second volume will contain the time period from the formation of the Chamber through World War II. That was the small farm era. After the War, the Valley struck its present stride of suburban/urban growth—a possible third volume.

Wherever it seemed appropriate, the growth beyond formation of the Chamber is detailed in the in-depth articles. Because such a history cannot be written in one week or even one year, it is important for the reader to know when a given article was written. Therefore the date of writing is at the top of each article. When there is already much printed material detailing a specific phase of Valley history such as is available about the Mullan Trail, or if there is already a detailed volume about an area such as *Otis Orchards* by Mary Berglund and *Memories of Liberty Lake* by Brereton and Foedish, I have chosen not to include an in-depth article about those subjects.

There is no doubt that the Spokane Valley known to early settlers has disappeared. This volume is meant to preserve those early lives and times.

---

*Whether to spell *Spokane* with or without the "e" in the early years poses a special problem. It is an Indian word that was foreign to white pioneers. Trappers and explorers wrote the word as they heard it pronounced. The result was a variety of spellings: Spoken, Spokein, Spokain, Spokan, Spokane; but most commonly, *Spokan* or *Spokane*. Those who added the "e" added it because they heard the word pronounced as three syllables, Spo-kan-ee, the final syllable having a *schwa* sound that was often lost to the untrained ear. Thus, regardless of spelling, the Spo-can pronunciation was retained.

When Francis Cook published the *Spokan Times* in 1879 in the small town of Spokan Falls, the spelling problem assumed political proportions. Cook was adamant that the word be spelled as it was pronounced—without the final "e". In fact, as a member of the Legislature

from Pierce County, residing in Spokan Falls, Cook actually opposed the bill organizing Spokane County out of Stevens County because, in the bill, Spokane was spelled with an "e".

However, it is said that "The Big Three"—Cannon, Glover and Browne—who were Cook's political opponents, not only continued the spelling with the "e", but brought a printing press and type from Portland and started an opposition paper, the *Spokane Chronicle*, in the pages of which *Spokane* was consistently spelled with an "e".

The controversy over the spelling was settled November 29, 1881, when Spokane Falls was officially incorporated with the final "e". In 1890 the "Falls" was dropped. The author has chosen to add the "e" in most instances for ease of reading.

Synopsis of Early Spokane Valley History

[From *History of the Spokane Valley Chamber of Commerce* by Tom M. Smith, published by the Chamber of Commerce, October 1, 1971]

The Spokane Valley is assumed to extend from the east city limits of Spokane City eastward to the Idaho line and from foothills on the south to the foothills on the north. Actually it extends on east to Coeur d'Alene Lake and also north and east, across Rathdrum prairie to Lake Pend Oreille. The Spokane River leaves Coeur d'Alene Lake to flow westwardly through the Valley, past the city and the falls and then west and north to the mighty Columbia River.

Prior to 1810, the only people to see the Valley were the roving bands of Indians. These people pastured their herds of horses on the luxuriant grass, dug roots of camas and camped at various places for such time as suited their purpose. After 1810, the fur traders followed over the old trails and about 1850, miners and the pack horse trains that supplied them, crossed the Valley.

This traffic brought about the establishment of the first commercial enterprise in the Valley. About 1853, Antoine Plante started the operation of a ferry across the river near a much-used ford on an old trail. This was located about two miles upriver from the present Argonne bridge. With produce from a small farm and orchard on the north side of the river and horses from his large herds, Plante was able to supply the needs of the travelers as well as ferrying them across the stream.

Ten years later, a second place of business was established when a toll bridge was built across the river, just west of the present Idaho line. Here a store and trading post were built and, in time, were added a blacksmith shop, a place for travelers to spend the night and a post office which was opened in 1867. This was the second post office in

all of the area north of Walla Walla and east of the Columbia River. The first post office was at Fort Colville on Marcus Flat, which was a hundred miles to the north. This little settlement, called Spokane Bridge, was the first of its kind built north of the Snake River, between the Columbia and the Rockies. This does not include the Hudson Bay posts, the first of which was built at Spokane House in 1810 and moved to Kettle Falls (Fort Colville) about 1826.

The Northern Pacific Railroad reached Spokane city in 1881 and construction was carried on east through the Valley during the following year. A few years later, the Oregon Railroad and Navigation Company entered the Valley from the south.

Near this point, a depot and little town of Chester were to be built. At Dishman another depot was established, followed by a new settlement. At Irvin, on the NP, a depot and store were built. This was near the location of the old Plante Ferry which had been abandoned many years before. Ranchers were now coming into the Valley and the Valley's commercial life was growing.

A radical change came to the Valley in 1889 when the Spokane Valley Irrigation Company built a ditch from Liberty Lake, six and a half miles north and west, to a place to be called Greenacres. The Corbin brothers who planned the project were interested in sugar beets. Later they withdrew, but the company continued as the Spokane Valley Land and Water Company with water rights to Spirit, Sucker (Twin), Hayden and Mud (Hauser) lakes. In 1904 an agreement was reached with the Washington Water Power Company to take river water from behind Post Falls Dam.

In 1905, water from Newman Lake was used to develop Otis Orchards. Also in 1905, the Modern Irrigation and Land Company developed 3,000 acres by putting down several large wells to tap the Valley's underground water. They platted Opportunity and stores sprang up at what is now Pines and Sprague. The district also extended west to Dishman where more commercial buildings would be built.

The success of the development of the canals from the lakes and streams soon brought a large population to settle on ten-acre and other size tracts. Apples were to be the principle crop but hay, vegetables and small fruit were also raised. There were a number of different plats laid out and given such names as East Farms, Hutchinson's Addition, Opportunity, Orchard Avenue, Vera, Otis Orchards, Trentwood, Kokomo, and others.

It is interesting that none of these communities was ever incorporated as a town. There were a number of little shopping centers, each carrying the name of the plat or community. Later a large paper mill on the river built a town, Millwood, which was incorporated. Schools were located in the larger districts and rivalry sprang up, not only from the ball teams but also between the citizens and merchants of the several communities. The census figures for 1900 gave the Valley 1,051 inhabitants. By 1910 this figure had grown to 3,503, and in 1920, it had reached 6,541.

People living near each other sooner or later form a club. The Valley was no exception. A Women's Club was organized at Newman Lake in 1900. The first grange in northeast Washington was established as the "East Spokane Grange" in 1904. A commercial club was organized at Otis Orchards in 1914; Orchard Avenue had a community club in 1917. Other clubs of this type were organized in the various communities from time to time, and over the years some were reorganized a time or two. The clubs filled a very definite need and were backed by the public-minded citizens of each community.

About this time a number of Valley men got together at different times, to discuss the problems of the Valley. They lived in different communities but all shared a strong interest in the present good and the future growth of the Valley. They felt that a Valley-wide organization should be formed representing all of the communities. By developing cooperation, such an organization could work for the good of all of the people and build up the development of the Valley. United they could also develop the strength necessary to deal with county, state, and federal government and legislatures. . .

Note: The Chamber was formed in 1921. It is with that historic decision that this volume of the Spokane Valley story concludes. Volume II will continue the story from 1921-1945.

The Land as it Was

The Indian, the explorer, the trapper and the fur trader "owned" the land by right of possession, squatter rights — until the coming of the surveyor.

Prehistoric Time

[From *The Spokane Valley* by Orville C. Pratt, 1951 (manuscript)]

Chiefly two geologic forces caused the Spokane River Valley to be as it is: the repeated flows of lava millions of years ago when the Cascade Mountains were rising, and repeated advances and retreats of ice from Canada during the last million years.

Sometimes the lava raises the surface; sometimes liquid lava spreads out over the surface. The first of these pushed up the mountainous parts of Northern Idaho and Northeastern Washington, including the Spokane Valley. Long geologic time wore down and sculptured this mountainous region and cut the Spokane Valley down to a thousand feet below the present level.

Then followed a million years of at least four advances and retreats of glaciers which filled the Valley with sand, gravel and rocks brought down from the north. Previous to this glaciation, Pend Oreille Lake was drained to the southwest into the Spokane River, a thousand feet lower than its present level. The glacial debris filled up the valleys of the Spokane and Pend Oreille rivers and turned the Pend Oreille River north.* The Spokane River flows on the surface of this glacial deposit.

However, the original V-shaped valley is still there and in it the water from Pend Oreille Lake and River still flows to a considerable extent. This is the underground flow of water (aquifer) which supplies the City and Valley of Spokane.

---

*Numerous floods towards the end of the last ice age (15,000-12,800 years ago) scoured the Spokane Valley. These floods, known variously as the "Spokane," "Missoula," or "Bretz" floods, had a catastrophic effect on the land between Missoula and the mouth of the Columbia River. *See* Allen and Burns, *Cataclysms on the Columbia*, Portland (1986).

Early Government

CHRONOLOGICAL HISTORY

1846 The Oregon country that included the land later to become known as the **Spokane Valley** was officially taken over by the United States in a treaty with Great Britain.

1848 The **Territory of Oregon** was established.

1853 March 2: **Oregon** region was divided at the 49th parallel and **Washington** became a territory. **Isaac Ingalls Stevens** was first governor.

1854 Congress appropriated $30,000 for a military wagon road to be built from Fort Benton, MT, to Walla Walla, WA. **Lt. Mullan** (later **Captain Mullan**) was put in charge. The finished road ran across the Spokane River near the Idaho line at **Spokane Bridge** in the Valley.

1858 January 29: **Spokane County** was created by the **Territorial Legislature.** The county included all of **Washington** east of the **Cascade Mountains** and also **Northern Idaho** and **Western Montana** — about 75,000 square miles.

1862 May 20: **Homestead Act** passed. Claims could be filed for not more than 160 acres of public domain by persons meeting specified qualifications. (See article, "Land Rights".)

1867 December: County name changed to **Stevens, Washington Territory.**

1869 **Spokane Bridge** (see article) became the precinct voting place for the area including the town of **Spokan Falls** (now **Spokane**).

1879 October 30: **Spokane County** organized out of part of **Stevens County.** The county seat was temporarily at **Spokan Falls.**

1889 February 22: **President Cleveland** signed an Act of Congress authorizing statehood for **Washington.** A convention to form a constitution met July 4. **Washington** officially became a state November 11, 1889.

1890 **Spokane County** passed a law stating that the county be notified of burials. Some Indians had been burying their dead on a small knoll near what is now

Thirty-Second and Chapman roads. Those Indian Burial Grounds were then donated to the Saltese Cemetery Association.

1898 The U.S. Government proposed making the Spokane Valley into an Army encampment ground. This never occurred.

1908–09 A.M. Sommer of Veradale, Jim Felts and Harry E. Nelson of Opportunity worked to organize a township with governmental functions. The legislature passed a law authorizing such townships. (See article, "Early Government," volume 2.)

1909 President Taft rode up the Spokane Valley by electric train to Coeur d'Alene and Hayden Lake. He stopped at most every station in the Valley and waved from the rear of the platform.

1917 April 6: War declared against Germany.

1918 November 21: World War I ended with the German surrender at the Firth of Forth.

1919 January 16: 18th Amendment ratified. National Prohibition went into effect at midnight, January 16, 1920. Prohibition had begun in Spokane County January 1, 1916.

1920 The 19th Amendment gave women the right to vote.

1921 Spokane Valley Chamber of Commerce was organized from the many community clubs in the Valley. First meeting was held at the Opportunity Bank office. Terry Grant was first president. (See article, "Chamber of Commerce.")

Trails

[From the "Memories of Nellie J. Lancaster" with permission of her grandson, Lloyd D. Lancaster.]

We arrived at Spokane Falls, Washington Territory, in the spring of 1879 and we stayed near Coeur d'Alene, Idaho. Bonanza was the name of the settlement at that time.

Mother cooked fish for travelers coming from Colville on the Indian trails which crossed what was later our farm on Pleasant Prairie. These trails were three to five feet wide and some places were worn deeper than cayuses' knees. That must have taken many years of horseback travel! The trails were wide enough so that Indians could travel easily with a pack horse.

We traveled these same trails to school, which was an old log building a mile north of what is now Trentwood. If we saw a herd of cattle coming (they were all wild), we would duck down low and go far around them to keep out of their sight.

Charles A. Frederick and I [Nellie J. Lancaster] were the only two kids from Pleasant Prairie. Other children I remember attending the Valley school were Albert and Del Fry; Addie, Ethel and Len Falkner; Malinda and Louise Keyser. The log house was on the place that Mrs. Ryan owned later—and her sons were James, Sam and George.

When we traveled the trails to school, we often met three or four Indians riding side by side. Some squaws carried babies on their backs. They were friendly.

Indian Trails

[By Seth Woodard, *Spokane Valley Herald,* April 10, 1936 (Excerpts)]

Sometime ago I asked the owner of a beautiful and valuable farm how and when he acquired the farm. He told me he homesteaded the land in 1880.

"Well," says I, "There were no wagon roads here then, so how did you get here?"

His answer was, "I followed the Indian trails."

When Governor Isaac Stevens traveled down the Spokane Valley on his way to Olympia in 1853, he says in his memoranda: "We traveled a well beaten trail on the north side of the Spokane River and camped by a spring where there was sparse grass. The next morning we found that if we had gone on two miles farther, we would have had a much better camping place and an abundance of feed. The trail runs between the river and a high, rocky point."

The spring was the one on the Myers Place and the rocky point was Myrtle Point where the Riblet Mansion [Arbor Crest Winery] is now located.

Away back as far as we can find any records, the early travelers or explorers speak of the Indian trails. Lewis and Clark, in their memorable trip of exploration across the continent in 1804, were guided safely through the Rocky Mountains by an

Indian woman who, the records say, "knew every trail."

Marcus Whitman, Jason Lee, Samuel Parker, and other pioneer missionaries speak of the splendid Indian trails over which they traveled. The Indians had an almost uncanny knowledge of locating the best and most direct routes. They knew all the mountain passes and the river fords. If they came to a river too deep to ford, they would float their children and camping equipment across in buffalo hide canoes and swim their horses over while the ordinary white man would be figuring out "ways and means."

The American buffalo, which formerly roamed the plains in untold numbers, was the chief—and also favorite—food supply of the roaming Indians. For some unknown reason, the buffalo never existed in any appreciable numbers west of the Rocky Mountains. Neither did the wild turkey. So, to get their coveted supply of meat, the various tribes of Indians west of the mountains made regular pilgrimages across to Montana and the Dakotas.

In making these journeys, very naturally, the trails were worn smooth. Some of these trails were still in use and most of the others were distinguishable when I came in 1882. There were trails to the shore of Saltese Lake (and it was a real lake at one time) where a camas field flourished and the Indians camped to dig camas roots and dry them for food.

When the Inland Empire Paper Company built on the south bank of the Spokane River, workmen found salmon traps spread out into the river and drying racks along the shore.

Ross Cox, a fur trader, is said to have related to his descendants tales of Indians holding races "on the plains between the Coeur d'Alene and Spokan lands." This would undoubtedly have been the Spokane Valley. These facts substantiate the belief that there were camps of the once powerful and numerous Spokane Indians throughout the Valley and that their activities are responsible for so many of the old trails.

One of the main trails the Indians followed "to buffalo" was from Colville and western points up the north bank of the Spokane River, taking the general course of what is now the Northwest Boulevard and Illinois Avenue in Spokane, thence on up through what is now Pasadena Park, past Myrtle Point, keeping almost due east of Trent.

From there it continued in a general easterly direction, coming near the river at Spokane Bridge, and again at Post Falls, thence following the river to the lake and on through the mountains to Montana, on nearly the same route that was followed by Lieutenant Mullan with his famous government road.

Other trails led into this one. One from the Colville country came across Peone Prairie, striking Pleasant Prarie almost north of Millwood, crossing the prairie near Collin Farm and connecting with the main trail about one and one-half miles northeast of the Trentwood store.

Another trail from the southwest hit the Valley near Edgecliff and took a direct northeast course through what is now Millwood, crossing the river at the old ford and connecting with the main trail at Myrtle Point about three-fourths of a mile northeast of the cement plant. This was the first crossing used by the Mullan Road.

Still another Indian trail remembered by the writer came from the south, passing the old Linke and Courchaine farms and entered the Valley on the west side of Saltese Lake. This trail crossed the river at a ford about a mile east of the Liberty Lake bridge and at another one farther up the river. These old trails were worn smooth by the passing of thousands of Indian ponies every year.

There were several fords on the river and these still can be forded today as in former years. But the Spokane River was never a safe river to ford, partly on account of the rapid current and partly on account of the rocky bottom. Indian ponies could swim like ducks and pull their riders out if they lost their footing, but I would not advise anyone to try it on the clumsy steeds of today.

Land Rights: Squatting, Pre-emption Rights, The Homestead Act

To completely understand pioneer history and these stories of early-day Spokane Valley, it is necessary to understand the happenings of the day in national, state, and local government, especially the laws enacted regarding the private ownership of land.

Before the American Revolution it was held that all rights in land resided in society. Thus, when land was turned over to private parties, society reserved such rights as were necessary to the proper functioning of government. Hence the belief that existed in the pioneer era and still exists today: that the government has the right to levy land taxes.

At the time of the Revolution, it was generally agreed that the government, to raise revenue, should sell most of the public land to private parties. Government regulations of land sold were to be kept to a minimum, leaving the individual as much freedom as was practical in the exercise of his rights.

After the war, land that belonged to the British Crown went to the thirteen states. No one questioned the right of each state to the unsettled land within its border. However in regard to western land not within established borders, several questions arose: Who would have charge of settlement of this territory? What rights would the settlers hold in the land? Who would govern this territory? What form of government would be established?

These questions were heatedly debated and as a result, the Northwest Ordinances of 1785 and 1787 outlined the way land would be disposed of, the rights of the settler in the land, and the way new states would come into the union.

It was provided that land would be laid out in six-mile square townships and sections of 640 acres. The first tracts surveyed would be drawn by lot for the military bounties promised soldiers and sailors under earlier legislation. Then the land would be offered for sale by whole townships and smaller lots, at one dollar per acre. Certain lands would be set aside for educational purposes, and one-third of the gold, silver, lead and copper rights would be reserved. The recipients of this land could transfer by deeds which would be recorded locally.

From the end of the war to 1800, because of the urgent need for money, the federal government sold the public domain in 36-section townships and 640-acre sections for the minimum price of one dollar per acre, but allowed the selling price to be paid sometime within a year. Disposal was slow.

As a consequence, from 1800 to 1820 the minimum area was reduced to 320 acres, and land was sold on credit at two dollars per acre with payment extended to five years.

Credit encouraged speculation and the process was abolished in 1820 after more than 19 million acres had been sold. An 1820 act further reduced the minimum size to 80 acres and the price to $1.25 per acre, no credit allowed.

Many settlers had no funds and occupied land and established homes without acquiring title. This was called *squatting*. The *squatters* pressured the government for land free of all charges.

The **Pre-emption Act of 1841** acceded to the wishes of the squatter by giving him the right to settle upon surveyed public lands before they were offered for sale and by giving him the first opportunity to buy his claim up to 160 acres. In 1854 squatting was legalized upon unsurveyed lands for which the Indian title had been surrendered. However the minimum price of $1.25 per acre continued and was a deterrent to purchase for many settlers, although land speculators flourished.

The philosophy of land legislation in this period was based on the belief that the public domain belonged to the people and that each head of a family was entitled to a home or farm, the possession of which should be protected against seizure for debt. The theory developed gradually for half a century after 1785. Earlier laws were intended primarily to procure revenue for the government, and for several years before the financial panic of 1837 were successful in that regard. But during the financial panic, there was increasing clamor to provide legislation that would help farmers and laborers.

The **Homestead Act** of May 20, 1862, offered free 160-acre tracts to persons who would settle upon and improve them over a period of five years. It was this offer of free land that drew to the new West hundreds of thousands of peasant farmers from Europe and many discouraged debt-ridden farmers and tenants from older parts of the United States.

In 1873, the **Timber Culture Act** allowed a farmer 160 acres additional land if he would grow trees on one-fourth of his farm.

Now let us see how these laws worked for settlers in the Spokane Valley and how, in turn, the courage and fortitude of the settlers laid the foundation for the Spokane Valley of today.

Note: The facts for this article were gleaned from various volumes of the 1959 edition of the *Encyclopedia Britannica.*

Fur Traders, Settlers, Homesteaders

"Mullan said that Plante spoke both French and English and that in his small field he raised corn, wheat and vegetables. From the river, in season, he took salmon in quantities which were dried for winter use. His cabin on the hillside sheltered for days at a time the Great and Mighty of that period. The spring by the cabin unfailingly administered to the wants of travelers of all sorts, from the squaw to the chief, from the bearded miner to the governor of the Territory.

"Today the field is still there [1930s]. A part of his cabin, a broadaxe masterpiece, still stands. The spring still bubbles forth. But the glories of those early days 75 years ago are gone forever. No sign of the Indian band which once dashed across the ford; no glint of polished steel of the military escort to Governor Stevens; no sign of the grave semi-circle of Indian chiefs in council; nothing to note the passage of Mullan's engineers, of the mail courier, the miner, the pack train, the settler. All are gone long ago."

["Valley of the Sun," Story No.5, *Spokesman Review,* April 7, 1930]

Fur Traders, Settlers, Homesteaders

Chronological History

1783   **Fur Traders** of the **North West Company,** organized in Montreal, Canada, are known to have looked upon the Valley about this time. **Louison LaLiberte,** a relative of **Steve Liberty** who founded **Liberty Lake,** was probably one of these.

1815   Indian families were known to have been camped on the banks of **Liberty Lake,** at the site of the present **Paper Mill** along the Spokane River, and at the site of **Spokane Bridge.**

1826   Formal trading posts of both the **North West Company** and the **Hudson's Bay Company** were abandoned although the **Hudson's Bay Traders** continued to travel up and down the Valley.

1849   **Antoyne Plaenit (Antoine Plante),** known as "Old Mountaineer," maintained a small **Hudson's Bay Company** station at his home. He, his Indian wife and family lived in a cabin on the north side of the Spokane River a short distance above the present **Plante's Ferry Park** and across the river from the **Ideal Cement Plant.** In the 1850s he built a cable ferry across the river. **Captain Mullan** wrote in his diary that the ferry was "worthy." The charges were $4 for each wagon, carriage or vehicle with two horses attached; $3 for each pleasure wagon with two horses attached; 50¢ for each additional animal; $2 for each cart, wagon, carriage with one horse attached; $1.50 for each man and horse; $1.50 for each animal packed; 50¢ for each footman; 25¢ for loose animals other than sheep or hogs; 15¢ for sheep, goats, hogs. (See article, "Antoine Plante".)

1858   **Colonel George Wright's** troops destroyed hundreds of horses at **Horse Slaughter Camp** just west of the Idaho line, on the banks of the **Spokane River.** (There is a monument at the weigh station on I-90.)

1860   **William Newman** came to the area as escort to boundary surveyors in the United States Army. In 1864 he settled and farmed on the shores of **Newman Lake,** later named for him.

1861   **Connors** built a cabin where **Rathdrum** is today. In 1872 it was sold to **Steve Liberty** and subsequently sold to **Frederick Post** for $1500.

1862   **A.C. "Charley" Kendall** built a cabin and established a trading post on the north bank of the Spokane River.

1862   **Antoine Camille Langtu** lived at Faulkner's (Faulconer's) Gulch across from Antoine Plante.

1864   **Joe Herring, Timothy Lee** and **Ned Jordan** built the first bridge across the Spokane River at **Kendall's** place. A small village and trading post, known as Spokane Bridge, grew up near the bridge.(See article, "Spokane Bridge".)

1865   **Thomas Newlon** came up from Riparia on the Snake River and built a bridge near where **Trent** is today. After two years he left for Montana to mine.

1866   French Canadian **Daniel Courchaine** settled in the **Saltese** area. He lived in peace with local Indians encamped there, bought land from them, and began to build a home in 1867. He brought the lumber for his home from Walla Walla. It was shipped via wagon train along the **California Trail** which passed through his land. It took over a year to transport the lumber and eleven years to build the home near present **Linke Road** and **Thirty-Second Street. Chief Saltese** was his friend.

1868-69   **"Old" Pete Barnaby** from Oregon settled at **Rathdrum.**

1869   **Steve Liberty** lived at **Rathdrum.**

1869   **Charles Kendall** bought **Spokane Bridge** and operated the bridge, store and log hotel until his death when **Michael M. Cowley** took over.

1870   **Knight** owned the **California Ranch.**

1871   **Etienne Eduart LaLiberte** (Stephen Liberty), wife Christine and nine children settled on the west side of **Liberty Lake.** The lake was named for him. **Joe Peavy,** his inseparable friend and the first blacksmith in Spokane, homesteaded on the northeast side of the lake. Both carried mail across **Pend Oreille Lake. Steve** died in 1911 and **Joe** in 1918. Both are buried in **Fairmont Cemetery** in Spokane.

1871   **Walter Linke's** parents, the **Herman Linkes,** came to **Rathdrum** and settled near **Saltese Lake** in 1875. **Herman** specialized in raising wheat and developed a hybrid strain known as **Linke** wheat.

1872   **Frederick Post** was living at **Rathdrum.**

1872   July 4: **M.M. Cowley** established a cattle business at **Spokane Bridge.** With **Tom Ford** as partner, he bought the bridge in 1877 when **Kendall** died. The following spring **William Tecumseh Sherman** came to **Spokane Bridge** and selected 999 acres on **Coeur d'Alene Lake** for **Camp Coeur d'Alene,** later named **Fort Sherman. Cowley** lived at the bridge seventeen years, furnishing supplies to **Fort Sherman.**

1873   **Maxime** and **Peter Mulouin** had preempted land near **Mica** six or seven miles south of **Dishman.** In 1876, they acquired that part of the **California**

Ranch astride **California Creek** east of their property. **Hiram Still** purchased the major portion of the original **California Ranch** from **Knight.**

1880   **J.C. Myrtle** homesteaded 160 acres of land north of the Spokane River on a bluff now known as **Riblet's Point,** but then called **Myrtle's Point.** With **L.W. Arthur** he put in a ferry at **Trent (Irvin)** and operated a boarding house and store for the convenience of ferry users.

1880   **Albert Edmond Canfield** and **Wife Matilda** and **two sons** came by covered wagon to be the first settlers in **Otis Orchard** near the south entrance of the area to be known as **Canfield Gulch. Canfield** had 160 acres on the west side of what later became **Campbell Road.**

1880   **Benjamin Lewis,** a Civil War veteran, settled on property in **Millwood** subsequently acquired by **Seth Woodard.**

1880   **Joe Goodner,** a fruit buyer in the **Walla Walla** area homesteaded 160 acres just west of **Canfield Gulch.**

1881   The family of **J. Clayton Smith** settled in south **Vera.**

1881   The **Esch** family homesteaded 160 acres in **Otis Orchards.** They later purchased 800 acres of grazing land and raised livestock.

1881   A **Mr. Edwards** settled at **Trent.**

1882   **Joseph Woodard** and family of nine left Kansas in two covered wagons in April and reached **Spokane County** in October and settled in the Valley. **Seth Woodard,** for whom a school was named, was one of the nine children..

1882   **Wesley P. Mahoney** homesteaded 140 acres in what is **Mirabeau Park.** He lived in his 16 x 20 shack forty years, carrying water 500 feet from the river.

1883   The **William Pringle Family** arrived in the Valley with **Fred Myers** and settled twenty acres at **Otis Orchards** in the **Harvard Road** area. Dry farmers, they planted the first crop of oats in the Valley. Between 1884-1887 **Pringle** did practically all of the freighting for **M.M. Cowley** between **Spokan Falls** and **Spokane Bridge.** They knew **Quinemosy** well. "There were no settlers in the main part of the Valley on either side of the river from **Millwood** to **Spokane Bridge.**"

1883   **Cornelius Harrington** arrived from Butte, Montana, and homesteaded near **Mica. Harrington Addition** in the **Valley** was named for him. In 1897 he bought part of the **Nosler** homestead and moved onto that, a bit northwest of **Dishman.**

1884   **John P. Sullivan** homesteaded near **Vera. Sullivan Road** is named for him. On election day,1886, he rode his horse into Spokane and voted on the question of returning the county seat from Cheney.

1884
Will and Louis Thompson came to Newman Lake. Thompson Creek is named for Louis.

1884
May: Titus, Antone and Isadore Blessing, Joe Ulowitz, John Korles all took up homesteads or bought property along the Spokane River where Sullivan Road is today. They hired two box cars to bring their families and belongings from Minnesota. In 1942, 81 acres of the original Ulowitz property and 220 acres of the original Blessing property was sold to the government for the Naval Supply Depot at Velox. (See article,"Naval Supply Depot," Volume II)

1884
Joseph Daschbaugh (or Daschbauch) built a home at Pines and Apple Way.

1885
Ignatius Fox came to Newman Lake and was the first constable.

1887
F.N. Muzzy bought a preemption of some railroad land at the head of Newman Lake where he farmed hay and beef cattle. James Muzzy pioneered in that year also.

1887
June: Henry Wendler rented 160 acres at Newman Lake for $200 a year from Mr. Stevens with option to buy for $3000, which he did.

1888
McCanna homesteaded at Vera.

1888
J.B. Myers arrived in Spokane from Buffalo to look over land in the Valley. He bought a ticket on the Northern Pacific to Trent. When he got off the train, there wasn't a house in sight. He saw smoke under the hill to the north and went in that direction. At the house he inquired for the town of Trent and was informed he was in the Trent Post Office, the only building in town. He purchased and farmed 80 acres of school land and 80 acres of railroad land near Trent.

1889
Indians still roamed the Valley and were frequent visitors to Valley homes. Wild animals still roamed the hills.

1890
J.S. Woodard purchased land in Millwood for $5 an acre from Northern Pacific Railroad.

1891
October 2l: Gail Muzzy was born in a log cabin next to the Frank Muzzy's on the Newman Lake farm purchased from the widow of Barton Mills.

1895
Pleasant Prairie Cemetery became officially recognized even though it had been used since 1882, the date of the first burial.

1895–1900
Peter Morrison began the draining of Saltese Lake to get at the rich soil underneath.

1898
Stegners bought the Dart place at Trent which took in the west shore of Plante's Ferry area. (See article, "Stegner Store.")

1899
William Anderson settled on a farm near Trentwood.

1902   Tom Hatch moved onto a 22-acre parcel on the **Wells Tract.**

1902   **Milton Dishman** was reportedly the first white child born in the area. He later built a landmark home at 315 N. **Willow Road.**

1902   **Holsclaws** lived at the top of a point of land west of **Barker Road** on the south bank of the **Spokane River** in **Greenacres.**

1904   **Louise Johnson** lived across from **Pringle.**

1907   **Mildred Beck's parents** came to **Moab (Newman Lake).** She was born at the **Taylor Ranch** there. Her uncle had arrived in 1903 and worked for **Peter Morrison** on **Saltese Flats. Mildred's father** drove stage for **Taylor Ranch** from **Moab** to the lake.

1907   **Harry Beck** and wife came to **Moab,** a thriving town that fell on hard times when the huge sawmill (basis of the town) shut down. Harry worked as a delivery boy in the **East Valley** area and delivered milk by boat around **Newman Lake.** He moved to **Greenacres** in 1927 and later began **Beck and Sons Service Station and Garage.**

1910   **Pines Cemetery** incorporated.

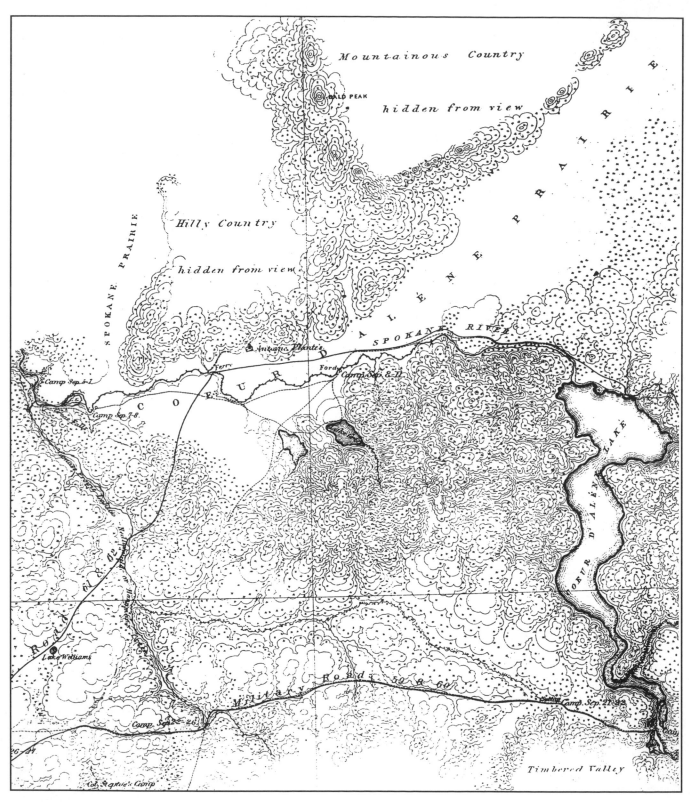

This map showing the Spokane Valley (the lower portion of the "Coeur d'Alene Prairie") was prepared under the direction of Lt. John Mullan, U.S. Army, during his reconnaissance of the area between 1859 and 1862. Note the ferry near Antoine Plante's in the Valley center, as well as the ford at the east end of the Valley which would later become Spokane Bridge.

Antoine Plante
First Permanent Settler in the Spokane Valley

[Waldo Emerson Rosebush, a manager of the Inland Empire Paper Mill at Millwood, researched Antoine Plante's life by corresponding with Plante's descendants. From 1930-1934 he published his findings as "The Valley of the Sun," a series of articles on early Valley history that appeared in the *Spokesman-Review.* The facts of Antoine Plante's life contained in this story are based on facts in Rosebush's articles.]

I wanted to see it again—the most imposing and historic monument in the Valley, the great piece of granite in Plante's Ferry Park that details the early history of the area.

It wasn't hard to get there. I followed Upriver Drive from Argonne Road toward Sullivan.

It was spring. The grass on Plante's Ferry Park hillside was green. The sky was blue. The water sparkled at the bend in the river and eddied around the rocks on the river floor.

I understood why Antoine Plante, who knew the Northwest well, selected, of all the places he had seen in his travels, a piece of land not far from this spot for his Valley home.

There were many beautiful spots along the Spokane River, but this one was practical as well as beautiful. The ford was navigable in almost all seasons.

Years earlier, Indians had discovered the spot. Antoine Plante rediscovered it, built a cable ferry across the river and made there a living for his family.

His ferry and his facilities at the ferry were used by Isaac Ingalls Stevens, the first governor of Washington Territory, and by trappers and explorers who wrote of the Spokane Valley in their journals and diaries.

In one sense Antoine Plante might be called the "Father of the Spokane Valley," for he was the first permanent "settler-businessman" in the Spokane Valley.

His grandchildren believe their Grandfather Antoine was born about 1800 or 1805 in Montana and they say that he was part French-Canadian and one-fourth Gros-Ventre, the easternmost tribe of the Blackfeet nation, then located between the Milk and Missouri rivers.

Waldo Emerson Rosebush in his "Valley of the Sun," Series III, said that the first historical reference he found regarding Antoine Plante was in the Journals of John Work, a chief trader for the Hudson Bay Company and one-time occupant of Spokane House. Plante was employed as a trapper on a beaver-hunting expedition for Work in the autumn of 1831.

The expedition started in August from Fort Nez Perce (Walla Walla) and traversed the Bitter Roots, western Montana, southern Idaho and eastern Oregon.

"Antoine Plante, however," says Rosebush, "did not stay with the party after October 24, 1831, but hunted and trapped on his own account thereafter. In this way he gained such intimate familiarity with all of the Indian trails and routes and with the general character of the intervening country that, as a guide in 1853 and 1855 for the parties of Governor Stevens and for others, he made himself known as a reliable man."

About 1834, Antoine married Mary Therese, a Pend Oreille Indian, and, as nearly as can be determined, they traveled up and down the country with the seasons. To Antoine and Mary Therese were born two children, Julia in 1836 (died 1917), and Frank or Francis, born in 1838.

"Plante parted from Mary Therese about 1840," says Rosebush, "and shortly thereafter married his second wife, Mary, a Flathead Indian. They had only one child, 'Charley,' born in 1841."

During this time descendants say that Plante headquartered with his relatives in the Colville country—probably 1835-1845. Also at that time, according to reference in Governor Stevens' reports, there were large bands of horses in the Spokane Valley and Antoine Plante himself was said to have been the owner of a considerable number. Since Indians were known to have acquired such herds in California; and because, in 1853, Plante and all of his friends and relatives are known to have returned from California, it is reasonable to assume his horses were the results of trips to California where he also panned for gold.

Shortly after their return from California in 1854, the Plante family settled on the Spokane River near Irvin (Trent).

At this point in Plante's life, our knowledge is from contemporary accounts.

His first "home" on the Spokane River was an Indian lodge or tepee. He next built a commodious log house and after that burned, built a squared timber structure. Antoine himself kept on the move much of the time trading in cattle and horses, trapping and hunting or acting as a guide (for Stevens among others).

On July 27, 1853, he is known to have been in Walla Walla when one of Governor Stevens' surveying parties engaged him to guide the party north through the Spokane country, over the Bitter Roots, to Fort Benton.

"In 1854 Plante had a carpenter who lived across the river (probably Camille Langtu) build him a substantial home near the Spokane River at Irvin," says Rosebush. "While he was away trapping, for some reason, the family became alarmed and fled into the hills. They took what gold they had in the house. While they were away, everything was burned—crops, apple orchard (the first planted in the Valley) and all. The Coeur d'Alene Indians were suspected."

Maggie McDonald, a granddaughter of Antoine Plante, stated in a letter to Rosebush that a simple home of two rooms replaced the nice one which had burned, and that she and her cousin, Isabel, recalled a substantial ferry as far back as they could remember. They always understood this to have been operated by Antoine Plante in partnership with Camille Langtu.

Duncan McDonald, a brother-in-law of Maggie, remembered the ferry in 1856 when, as a lad, he visited the place with his father and mother and sister, Christine.

Rosebush continues the story: "Captain John Mullan, while building his military road, arrived at Antoine's ferry June 1, 1861. In his report he says 'The ferry at Spokane is a good one, consisting of a strong cable stretched across the river and a boat 40 feet long. It is kept by a very worthy man, Antoine Plante, a halfbreed Flathead Indian, who speaks both French and English. He has a small field under cultivation on the left (south bank) near the ferry, from which he obtains corn, wheat, and vegetables; these with the salmon from the river form an abundant supply for his Indian family.'

"From about 1855 until 1864, Antoine had a free hand and undoubtedly made money from the miners, the packers, the boundary commissionmen and especially after the Mullan Road crossed his ferry in 1861. But Kendalls's bridge crippled him in 1864, and Newlon, who built a bridge near Trent in 1866, added to his trouble. The latter bridge probably became Schnebly's Bridge in 1867, for A.J.Splawn, a pioneer trader, wrote that the Mullan Road crossed by that bridge to the north bank of the Spokane in 1867.

"In early 1872 Antoine probably had less than 15 white and French-Indian neighbors. At the close of 1873, Antoine's neighbors had increased in number many times. By this time civilization was pressing Antoine pretty hard. He found his freedom of activity restricted on all sides and his means of existence were undoubtedly suffering accordingly.

"Mr. Boughton Masterson of Rathdrum states that when they first settled at Trent (Irvin) in 1876 there was no ferry then at Plante's old crossing and that there were very few traces of the ferry left. Mr. James LeFevre, the son of Andrew Lefevre, states that Antoine was running the ferry in 1873. He says that Antoine did very little business, operating it more as an accommodation to his friends than anything else. It was then called a 'cayuse ferry', operated by rowing a small boat across the river.

"Allan Scott, present county engineer [1930s], located with his people at Plante's old ferry on the north side of the river in 1884. At that time, he says, the old ferry post, a huge stick about 16 inches square, was still in place. His father cut it up for fuel.

"In February, 1890, Antoine Plante died in Montana, being visited frequently in his last days by Father D'Aste. He was taken ill while cutting his winter's supply of wood, the immediate cause of death being Bright's Disease.

"There does not seem to be any picture of Antoine in existence. From descriptions of those who knew him, he apparently was a large, dark man, over 6 feet tall, weighing about 200 pounds, perfectly bald and clean shaven. Duncan McDonald recalls that Plante had his hat trimmed with feathers which were stuck in the hat band and that he always dressed in white man's clothes. He was rather genial by nature, well liked and at times rather openly exuberant as described by members of Stevens' party in 1853, wherein he aroused the camp in the morning with a war whoop or the joyous shout of the voyageur.

"At other times he was rather quiet and reticent. Antoine was devout also. Mary Therese, his first wife, in her last years described to the children how mystified she was when she first saw him kneel in prayer. As he is said to have been brought up by a white family (probably his French-Canadian father's), he was well versed in the ways and habits of civilization and could read and write. He was fluent in both English and French as well as in Indian dialects.

"Says Saxon, a lieutenant of Stevens' party, 'His service was invaluable. He guides our little band through this unbroken wilderness without a trail as true and unwavering as the needle to the pole.'"

M.M.Cowley

[Excerpts from a short biography of M.M.Cowley as told by his daughter, Eleanor Cowley Smyth, "Valley of the Sun," Story No.7, *Spokesman-Review*, April 14, 1930.]

One of the earliest permanent settlers of the Spokane Valley was my father, M.M.Cowley. He was born at Rathdrum, Wicklow County, Ireland, May 9, 1841. He received his education in the monastery of Clondalkin, finishing when he was 15. Being the youngest boy in a large family, he saw no future for him in Ireland, so shortly after finishing school, he left for America.

For five years Father did various jobs in the East and Midwest while heading for the West.

In 1861 he came to Portland, then Walla Walla where he took up a ranch. Going into Walla Walla one day, he found an auctioneer selling a horse. He had $20 in his pocket and bought the horse and saddle for $18.

That night he baked bread and beans and the next day started for Florence, Idaho, 300 miles away. The trip took seven days and on arriving, he sold the horse for $75 and went to ground sluicing at $7 a day and his meals.

In the fall he returned to Walla Walla, sold the ranch and went to packing merchandise.

The route was from Walla Walla through the Spokane country on into northern Idaho down the Kootenai River across the boundary to Wild Horse Creek, B.C.

The pack trains consisted of 80 or 40 pack mules, each carrying an average of about 300 pounds of merchandise, for which they received an average of $1 per pound.

In 1867 Father established a trading post at Bonners Ferry. With only axes he and some other men hewed out lumber for a ferry boat, which he ran across the Kootenai River. He stayed in business there for five years, buying furs from the Indians and selling merchandise to the miners.

July 4, 1872, he landed at Spokane Bridge. He found there Thomas Ford and A.C.Kendall, the latter the proprietor of a trading post. Owing to ill health, Kendall disposed of the post to Ford and Father. Kendall moved to the south side of the river, where he died in May, 1873, and was buried on a bluff overlooking the river.

While Father was at the Bridge, he ran a ferry,

later replaced by a toll bridge. Three times the toll bridge was swept away by spring high water and each time replaced, to be sold at last to the county when the county took over the roads.

In his wanderings through the country, Father had learned a jargon of English and Indian, by which the white man talked to the Indian.

In talking one day to a Coeur d'Alene chief, the chief advised Father to learn their language as the interpreters were "unreliable and only made trouble."

The Indian procured a boy of 5 or 6 who taught Father the language in return for being taught English. As soon as he learned their language, Father scolded the Indians for not trapping fur. He promised them $10 for every prime marten brought to him. The first year he bought $1500 worth of furs, the second $6000 worth and so on in increasing quantities, until the Government moved the Coeur d'Alenes onto the reservation when trapping ceased.

At the time of the Nez Perce War, in 1877, the Government started a post at Coeur d'Alene, called Fort Coeur d'Alene. This gave Father a chance for further activity. He took contracts for hay and grain for the Fort. During the Indian uprising, Father had the pleasure of entertaining both General Howard and General Sherman.

While in Walla Walla, Father met Annie Connelly. She had come from Ireland at age 13. Father married her October 7, 1873. After the wedding, Father and Mother drove in a light spring rain from Walla Walla to Spokane Bridge, a trip of almost five days.

In the beginning of 1873, Ford and my father had built a new store, as the log one they had was too small and too cold. This store cost them $1500, an immense sum for those days when there was everything here but money. It was to this log house, however, slightly remodeled, that my mother came on her honeymoon. There my sister and I were born.

Shortly after this, Ford also married. His wife, Sarah, did not like the existence at a trading post and on July, 1880, a deed is on record, selling to my father one-half of the land held by Mr. Ford. It was 37.35 acres and cost $40. On June 11, 1881, Father bought the second half for $50. In 1889 Father bought from the Northern Pacific Railroad 139.61 acres for $628.25.

Since 1872 the Northern Pacific had been promising to run a line to Astoria. It was not until 1882 that they actually did build. Our station was Idaho Line, four miles from our home and a little east of where Moab now stands. When we wished to travel, we went to the station and, as there was no telegraph operator, we sat until we heard a train approaching, grabbed a red flag and flagged the train. When it proved to be a freight, we would wait some more. Such was pioneer life in the Valley.

As to weather conditions, from all I can learn from letters I have which my father wrote to my mother before their marriage, it was as erratic as now.

In December, 1872, he writes of the beautiful sunshine, warmth and lack of snow being a blessing to him, as the cattle can still feed on the bunch grass. In June, 1878, he writes again to my mother, telling her of the detestable weather, raining one moment, snowing the next.

Just a word about my father's relations with the Indians. They always had the utmost confidence in him and affectionately called him "N-Upsin," meaning "Long Beard." He bought furs, hay and grain from them, selling them all kinds of merchandise, including beads, bright calico, blankets, and paints for their faces, besides all the necessities, and never once did he have a dispute. Until his death in 1915, whenever an Indian came to town, Father visited him and whenever he met them he gave them a word of welcome.

Below is a letter found in father's effects. On the face of it is written, "Paid Oct.8, 08." Daniel evidently kept faith absolutely by paying as promised. Daniel was the son of the original Quinemose, a Spokane subchief.

"Dear sir, I am going to say a few words to you. I am in very bad fixed because my little girl died a weeks ago and I am going to put up a big dinner for my little girl died. You know how the Indians does, and I wish you would give me about $100 or $50 if you please and I will pay you this fall some time. From your Truly Loving Friend Daniel Quinemosey.

The record of sale of railway land to the old chief gives his name as Quin-a-mo-see. The spelling of Indian names in English has interesting variations. Saltese, for instance, has been spelled in seven or more ways. Mullan spelled it Seltisse. Another common form is Seltice.

The Cowleys, the Pringles and the Myers Come to the Spokane Valley

[Condensed from the reminiscences of Adelaide Myers-Smith published in the "Valley of the Sun," Story No.10, *Spokesman-Review,* April 23, 1930.]

When the Civil War broke out, Frederick Franklin Myers, with a number of others, enlisted in the Oregon State Military Forces. He was made captain of his company. It was detailed to border defense against the Indians. It was while on this service that Mr. Myers first saw the Spokane Valley in all its wild beauty.

Looking down from the mountains, he said the Valley was the most beautiful sight he had ever seen and wished it was possible for him to make a home there.

Not long after, while helping to put skids on a heavy wagon in a wagon train, a wheel passed over his foot and badly crushed it. This put a stop to Mr. Myers' outdoor activities for a while. He had to go to San Francisco for medical attention and for two years [the man who would become my husband] was on crutches.

In 1863 in San Francisco he went into business handling building materials for, strangely enough, the Washington Brick, Lime, and Cement Company, [active in the Valley] and the first importer of Portland Cement.

In 1873, Mr. William Pringle started to work for Mr. Myers.

California, in the early 80s, became greatly agitated over the Chinese and other questions which affected business. So, when a friend named Michael Cowley whom Mr. Myers had met 25 years before, appeared in 1862 with glowing tales of the cattle business in the Spokane Valley, Myers was greatly interested.

He successfully disposed of his business and most of his property and April, 1883, found him and Mr. Pringle and Mr. Cowley in the Spokane Valley.

In August Mrs. Pringle and the three Pringle children, and Mrs. Pringle's brother, John Cowley (brother of Michael) arrived in the Valley also and found that the men had built two houses for them, one on the Myers homestead and one on Pringle's preemption which adjoined the other on the east.

In December Mr. Myers returned to California on business and while there overruled my parents' objections to my going into the wild Spokane Valley country with him. We were married in February and arrived at the little station called the Idaho Line in March, 1884.

A girl friend, Nellie O'Brien, who had been ordered to seek a complete change of climate, accompanied us.

In the Valley there had been an ice break-up and a freshet; the ground ran with water. Sam Walton, who lived at the station and carried the mail across the prairie to Spokane Bridge post office, put a plank from the train step to the platform of the little station — making it possible for us to leave the train.

Mr. Pringle met us with a big teamster wagon with its lofty seat. Again the plank was used to get us on the wagon. There was no road at all. When we struck a big rock, we clung together expecting to go off into the mud and water. The driver would call out, "Ladies! Keep your seats!"

The night was very dark and the March wind coming off snowcovered mountains cut our city flesh like knives. We kept our furs close and peeked out to see if we could make out anything of the place to which we had come. Once I thought I saw an orchard, but when I called up to ask the men, they laughed so long and loud I asked no more questions until they told us we were nearing Spokane Bridge—the post office and store.

Mr. Cowley tried to get us to spend the night at his place, but the men thanked him and said they would go on as they wanted to get our baggage under cover. The road got some better and presently we saw a bright light ahead.

Fred Myers, now my husband, reached back and said we were nearing "home, sweet home."

Then we saw that Mrs. Pringle and her brother had lit a big bonfire to welcome us and also had prepared prairie hens and all the good things they could find to eat.

We made many good friends. Tears fill my eyes as I remember the kind motherliness of Mrs. W.H.Black. The Black ranch which included the old cabin of Antoine Plante was nearby. Mr. Black set out a wonderful orchard for those days. One day Mrs. Black and her daughter came driving up to our place laughingly saying they had something to brighten the eyes of an old Californian; and, sure enough, it was a lovely basket of fresh home-grown cherries.

THE BLIZZARD OF 1884

The winter of 1884 was one of the worst in many years. The temperature remained around zero for six weeks, with terrible blizzards. Long, temporary cattle sheds had been built at Pringle's and Fred thought he must go every day to check the cattle — a mile from home. He left in the morning and didn't return until after dark.

In those six weeks I never saw anyone else. The drifts closed what traffic we had. I lived in fear daily that his horse could not make it.

We had been told there was little of the winter that cattle could not find tall bunch grass, but the hay ran out and the men had to go to Newman Lake and get wild hay at $25 per ton. They had to break all the roads. The train could not get through, so there was no mail and no newspapers.

We had plenty of needed provisions, but had expected to get some extras for Christmas at Spokane as the store at the Bridge did not carry everything.

So Christmas was a homesick day and bitterly cold. I wanted things nice for our first Christmas in our home. Everything went wrong. I went to make a cake; the eggs were frozen, so I gave up and cried.

In the middle of February the weather broke. The chinook winds cut the snow off. The green grass started, then the buttercups.

When the trains got through, we were flooded with mail, newspapers, two boxes by freight with California good things. We certainly had our Christmas then.

Everything was most beautiful. The wild flowers, the mountains all looked like California. The evergreen trees stood guard like old friends along the river. Everything was so perfectly beautiful out-of-doors that I begged for a small piece of land to be prepared so I could grow vegetables.

I planted lettuce, peas, early potatoes, turnips, cabbage, rutabagas, carrots and onions. How they did grow! Thus it was I raised the first garden known on the prairie.

Lizzie Esch drove over one morning with some hollyhock roots, a few gooseberry and currant roots. She said it would do no harm to see if they would grow. They certainly did and the dear old hollyhocks went right to blooming. Their great-great grandchildren are here yet.

The second Christmas we had turkey and all the trimmings.

There were many other problems to solve, but I knew in my heart they were nothing to what was endured by the brave women of the covered wagons. In 1896 we had saved enough from our dairy and poultry business to get a well and an addition on the east end of the house. The first bathroom in the country!

Life at Spokane Bridge

[*Spokane Valley Today*, November, 1988.]

Spokane Bridge, the earliest recognized community in the Valley, grew up along the Spokane River about eighteen miles from Spokane and twelve miles from Coeur d'Alene at the site of the present Port of Entry weigh station and rest stop.

When I-90 was built in the late fifties, the last remnants of Spokane Bridge were buried under asphalt. But a marker behind the rest rooms declares: "600 feet north of this monument was located the first post office in what is now Spokane County established in 1867, first post master Timothy Lee, also first bridge across the Spokane River built by Joe Herrin and Timothy Lee in 1864."

Although the buildings have disappeared, there are in the Valley residents who lived at Spokane Bridge and remember the people who once worked and played and went to school there. I was able to talk to four of them. All echo the sentiments of Amanda Millsap Streit, now past 90 years old, who said over and over, "It was a wonderful life."

Amanda's parents and their four children moved to Spokane Bridge from Arkansas in 1901 when she was six years old. She lived there until she was married in 1912. She walked to the one-room State Line School in all kinds of weather and remembers drying her clothes at the old pot-bellied stove. For lunch, the teacher made a pot of "something like stew" and the students brought potatoes that they baked in the stove while the lesson was in progress. Two students were assigned the duty of pumping water for the school at Holland's farm not far away. They brought the water back in galvanized pails and "we all drank from the same dipper and never got sick!" exclaimed Amanda.

She finished eighth grade but didn't go on to the high school at Otis because it was too far away.

Amanda knew Orange (Bert) Humphries whose family moved to Spokane Bridge in 1902. The Humphries' house is still standing — the first house on the left after leaving I-90 at Exit 299 and traveling south. Bert's mother, Ingrid, was Swedish and "the best cook in the area," remembers Amanda. "I liked to walk past their house. Bert's mother always invited me in for a slice of cake or homemade bread or pie. People were like that in those days, friendly."

Bert entered the Spokane Bridge School in 1912 when he was six years old. However *he* didn't stay for lunch. His family built a bunkhouse for railroad section workers and took in boarders — section crew workers and travelers. Bert was expected to be home at lunchtime to dry dishes. "There was a gravel pit where Jacklin Seed is today," said Bert. "When railroad crews came to load gravel, we had anywhere from ten to fifteen boarders. Mother charged 25¢ for dinner on week days and 35¢ on Sundays. She was well known for her Swedish recipes."

The first bridge across the Spokane at the state line was built in 1864. By 1869 the small trading center had grown up near the bridge and it was the precinct voting place for all area voters including the town of Spokan Falls.

When Bert Humphries arrived, the trading center included Hewitt the shoemaker, Pat Senters' livery stable, and Rice's grocery that was subsequently purchased by Mrs. Finch who added a second story dance hall to the building. She and her husband operated the store and locker plant and post office until the early fifties.

"I was too young to dance," said Bert, "but my sister, ten years older, had a good time there. There was a blacksmith shop too. I remember that because I was afraid of the blacksmith's dog. Mrs. Finch also ran the post office. Her brother, Fred Galloway, carried mail out of the Spokane Bridge office from 1907-1939. He had two horses, one for his morning route along the State Line to Liberty Lake, and a fresh horse for his afternoon route north of the river.

"My dad, Joe Humphries, was a hog farmer. On his 75 acres he also grew wheat, hay for his six milk cows, and potatoes. There was a sand pit on our land. The last four miles of the Appleway was built from that pit.

"Spokane Bridge was a rich little district. The Milwaukee Railroad and the electric train both came through south of the river. The electric train had a depot, but the railroad was a flag stop although there was a large loading platform and warehouse for its customers. Near the railroad was a saw mill."

Bert remembers an Indian burial ground across the railroad tracks south of the river. Both he and Amanda remember Indians tethering their ponies in the meadow and coming to their farms to pick raspberries.

About 1911 or 1912 there was excitement at Spokane Bridge. One of the settlers who was furnishing supplies to mountain moonshiners robbed the Martin mercantile. With the law on his trail, he skipped to Tennessee "leaving a good wife with a large family."

State Line School and Spokane Bridge School often had their Christmas programs together. There were Decoration Day programs and picnics at the Pleasant View Church after it was built in 1910. And CHIVAREES! "They were something," said Bert. "I always was afraid I'd be chivareed when I got married. The settlers came to the house of the newly weds in the night banging pots and pans and a big round buzz saw until the young couple invited them in for refreshments.

"The settlers traded help. We used to go to Hollands and help them tramp down silage and they would come down and help us bundle our wheat. Transportation was all hacks and horses until 1920 when Dad bought a Buick. What a day that was!"

Norman Bye and Lucille Branson today live in the Valley only a few blocks apart. In 1923 Norman's family moved to Spokane Bridge and In 1926 Lucille was his teacher at Spokane Bridge School. She taught there for only one year but "that was the best year of my life up to that time," she said. "I was making money and having a good time doing it. I was only nineteen, played ball at recess with the kids, felt important ringing the old rope bell each morning and was overjoyed with my pay check of $110 a month. From that sum, I paid the custodian, Mr. Hickey, $10 for building the fire, sweeping, and putting up the flag each day. Mr. Hickey was also the clerk of the schoolboard and a good friend of mine.

"I commuted each day to my home in Spokane. At dusk I lighted the candle that sat on my desk in an empty fruit can. I extinguished it when I saw the bus coming down the hill across the road. My 'teaching dress' was one I had remodeled from Mother's wedding dress."

In the 1800s at various times there were four wooden wagon bridges built across the river at the state line location. The fifth one, built in the fall of 1911 by O.H. Stratton, length 366 feet, at a total cost of $19,400, was of steel with wooden flooring. This is the bridge Norman Bye remembers crossing every day on his way to and from school.

"We moved down from four miles south of Spokane Bridge to one mile west. The first year we four kids went to Spokane Bridge School. But Dad thought the discipline was bad; so after that, we all went to Otis. Miss Creighton (Lucille Branson) taught in 1929 at Otis and was my fifth-sixth grade teacher there.

"The curves at both sides of the bridge were sharp. Many mornings, walking to school, we saw accidents or the results of accidents at the bridge.

"Dad had a dairy farm. I herded cows for nine years, even stopped cars on the Appleway getting the herd across it. Our family milked the cows by hand and cooled the milk in the river until the practice was condemned by the health department. After that, we cut blocks of ice from Liberty Lake, packed them in sawdust, and stored the milk on the farm. Transporting the milk led to the establishment of a freight company called Pleasant View Auto Freight with L.G.Perigo."

The Bye farm was on land originally owned by Mr. Galloway and earlier had been the site of the famous slaughter of 700 horses ordered by Col. George Wright.

There were sad times in the little community. Norman's twelve-year-old brother drowned in 1925 while wading in the Spokane River. Amanda and Bert remember how caring the community was when the mother of six children died giving birth to twins. Four of the children were immediately adopted by neighbors.

As neighboring communities grew — East Farms, Otis Orchards and Post Falls — and World War II brought its influx of residents to the Spokane Valley, the importance of Spokane Bridge as a town decreased. Little by little the trading center was abandoned, new roads were built, and the railroads torn up. But the roots laid down by the early settlers remain. And there are the memories of "a wonderful life."

An Early Settlement: Trent

[From *An Early History of Spokane County* by Jonathon Edwards, W.H. Lever, publisher, 1900, p.279]

Situated nine miles east of Spokane, on the Northern Pacific Railway where it crosses the Spokane River. The land in this section was settled upon nearly twenty years ago, the first settler being a Mr. Edwards. Mr. G.P. Dart, now of this city [Spokane], resided here for some years and was the owner of the townsite until about two years ago. About ten years ago Mr. J.A. Stegner opened a general merchandise store. After his death the business was conducted and continues to be controlled by his widow, now Mrs. J. Narup. There is a good district school house with an enrollment of about forty scholars. East of Trent a few miles are some of the oldest settlers in the county, Messrs. Esch, Goodner, Myers and others.

Cowley Bridge is an old landmark. It is on the Spokane River near the Idaho line and well known to all the old settlers.

[From "The Valley of the Sun," Story 7, *Spokesman Review*, 1930-34]

At one time Trent was an active contender with Spokane Bridge and Spokan Falls for the town leadership of the Valley. Frederick Post of Rathdrum and Post Falls had considered locating a milling enterprise at Trent, but Mr. Glover, with a subsidy of forty acres of land near the falls, induced him to come instead to Spokane and build a flour mill.

In 1879 Calloway Hodges homesteaded at Trent. His son-in-law, Mr. Michaels, settled the same year at the foot of the hill, three-fourths of a mile southeast of the Trent school.

Another son-in-law, J.C. Myrtle of Eugene, Oregon, located on the north side of the river in 1880. With J.W. Arthur, he put in a ferry. Seth Woodard says this ferry was on the site of Plante's old ferry.

They operated it in connection with a store and boarding house for about two years. Then Myrtle homesteaded 160 acres on the north side of the river and built a log barn and a cabin with a sod roof. These buildings are [1930s] still standing below Myrtle Point, where R.N.Riblet built his beautiful home.

The first Trent bridge was built for the county in 1890 by the San Francisco Bridge Company for about $7000.

Mr. and Mrs. Narup, mentioned above in Jonathon Edwards' notes, were greatly interested in all plans for community growth including light, power and water systems. She became postmistress, was a staunch supporter of the church organized by the surrounding settlers in 1889 and with her husband purchased and operated over 700 acres in that vicinity.

As population increased, the Trent area [Irvin] had several plattings. The first platting was the town of Trent, located astride the Northern Pacific right-of-way. Some old-timers say "Trent" was Stegner's wife's maiden name and that the platting was named for her. What later became Pines Road originally was Dart Road, named for another Trent pioneer.

The platting of Trent was vacated and later followed on the south side of the right-of-way by the plat of Louisville. That name was possibly selected by the Kentuckian who built and operated a distillery at Trent Bridge.

In addition to Louisville, there was also the plat of The Palisades, which covered the area west of Louisville and south of the railway. Both of these plats were later vacated.

The Irvin church stands [1930s] on lots originally part of the vacated town of Louisville.

The J.A. Stegner Store

[From "Echoes from Yesterday" by J. Howard Stegner, *Spokane Valley Herald*, April 8, 1954]

Unlike many of the early pioneers, the J.A.Stegner family came west, not by covered wagon, but over the Northern Pacific, which had been built five or six years before. We came from St. Paul, Minn., traveling deluxe. Our berths were comfortable with beds made of straw. The sleeping cars were equipped with a range in one end to cook meals on, so that was like sleeping in the kitchen.

The year was 1889, the month was August, our destination was Spokane Falls, Washington Territory. This was rather an historic time. It was the year of the great Spokane fire and the year that Washington became a state. On arriving I wonder just what my parents' thoughts were. The smoke of Spokane's great fire had cleared, and there stood the ghostly ruins of 32 square blocks, with tents where business houses once stood.

Father placed mother and us three children in one of those tents that represented a former hostelry. He proceeded on foot to locate a college friend, Monroe Denman, who had a homestead about one mile northeast of what is now Hillyard. Toward evening father came driving in to town with the Denman team and buckboard, and we were soon happily situated with the Denmans.

We soon decided to move to Latah, a new town on the OR&N railroad. There we started a "racket" store, now called a dime store. However, Father was a commercial salesman and soon had a position with the Singer Sewing Machine Co., while Mother ran the small store. In my father's journeys between Coeur d'Alene and Spokane Falls, he visioned the possibilities of the Valley.

With the coming of spring, 1890, we moved from Latah, to Trent, now known as Irvin. My parents purchased some lots from G.P. Dart, in Palisades Addition where we started the only store between Spokane Falls and Spokane Bridge.

This was located about one block west of where the Trent School now stands and on the south side of the NP railroad. G.P. Dart had the post office when we came and that was located about where the laboratories of the cement plant are located now. In 1891 or '92 we took over the post office which supplied most of the Valley, Foothills, Pleasant Prairie, Newman Lake, and even Saltese Lake. We found that this was quite an asset to our general store, that when people came after their mail, they would do some trading.

Now if you took away roads, cars, telephones, radios, electricity, water supply and put in about three one-room school houses, that would be the Valley in the early nineties. Transportation was by saddle horse, horse drawn lumber wagon, buckboard, hack, and oxen. If in summer you saw a cloud of dust, you might expect to see some Indians with one or more travois. News traveled slowly. We took the twice-a-week *Review,* and if any one got hold of any news, around our store stove was the place to tell it.

Our store didn't amount to much, but we sold groceries, flour, feed, plows, barbwire, and later McCormick binders. We sold both Arbuckle and Leon Brothers coffee for 15¢ a pound, put up in one pound sacks and had to be ground.

I recall one humorous incident in connection with our drug department. Mother, a licensed pharmacist of those days, also sold patent medicines. She was a staunch prohibitionist and positive in her convictions. However, she had upon our shelves a goodly supply of flavoring extracts.

Some of our Spokane Indians had learned that these innocent appearing liquids had purposes other than glorifying desserts.

One morning a fine looking Indian rode up to our store and tied his horse to the hitch rack, walked leisurely into the store and glanced casually about the room. He quickly observed the shelf of extracts, and pointing to the vanilla inquired, "How much?" He then took from a long buckskin bag the price of vanilla and slipped silently from the room. Throughout the day, the Indians came steadily until the supply of extracts was exhausted.

When Father came home from his usual selling trip, he told of a number of Indians going on a rampage at Spokane Bridge. Mother remarked that they probably had been over to the new distillery. Father laughed and said, "Maybe so." At any rate this incident ended the extract business at the Stegners.

By 1895 our family had increased to three boys and two girls, but that would soon change.

Mother made a trip to Minnesota taking two sisters and baby brother Guy.

While mother was on this trip, my father became very ill, and my mother was sent for. Dr. Allison pronounced it appendicitis and father was taken to Spokane Falls in our grocery wagon with a bed spring to lighten the bumps. He was operated on in the Pedicord Hotel. Five of the best doctors were there. He died July 18, 1895, and was buried in the new cemetery on Pleasant Prairie, opened in '94. Now, for a widow with five children to run a store and keep the wolf away was no small matter.

Mother hired a lady to help with the house work. Father left $2000 insurance and that money would buy a lot in 1895. She bought 160 acres of land in what is now Pinecroft for $800 and after the electric road came in, she sold it for $16,000.

J.A. Narup, who started a blacksmith shop at Trent in 1894, rented this farm of my mother and in 1897, Thanksgiving Day, he married my mother. This was indeed a Thanksgiving Day for he was a fine man and we were all his children. From this marriage we gained two more sisters.

My folks, now known as the Narups, prospered as most people do in the Spokane Valley. In 1898 they bought 160 acres on Trent Road, with a new store building on it, from the Darts.

The Darts had started a store in competition, but somehow they didn't make a go of it, perhaps because we had the post office. Mother and my oldest brother ran the store and my stepfather the farm and it wasn't long before I was a lot of help to him.

With the sale of the land that our mother bought in what is now Pinecroft, we bought more land along Trent road, this included the land and the buildings of the Spokane Distilling Company located near the Trent bridge. We didn't go into the distilling business, but there were less drunks around after that.

Finally our holdings extended from Trent River bridge to the Paper Mill on the west and included all of the following additions: Grandview Acres, Fairacres, Palisades Addition, Fruitland Addition south of the NP Subway and 100 acres on the Palisades where Mr. Riblet has his castle.

We closed our store business in 1907 after 17 years to take care of our real estate holdings.

Mrs. Stegner's Recipe for Suet Pudding

[From *Treasured Recipes from Spokane* by Mildred Sager, 1948]

Suet Pudding
Mrs. J. Howard Stegner
Mix well, put in greased mold or can and steam 3 hours. Serve with sauce (hot).

1 cup suet, chopped fine	2 level teaspoons baking powder
1 cup brown sugar	¼ teaspoon salt
1 cup milk	1 cup raisins
2 cups flour	

Add nutmeg or other flavoring.

Sauce

½ cup sugar	1 tablespoon butter
1 heaping tablespoon cornstarch	2 cups water (more if desired)

The Cayuse

[From "Echoes of Yesterday" by J. Howard Stegner, *Spokane Valley Herald*, November 4, 1954]

A common sight during white winters of Valley pioneer days was the Indian pony, or cayuse, pawing at the snow to get to the grass beneath.

When we came to the Valley in 1890, there were no herd laws. You had to fence your crops instead of your stock. There were hundreds of acres of fine bunch grass from 12 to 24 inches high. This was before the cheat grass era.

The cayuse ranged all winter. With an extremely hard winter, these horses had a hard time to survive and many of them didn't. The genuine cayuse would survive where an ordinary horse would starve. These cayuses somehow had the knack of pawing the snow away to get the taller grass.

About the latter part of a winter, the snow would melt first on the railroad track fills. Seeking their first square meal in months, horses would get out there in large numbers. If you heard a lot of tooting, you would know that there were horses on the railroad track.

Around on the prairie near Trent, there were two large bands of horses known as the Webster and the Clark bands. My folks often traded for horses and sometimes it was necessary to take a horse on a bad debt or grocery bill. Our surplus stock generally ranged out with the Clark band. It was a pretty good idea to have your stock branded as there were those who made a practice of picking up slick ears or mavericks.

You could break a cayuse to ride or drive and if you turned him out for a week or so, then gave him a feed of oats, you would have to break him all over again. I have often wondered if the expression, "feeling your oats," didn't originate with the cayuse.

One time we traded for a cayuse mare and she had a mare colt. It seemed like it wasn't any time before we had four head of horses. There wasn't much of a market for the small horses just then, but we traded the four head to Frank Hanson, who had a place near where the Northern Pacific yard office is now located. We also gave him 40 feet of rope out of our store to catch them with.

In trade we received a dozen thoroughbred light Brahma chickens and a rooster. These chickens were the largest I ever saw. We sold the eggs for $1 a setting. This trade worked out fine for both parties concerned.

These cayuses were tough, wiry ponies with an average weight of 750 to 800 pounds. They would readily ford a stream and could swim like a duck; 40 or 50 miles a day was easy for them. Most were bays, some were pintos. If used for work horses, it took about four of them to pull a 14-inch walking plow.

The early day schools all had hitch racks as many of the students rode these Indian ponies to school.

Pioneers ate cayuses as well as used them for transportation.

Colonel George Wright's slaughter of hundreds of Indian cayuses near Spokane Bridge during the Indian War is a story that is remembered by a marker at the weigh station on I-90.

Without the use of many cayuses, which they were able to obtain from the Indians, the Lewis and Clark Expedition might not have been a success. This could have changed the course of history.

Another Cayuse Story

About 1901 or 1902, three or four years after we moved over on Trent Road, our vacant store building was used for church socials. (This was before the Congregational Church was built.) The Will Anderson family moved out here from Minnesota and located at East Trent. They were quite a support to our struggling church.

One evening the Andersons tied their team to a board fence while they attended a social. When Will went out after the show to where he left the horses, he found they had broken loose taking part of the board fence with them. They ran west through what is now Fairacres.

Several of the men looked all night and at daylight found the team in Harry Salmons' pasture which would be a little west of the south end of where the Argonne Bridge is now. They had run through eight or nine barbed wire fences to get there. Seems like they had to shoot one and the other wasn't any good after that.

Grace Anderson, who a short time after, became

Mrs. Alfred Shaw of Vera, wrote to some friends in Minnesota that the cayuses had run away with the hack. They wrote back and wanted to know what cayuses and hack were.

Albert F. Chittenden's Story

[Excerpts from "Of Life in the Valley 69 Years Ago" by Albert F. Chittenden, *Spokane Valley Herald*, November 11, 1954; August 4, 1955]

In the summer of 1885, with her five young children, ranging from eight to 13 years of age, my mother left New York for the new Territory of Washington. Here, in due time, she filed on and acquired a pre-emption, timber claim, and homestead on the height of land at the eastern edge of Pleasant Prairie, about three miles north of the present Kaiser Aluminum plant.

We left tenement-lined canyons paved with cobble stones. We came to woods, wide open prairies, mountains, rushing streams, a vast multitude of exciting wild life. For the first time we tasted water from crystal springs, breathed pine-scented air, heard the lonesome call of the mourning dove, the scream of the coyote and cougar. We saw bear and deer destroying our vegetable garden from our cabin window. For long winter months, we were imprisoned with no radio, no television, no place to go — and loved it.

It is hard for anyone today to understand the clean refreshing psychology of the new land to which we eagerly came. Universal hope warmed the heart like the song of the myriad birds that filled the valleys and hills with enchanted melody. The pioneer was eager , hopeful and confident. In our case it was not only the great beauty of the countryside, not only the friendly, hopeful people we met, but also the contrast with what we had left.

We had broken the bonds of our eastern tomb and stepped into the dazzling sunshine of a new and better world. A world where no quarter was asked or given, where the welfare state was unknown.

We children almost immediately had to take an

adult's part in developing the farm. Before three years had passed, before any of us three boys were fifteen, a great deal had been accomplished.

Mother had proved-up on her pre-emption and moved on the homestead. We had four horses, two cows, a calf and pig, over 1000 chickens, some ducks and geese. But more, we had shelter for them all. We had several acres planted in wheat for their food and two garden patches—one for the table and another for market.

All this land was fenced with rail fences from our timber and we had done all the work ourselves, that is, excepting our pre-emption garden and cabin, with which we had help. The new homestead house, the shelters for our stock and chickens, were all built by ourselves. These were partly of logs but mostly of lumber cut from trees we felled and hauled some ten or more miles to the mill...

There were no schools in the locality. Receiving an education was a major problem. Mother solved this as far as possible by teaching us herself. During those pioneer days agencies sponsored, I believe, by groups interested in the proper development of the isolated pioneer, produced and sold reprints of historical, educational, and classical literature on cheap paper at a small fraction of their usual cost.

Of course Mother supplemented those she purchased by others borrowed from neighbors and friends. I do not believe that any public library existed in the Spokane Valley in 1885.

We had religious home services night and morning and grace at every meal.

Our neighbors called occasionally. I imagine many came to estimate how long we would last. They inspected Mother's chickens, her few ducks and lone goose, appraised the pig, garden and cabin, and other evidence of our work — decided that we intended to stay, and what was more, that we could stay.

They were friendly, and on their advice we added a root cellar in which to preserve winter food. In it we could store potatoes, turnips, beets, onions, and other vegetables.

As summer advanced, our neighbor, Mr. Esch, decided to fence. The line he ran, however, indicated that our cabin was some twenty feet on his property. Fortunately all our other structures were on our own land. Mother insisted that we have a regular land surveyor check the line. Because of the great quantity of survey work, this was not done until late spring of 1887.

Mr. Esch not only paid for all of this survey but informed us that he, together with other neighbors, would move our cabin, without cost to us, as soon as they could. Because of planting, summer work, and harvesting, this was not done until the late fall of 1887, and it was not until 1888 that we had lived on our land the required time and could file for pre-emption. Mother felt very insecure until we could file, of course we all did. Neighbor after neighbor, however, assured us, as did the land office, that we had nothing to fear.

We were told again and again that not only did our work and good intentions give us a legal claim but even if we had no legal rights no one would dare jump a woman's claim without risking tar and feathers and being run out of the country on a rail. In the rough Wild West a woman was even more secure than she is today — and a woman with children — well, they were sacred.

The problem of accurate property location was many times costly to the pioneer. Even at that time many corners could not be found — especially by the inexperienced settler. Experienced land surveyors were few and frequently stationed many miles away making their employment financially impossible. Because of these reasons laws of adverse possession were created.

During 1889 Mother proved-up on her pre-emption and filed on a homestead. She also purchased from the government a timber claim adjoining the homestead on the north. Residence was not mandatory on the timber claim but was required on the homestead. This made it necessary for us to construct shelter for ourselves and livestock on the homestead as well as move all our possessions to our new cabin.

A Pioneer Home in the Valley

Our cabin had proven too small so we built a real house on the homestead. It had a large kitchen 8x12 feet, and a still larger living room fully 12x14 feet. Upstairs we had two dormer bed rooms where we boys slept. The girls and mother slept in the living room.

On the north, dug into the hill, was a log lean-to. We built a fireplace of native stone in its north wall, which by leaning a little could have nestled against the hill which towered far above it. This gave us another lesson of where and how to build, because the fireplace had no draft and smoked atrociously.

We went upstairs by means of a ladder. We had forgotten the stairs in our plans, and when this error was discovered, we were never able to squeeze them in without making some other part of the building bulge out and impair the architectural beauty of the structure. We used the fireplace only once and then surrendered the lean-to to tools, small equipment and cords of wood. In spite of our mistakes, we had a far more comfortable home than our cabin had been, then too, we had a wonderful view from the south window.

When I was seventeen-years-old, with less than an eighth grade education, I began to teach in the public schools. In those days people read far more than they do today. Reading took the place of the radio, television, and movie. Owing to Mother's guidance, we children read far more than the average even at that time. I had completed mathematics at home, well into high school work, and all other subjects beyond grade school requirements. But I had not attended school more than two or three months since coming west.

Our work and necessary experiences on the farm proved to me, at least, that Mother's belief was correct that "true education is experience enlightened by knowledge"—not the reverse. Like veterans, who from experience at war are eager for more knowledge, we received our experience the hard way and after graduating from the farm, sought enlightenment in schools and universities.

The Saltese

South of Greenacres in the foothills of Mica Peak is an area known as The Saltese. Strictly speaking, it is not in the Spokane Valley. However, through the years its residents have been so closely involved with the Valley that, in the minds of old-timers particularly, it is part of the Valley.

The Saltese Meadows or Flats (both designations are used) was named for the great Coeur d'Alene Indian Chief, Andrew Seltice (or Saltese) who lived on the east side of Saltese Lake.

Chief Seltice was a friend of Steve Liberty for whom Liberty Lake is named. They had common religious beliefs: Liberty had studied for the priesthood and Seltice was a mission Indian.

THE COURCHAINES AND LINKES

Two of the pioneer families in the Saltese area were the Courchaines and the Linkes. Fred Linke says his grandfather settled there because of the good land on the hillside. Descendants of the Courchaines say it was the fine spring water ("best in the Spokane Valley") and the abundance of grass for horses and cattle that brought their pioneer forebears to the Saltese.

Sometime after 1850, Daniel Courchaine, patriarch of his family, joined an influx of French Canadian settlers from Quebec headed for the Territory of Washington. He arrived in our area and purchased a section of land in the Saltese from the Indians. In 1878 he built a house on the land, hauling the lumber by team from Walla Walla. His son, George B. Courchaine, was born in that house, and lived in it for more than three quarters of a century. The house was located on what is now Linke Road off 32nd, one ridge over from the south end of Saltese Lake.

Herman Linke, patriarch of the Linkes, and his wife, Henrietta, came from Germany to Illinois in 1869. After a time in California, in 1873 they came north and went to work on the Rathdrum Prairie ranch of Frederick Post, Henrietta's father and later the founder of Post Falls. Soon the two, under the Homestead Act of 1862, preempted 320 acres of land on Saltese Hill and built a log cabin there in 1877.

Through the years, piece by piece, Herman extended his holdings, buying chunks of right-of-way land from the Great Northern Railroad until by 1885 he had a ranch of about 1160 acres, one of the largest and finest in the area.

By 1890 Linke had completed a true farmhouse on the Saltese property and it became home for his wife and son, Walter, and Walter's wife and four children, one of whom is Fred.

Both families farmed extensively, raising their own food and food for their animals; but Herman specialized in seed wheat, introducing choice varieties into the country and developing a hybrid strain popularly known as Linke wheat. On the other hand, the Courchaines, in peak years, fed over one hundred head of mature Shorthorn beef cattle plus calves. Son Miles did most of the farming for his parents during the twentieth century.

It is said that before telephones, the families sent messages back and forth by pony. Both had many Indian friends. Walter Linke spoke the Chinook Indian dialect, a language invented by the whites to converse with the Indians and Daniel Courchaine's wife was part Indian. Indians frequently visited at the Courchaine ranch on their way home from Mt. Spokane to swap huckleberries for puppy dogs or to graze and water their ponies at the "wonderful" spring on the Courchaine property.

It is said that twice a year Herman Linke made a two-week journey to Walla Walla for supplies with his team and wagon. In the early 1900s just traveling the fifteen miles to Spokane was an all-day trip over the rocky, rutted road that was only a trace, not even graveled. To go to Spokane, he loaded his wagon the night before and left the next morning after breakfast if he wanted to be home in time for dinner. However, after the Electric Interurban Railway came through the Valley in 1903, he and other residents were able to journey more easily to Spokane and Coeur d'Alene.

The Courchaine place was a favorite camping ground for covered wagons. There was plenty of water for both humans and animals and grass for the horses. The road going by their home was so well traveled by settlers going from California

Creek to the Spokane Valley that it became known as a part of the California Trail, although today (1993) it is Linke Road.

George Courchaine has the Linkes to thank for his wife, Annie. She came to teach at Lone Fir School from Cheney Normal and boarded at the Linkes.

The Depression affected both families. The Courchaines sold off half of their land at that time. Fred Linke, who owned the Linke ranch during the Depression, said,

"We raised considerable peas and hogs and chickens during those years and sold cream and eggs and milked the cows; although I must say, we never had a crop failure and never went hungry."

It was then that Fred bought his two brothers' share of the estate that had been divided when father Walter died in 1927.

Fred was an advocate of soil conservation. He kept a pond near his home to hold back water stored for livestock. He always planted his gullies and ditches with grass and replenished the land with fertilizer and by using crop rotation. He farmed until late 1969 when he retired.

Both the Linke and Courchaine ranches were dotted with big barns. Barn dances at the Linkes were the social highlight of many settlers' lives.

Under Roosevelt's New Deal, Fred Linke worked in the '30s for the Agriculture Adjustment Administration. This program made commodity credit loans and reduced acreage because of wheat surpluses. In 1938 he became Federal Crop Insurance Inspector and was always active in community affairs such as the school board and Chamber of Commerce.

The present-day Courchaines and Linkes are of true pioneer stock. Herman Linke had no capital or friends and no knowledge of the langauge when he arrived in this country. But he had an inborn desire to succeed that was common to the early settlers. George Courchaine was parentless at the age of ten, but continued to improve the ranch and rally in the face of adversity.

The Saltese, like the rest of the Spokane Valley area, is involved today in heated controversy concerning development, land use, environmental laws, fire protection, and the advisability of density restrictions—problems Daniel Courchaine and Herman Linke never dreamed of.

Minnesota Pioneers: Blessings, Ulowetz

[From "Echoes of Yesterday," by J. Howard Stegner, *Spokane Valley Herald*, late 1950s and 1961]

There was quite an immigration from Minnesota into the East Trent area in 1884, motivated by extensive advertising by the Northern Pac ific Railroad.

That spring, two years after marriage, the Isadore Blessings teamed up with Isadore's two brothers, Titus and Antone, and Joe Ulowetz and John Korles for the long journey to their new home.

The five adventurers and their families arrived in the village of Spokane Falls May 29, 1884, five years before Washington became a state.

They first went toward Lewiston to look for free land, but finally came back and took a look at the Spokane Valley. They found lots of rocks and gravelly soil that caused them to be somewhat dubious they could make a living off the land.

All five settled in the vicinity of what was then called East Trent, now Trentwood, along the Spokane River, as the stream furnished water for the stock and the household, as well as driftwood for fuel.

Isadore Blessing homesteaded 160 acres and bought 160 more of railroad land at $3.25 an acre. In 1942, 220 acres of his land was sold to the government for the site of the Velox Naval Supply Depot, leaving 90 acres of the home place along the river.

Antone Blessing bought 223 acres of railroad land on the east side of the river near where Thomas Newlon built a bridge in 1866.

In 1886 Joe Ulowetz filed on a homestead relinquishment of 117 acres near the present site of Sullivan Bridge. Some 81 acres of his original homestead was later owned by the Naval Supply Depot.

Joe wrung a living from that rocky soil. "I hauled as many as 80 loads of stone from 20 acres of ground," Joe once told me. Clearing the land of its stony content was a prerequisite of farming.

Before being able to make a living off of the land, many wells were dug in the Valley and in Spokane Falls. Joe dug two wells when Gonzaga was out on the prairie and before the village of Spokane had water mains.

Joe farmed 117 acres and rented 100 more for many years. These thrifty German families who spoke very little English had the knowhow when it came to farming and helped each other get started.

There were no churches in the vicinity so services were first held in their homes. They were among those pioneers who assisted Father Barnabas Held, O.S.B., in the organization of St. Joseph's Church in 1891. (See article, "Parish Churches")

School was also conducted in the homes until the residents organized District 63 and built a schoolhouse.

Others who settled in the area were Mike Stitz and William Hofford who later sold out to Frank Bracht. They also had large farms now occupied by Kaiser Rolling Mill or the supply depot. (For more about early farming see article, "Breaking the Soil.")

Fire!

["Echoes of Yesterday" by J. Howard Stegner, *Spokane Valley Herald*, September 2, 1954]

The largest fire I believe the Valley ever had was caused by a train wreck. It happened at 1:30 a.m., Monday, May 21, 1900.

Shortly after 1 o'clock that night a log train coming from Thompson spur of Spokane stopped at Trent (now Irvin) for a hot box. The caboose was a little east of Pines Road, then called Dart Road. A lone engine in charge of J. H. Montgomery came up and was flagged. He stopped his engine a short distance behind the caboose of the log train, waiting to pull out.

Disaster in the form of an extra freight of about forty cars with Jake Palmgren as engineer was rapidly approaching from the east. Whether the two stalled train crews had a flag man out later became the question.

The railroad men claimed they had, but on account of the curve, he wasn't in time. Just as the approaching freight engine came across the high bridge which spans the river there, the engineer saw what was ahead of him. Quick as a flash, he sounded the whistle and applied the airbrakes. But he was too close — 150 yards — to stop a train of forty loaded cars on the downgrade.

Seeing there was to be a collision, the engineer and firemen of the approaching engine jumped.

The trains came together with a tremendous crash. As the engine of the freight struck the single engine, the latter was driven with terrific force into the rear of the log train. Such was the force that the lone engine was pushed right over the caboose of the log train, grinding it to pieces. This was followed by the mad plunge of the second engine which telescoped into the first. Ten seconds after the crash, the train burst out in a mass of flames that mounted hundreds of feet into the sky.

Six oil tanks near the engine contained some explosive liquid, some of which must have been thrown on the fire of the engine. A tremendous explosion resulted, throwing iron and scraps 300 feet into the air. Six other thunderous explosions followed.

Our store was about 175 yards away and we were sleeping above it. My mother and stepfather, J.A. Narup, had heard the whistling and rushed to the window and saw the crash. After the first explosion , we decided it was time to vacate and we all hit down the road west.

The heat was searing and we sure didn't expect to ever get back into our store and home again. Before we left, we let loose all of our livestock and drove them away.

There were several freight cars of merchandise on the track containing almost anything you might want to mention. Another engine crew came in from the east and pulled back all the cars they could get to without getting burned.

We spent the rest of the night over at our old vacant store west of the Trent School where the Oliver Edwards family was living temporarily. Don't think for a moment that we went to bed.

After the fire we dug out large lids off the oil tanks in our flower garden. If they had hit the house, they would have gone clear through it.

Yardley, Parkwater—East Spokane

Old records refer to the area just east of the city limits as East Spokane. Old-timers who lived there are more specific. They refer to Parkwater and Yardley. Parkwater is north of Trent Road, they say; and Yardley is south of Trent.

Actually the boundaries are more irregular than that, and unless a map is used, it is difficult to say off-hand what part of the area is actually Spokane and what part is Valley. Adding to the confusion is the fact that Spokane City furnishes the utilities for the two communities, but they remain a part of unincorporated Spokane County.

Their history as an industrial area dates back to the turn of the century when the coming of the Northern Pacific shops and the match block industry brought workers to the area.

Yardley was the name assigned the Northern Pacific Railroad switch yard and telegraph station just east of the city limits in 1902. On January 2, 1913, the Yardley Rural (Post Office) Station of Spokane was established. However, it was not until 1920, that the Post Office Department decided to upgrade the Rural Station to full post office status with a career postmaster in charge.

By 1920 a Spokane Valley Census shows 1200 people living in "East Spokane Township." Much of this population derived its income from the match block factories, the first of which was built at Sprague and Rebecca in 1915.

William W. Powell was the man who brought the match block industry to the area. The heart of match manufacturing interests was Pennsylvania. Powell went east after seeing the quality of white pine in the Idaho forests, and tried to convince the eastern match barons that it would be economically better to manufacture the match blocks at the site of western timber. They were not convinced.

Powell rigged up a home-made match block saw in an old planing mill and sawed out a carload of white pine match blocks. He shipped them to the Pennsylvania Match Company (which later consolidated with the Federal Match Company) and arranged to be there when the shipment arrived.

The tests he performed with the superintendent of the plant proved that those white pine blocks from the west were the finest match material ever put through the company's stamping machines and that manufacturing the blocks in the west from western timber would eliminate expensive freight charges on waste.

Thus came about the first match block factory on East Sprague. Within two years, the Diamond Match Company, the Ohio Match Company, and the Federal Match Corporation (later puchased by the Swedish Match Company, largest match concern in the world) had large plants in East Spokane.

Old-time residents say "it seemed like the whole area was nothing but timber." According to a *Spokesman-Review* article dated January 3, 1932, the manufacture of match blocks had become Spokane's largest industry.

In a February 2, 1929, article in the *Spokesman-Review*, the manufacture of match blocks was described as follows:

"Logs from the woods are shipped to the block factories east of the city and there the big logs are planed and sawed into small blocks the exact length of a wooden match and about six inches in diameter. These blocks are loaded into freight cars and shipped to the match factories in the east where they are cut up automatically into matches and their ends dipped in the firing solution.

"Every day 200,000 feet of white pine timber is utilized in Spokane for this purpose."

The contracts for the Northern Pacific shops, which also brought industry into the area, were awarded in February, 1912. Shops, a round house and icehouse at Parkwater would cost approximately $300,000. Most of the material was to be purchased in Spokane and all of the white pine to come from local forests.

With the arrival of industry, a large hotel was built at Yardley.

Girls at the Federal Match Factory at Yardley in the early 1920s cutting out pitch, knot holes, and other imperfections in wooden blocks from which matches were made. The grain had to be perfect. Residents of the area bought the waste from the factory for fuel. The old Federal Match office still stands on the north side of Sprague across from the site of the recently demolished Fred Meyer store. *Courtesy of Alice Anderson, a worker at age 15, shown at the rear in the line of girls.*

Family Life in Early Yardley— The Seehorns

[*Spokane Valley Today,* May, 1989]

The year was 1912. Milton Seehorn, proprietor of Brown and Seehorn, "the practical hatters," established in Spokane in 1894, sold his shop at 305 W. Riverside Avenue where he had a thriving business cleaning hats and making new hats and mourning bands. Solvent used in the cleaning process caused his health to deteriorate. Doctors recommended that he live and work where the air was pure.

Milton found a job at the Northern Pacific Yardley Railroad Shops in the Spokane Valley and moved his wife and two daughters onto five acres on Sharp Road about a mile and a half east of the shops. The home was on the city-valley line.

When the girls, Lois and Erma, reached school age, the parents had to decide whether their children should attend Valley or city schools. They chose the Valley school at Parkwater because the electric line stopped near their home and near the school. That decision established officially the school boundary line that is used today.

The girls attended the Parkwater School on Hardesty Road (now Fancher) for two years. Although no longer used as a school, the building with its outside fire escape still stands at the corner of Fancher and Commerce. For many years it was a nursing home, then Spokane Technical Institute.

The girls completed their schooling at Orchard Avenue School and the old West Valley High, later called Argonne Junior High and demolished in 1992. The site became an Albertson's Super Market in 1993.

Milton's wife, Zelpha, raised chickens on the five acre tract at Yardley—hundreds of them. According to a newspaper clipping in Milton's scrapbook, when a reporter visited the farm, she found "600 chickens ready to fry, 400 smaller hens, and a flock of several hundred laying hens of the White Leghorn variety."

Daughter Erma (White), who still lives in the Valley, says her family must have had the only well in the vicinity. She remembers that her parents furnished water to about twenty families. "One winter around 1918 when there was a terrible freeze, mother begged father to pump warm water into the well, but Father thought it wouldn't be necessary—that everything would be all right.

"The next morning the water was frozen. It took about two weeks before the water ran free again even though men dug holes and built fires to warm the ground."

Strikes, according to Erma, are nothing new. Her father lost his job at the NP shops because of a strike in the '20s. "Scabs took over and the regular workers were never rehired. Father found work at the Carstens Meat Packing Plant."

Erma's earliest memories of the Valley are of wide open spaces and severe dust storms. "That was before irrigation came to the Palouse," Erma said. "The dust would be thick and yellow and everything got as dark as night. Father rode his bicycle to work and Mother would have to put a light in the window so that he could find his way home — it was that dark. He couldn't even see the fence posts. I can remember Mother yelling to us to close all the windows as the yellow dust came over the hills.

"When we first moved to the Valley, we could see only two lights at night in the entire Valley."

So many of Erma's memories are about trains — those that came through in the Depression loaded with transients, and the "silk trains" that barreled through from Seattle to New York, never stopping, and puffing a stream of black smoke as the engineer tried to get his precious cargo to destination before the worms changed into moths. The moth, in emerging from the cocoon, would cut through the silk fibers and destroy the cocoon for silk reeling purposes, rendering it valueless.

"During the Depression, transients often swung down from the boxcars when the train stopped at Yardley," said Erma. "They came to our house for food. Mother helped them, but always made them work for whatever she gave. Going to school, my neighbor, Helen Russell, and I often saw tramps cooking over fires along the tracks. We were never afraid of them and they never bothered us.

"We lived at Yardley twenty-seven years. There were so many birds and flowers in the springtime! My father loved to sing and whistle. He could whistle like a meadowlark. I picked love darts where the pea factory is today just off Fancher.

Milton Seehorn came west with his family in 1880 from Missouri — by train to San Francisco, cattle boat to Portland, boat up the Columbia to Wallula and train to Spokane. His brother, Billy (Elihu) Seehorn also worked first for the Northern Pacific, on the right-of-way south and west of Spokane. He helped put in the grading at Hangman Creek when 1500 men, 1000 of them Chinese, were employed shoveling out the sand.

In 1885 Billy founded the Seehorn Storage and Transfer Company with a one-team dray. A year later he added a team and opened an "office" in front of the E.B. Ewing Company at what is now Trent and Howard.

As we talked, Erma's husband, Larry, who came from West Virginia in 1936 and worked at the Paper Mill, was practicing his golf strokes on their neatly groomed expanse of lawn. The house was filled with the tempting aroma of a chicken simmering for dinner — perhaps prepared from one of her mother's recipes for the "home-grown"variety.

SONG: "SOD SHANTY ON THE CLAIM"

[The Seehorn girls, Erma and Lois, knew it was time to get up when they heard their father whistling and singing in the garden. This was one of his favorite songs:]

I am looking rather seedy now while holding
    down my claim
And my victuals are not always served the best
 And the mice play shyly round as I settle down
    to rest
In my little old sod shanty in the west.

I rather like the novelty of living in this way
Tho' my bill of fare is always rather tame
I am happy as a clam on the land of Uncle Sam
In my little old sod shanty on the claim.

My clothes are plastered over with dough
Everything is scattered round the room
I would not give the freedom that I have out in
    the west
For any fancy eastern mansion home.

CHORUS: The roof is made of mud and straw,
The window has no glass
I hear the hungry coyote as it sneaks up in the
    grass
Round my little old sod shanty on the claim.

Author Unknown

Public Schools

"Education forms the common mind; just as the twig is bent
the tree's inclined."

ALEXANDER POPE

(Carved over the entrance way of West Valley High School, built in 1926.)

A class at the Millwood School about 1916. Students: Grace Hanshaw, Lucy Paladin, Madeline Cummings, Howard Harrington, Lucille Knowles, Frank Paladin, Raymond Niles (at board), Harvey Woodard, Everett ———?, Louise Williams, Henrietta Schaeder, Howard Stout, Marguerite Woodard, Andrew Byram, Stanley ———?, Marguerite McGinnis, Lucy Berns Boughton, teacher. *Courtesy of Marguerite Bartleson.*

Public Schools

CHRONOLOGICAL HISTORY

1853
    The **Territorial Legislature** passed the **Organic Act** which stipulated received from sections 16 and 36 of each township was to be used ⌐ support.

1854
    Governor Stevens urged the Legislature to pass an act establishing a mon school system for the state. It became the basic school law.

1855
    January: A Territorial University was authorized by legislation. The was the eventual establishment of the **University of Washington.**

1877
    Spokane Valley was part of school district #8. *A History of Spokane* defines the original boundaries of School District #8: from the mouth of ⌐ man Creek up along the stream to the Idaho line. Eleven children were enrolle in the district with an average daily attendance of four during a three month term. Four of the textbooks used were *The Pacific Reader and Speller, The Cornell Geography,* Davis's *Primer and Arithmetic,* and Greene's *Grammar.*

1887
    The **Anton Blessing** family and others helped build the **East Trent School** located near the south end of the wagon bridge near Trent and Barker. **Jacob Esch** hewed the logs for it.

1887-88
    School started at **Vera** with 32 pupils enrolled, but an average daily attendance of 20.

1888
    School District #76 was formed and a one-room schoolhouse was built by residents of communities later to be called **East Farms, Moab, Otis,** and **Spokane Bridge.** The one-room school between **Simpson Road** and **Malvern** about 600 feet north of **Trent** (now **Wellesley**) was for all eight grades. Thirty pupils were enrolled, average daily attendance, 17. **William Pringle** donated $20 to purchase lumber. The school was about ½ mile east of the **Otis Orchards Community Center** and affectionately called "The Little White School on the Hill."

1888
    A school was built at **Chester.** It measured 18 x 24 feet. **Cora Bussard** was the first teacher. She received a salary of $25 a month for a three-month term.

1890
    Spokane County Teachers Association was formed with **I.C. Libby,** president. Membership rules: pay dues of 25¢ a year, be accepted by a majority of

members, accept no employment in any school for less than $50 per month. A six-month school term was recommended.

1890-91
The following school districts were operative: **#25 Mica**, enrollment 23; **#71 Chester**, 59; **#39 Saltese**, 14; **#40 Vera (South Trent)**, 28; **#78 Liberty Lake**, 20; **#85 Pasadena**.

1892
Property at **Liberty Lake** was deeded for a school and the school was built shortly thereafter. It was demolished in 1960.

1893
School was held at **Newman Lake** in **Wallen's** house for two or three terms until a school was built.

1893
East Trent School relocated on **Sunshine Valley Road,** now **Flora. Trent District #118** was organized.

1894-95
Lone Fir District #128 in the **Saltese** area was formed with an enrollment of 18. **Fred Saltz** donated land west and south of the lake (near what is now **Chapman** and **Linke**) for the **Lone Fir School** and **Walter Linke** worked to get it started. In 1954 it was moved behind the **Vera Congregational Church** to serve pre-school children at **Vera.** The school building still exists in 1993 and is located at **Sprague** and **Progress** behind a used car lot where it is used for storage. Also in the **Saltese** area was the **Saltese School** on the corner of what is now **Thirty-Second** and **Linke roads.** It was later used as the **Greenacres Grange.** Another school in that district was the **Quinnemosa** at the corner of **Henry** and **Saltese,** near the south end of **Saltese Lake.**

1895
Prior to 1895 practically all school support was from the district or county. Then the state decided to make larger contributions and provided that $6 should be set aside for every person between the ages of four and twenty-one in the state.

1900
September 7: **Orchard Park School** opened — a one-room wooden structure 24 x 40, with an enrollment of 28. The schoolhouse was on the corner of **Orchard Avenue** and **Mission.** The **Orchard Park School District #143** included what now constitutes **Dishman, Millwood, Orchard Avenue** and half of **Yardley** and **Parkwater districts.**

1900
The **Bordon School** was built in **Canfield Gulch** and named for **Minnie Borden,** the first teacher. In 1908 this became **District #144.**

1903
30 x 40 foot school built in **Greenacres** at **Mission** and **Barker.** First classes had been held in one room of **Hatch's** three-room bunkhouse.

1905
New **Orchard Avenue School.** A two-story, four-room structure with basement, of solid masonry construction with cloak rooms and other facilities. Price, $6000. No electricity. Power lines were not extended to the area for 20 more years. In 1923 gas lamps were purchased for the rooms.

1905
A **Vera School** was built at **Sprague** and **Progress.** It was demolished in 1960.

1907   **Opportunity School District** was organized and the first unit of **Opportunity School** built at **Bowdish** and **Appleway.** There were 139 pupils, average daily attendance 96, four teachers at a salary of $60 per month. The unit was valued at $158,940. At the dedication **Estelle Cashett** buried a fruit jar in the cornerstone that contained, among other things, the names of students and teachers. In 1969 , when the school was demolished, the glass was cracked but the papers were intact.

1907   A two-story, four-classroom brick building was erected at **Greenacres.** It burned in 1922 and was immediately rebuilt.

1908   Bonding for school buildings was authorized by the **State of Washington,** making it possible for small areas to reduce their transportation problems by building new schools.

1909   The one-room **Moab School** was built 300 feet north of the **O'Brien Store** at **Starr Road** and **Trent.** It was used for two years until a new building was constructed on **Starr Road,** north of the **Northern Pacific Railroad.**

1910   **Otis Orchards School District #168** formed. 28 pupils. A school was built that was outgrown after only one year.

1910   A four-room brick veneer school was built at **Dishman** at a cost of $63,000; and a brick school was built at **Greenacres.** High school was attempted at the four-room building at **Orchard Avenue** in connection with the grade school, but abandoned. It was for freshman only. There was an average daily attendance of 4. **Greenacres, Opportunity** and **Trent** also tried high school about this time, without success.

1910-11   School District #172, **Spokane Bridge,** formed. Enrollment 14.

1911   The **"Cobblestone School"** was built at **Otis Orchards** and a high school program was introduced. The school was a three-room school with amenities such as a cloak-room and a full basement.

1912   **Vera High School** started but had a hard time because of small enrollment. In 1915 there were 30 high school pupils.

1912   A four-room school with basement of solid masonry construction was built at **Millwood.**

1913   Hillyard Townsite Company donated the site for a new **Parkwater School** and the contract was let but the building was not completed until 1923 because of money problems. It was to be a duplicate of the **Millwood School.**

1914   First high school graduation at **Otis Orchards** held in the **Spokane Fruit Growers Warehouse.**

1914-15   **Vera School District** undertook a successful high school program with 31 students enrolled.

1916–17   High school work accredited at **Millwood.** English, classical, and scientific courses offered.

1917   **Pasadena School District** annexed to **Orchard Park.** A one-room cobblestone structure erected at **Pasadena Park.** Sold at auction June, 1926.

1918   New wing added to **"Cobblestone School"** at **Otis Orchards.**

1919   All school pupils released to help pick apples.

1919   **Orchard Park District #143** became a second class district, with an enrollment of 597 and 20 teachers.

1920   A law was passed that provided that $20 for every census child in the state be set aside for education.

Looking south from Valleyway toward the Opportunity Schoolhouse at Sprague and Bowdish, 1908. *Courtesy of Patricia Smith Goetter.*

East Trent Schoolhouses

[Excerpts from "Echoes of Yesterday," by J. Howard Stegner, *Spokane Valley Herald,* September 9, September 23, 1954]

One of the first schoolhouses ever built in our Valley is still standing. This is the one-room East Trent Schoolhouse which was built around 1886 and did not close until 1950, a period of 68 years. Located on Flora Road about ½ mile south of Trent, it was built one mile west of its present location and moved in 1896 after district 118 (Trent) was organized.

It is hard to realize that this building was built in Territorial Days without county or state help. The sills were hewn by Jacob Esch. Those who participated actively in the building construction included the four Blessing families, Leopold Ziraprick, Joe Arbes, and some other settlers who bought railroad land or filed homesteads before or during the big wave of pioneers in 1884. The land was given by Joe Arbes and Joe Krupp. Size of the building is 18 x 30 feet.

My brother Conrad started to school there in 1891 and in 1892 my sister Mary also attended the East Trent School. The 2½ miles to travel was solved by boarding the teacher.

We furnished a horse and cart, the teacher doing the driving, so my brother and sister, ages 6 and 9, could make the five-mile round trip each school day. The teacher paid us $3 per week room and board.

There were many ponies tied to the hitchrack and in the woodshed. Students that walked, when the snow got deep, wrapped in gunny sacks, as there were not many rubbers or overshoes. Seats were homemade and as many as four of the smaller pupils sat in one seat.

Drinking water was carried a half mile. It was often necessary in the fall to skim the grasshoppers off of the water after it was carried to the school.

On July 8, 1893, District 118 was formed and on August 2, 1893, was reported to the commissioners. At that time the East Trent School was moved to its present location on Flora Road. During the moving one mile east, the movers got the building stuck in a mud hole. Before they could get it going again, the money ran short. So the building was blocked up right where it was and a dance was given in it. This raised plenty of money to complete moving the building.

An old vacant Methodist Church building about 16 x 24 feet located on the prairie about ¼ mile east of the present Trent School was used until a building could be built. The first teacher was Rosine Edwards, daughter of Rev. Jonathon Edwards, early day missionary. (See article, "Veradale, Veradale United Church of Christ, Rev. Jonathon Edwards.")

The new building was about 24 x 40 feet. It was known as No. 2 and was located on the north side of the present Trent School. Its cost was $725 with an additional $150 required to furnish it. This building was also used by the Trent Congregational Church before they built a fine building.

In 1896 thieves broke into the schoolhouse and stole the church organ, a very large Bible, large dictionary, case of maps, and about everything else, including the globe. Then in December, church was held at 2 p.m., and about 8 p.m. the school burned to the ground. The cause was no insulation under the stove.

Miss Elizabeth Johnson, the teacher, had a contract so school had to go on. My mother offered our old vacant store building and it was used until the fall of 1899. This building was called No. 3. Building No. 4 was built on site No. 2, same size as No. 2, cost $900. The District was bonded for $1000 and the property owners paid nine per cent interest on the bonds.

In about 1908 the Valley began to build up quite rapidly. For a while the Congregational Church that was built about 1903 was used to house the school's overflow and two teachers were hired. The church was known as building No. 5. Finally in 1909 the District was bonded and building No. 6, a four-room, two-story red brick structure was erected at a cost of about $12,000. This building was used until outgrown and No. 7 was started.

No. 7 has had several additions which you latecomers in Irvin or Trentwood areas know more about than I do.

[Note: In 1993 Trent is in the East Valley School District.]

First Orchard Park School, still standing at Mission and Park. *Photo taken in 1932 by Leo's Studio in the Valley.*

Orchard Park and West Valley Schools

[From *History of Orchard Park Schools and West Valley High School*, written by Arthur B. Ness and printed for the West Valley School District, 1950. Mr. Ness became principal of Millwood High School April 9, l920. The Arthur B. Ness Elementary School at 9612 Cataldo bears his name.]

At the dedication of Ness Elementary School October 10, 1957, Arthur Ness spoke as follows about writing the history of the schools:

"My last task in this school district, and it was a pleasant one, was to compile a history of Orchard Park Schools and West Valley High School. Aside from the purely statistical data gathered from annual reports and other sources, I read the minutes of every board meeting since the formation of the district in 1900 — 57 years ago. The reading of those minutes gave me a new insight into the struggles and problems of the early pioneers in this area.

"One of the most serious problems in the life of the pioneer is that of providing educational facili-

ties for his children. A fundamental trait of the trail-breaker is a passionate desire to prepare his children for the future, so that they may be better equipped than he to fight life's struggles. The only means he knows of to realize this aim is education. To the pioneers in Spokane Valley, this became a burning question. The problem was temporarily solved in the south-western area, now constituting the major portion of Orchard Park School District No. 143, by sending the children to Carnhope School in the outskirts of Spokane. But the distances were great and the trails and roads were poor, presenting difficulties and problems to both parents and children.

"In l900, fifty years ago, a bold step was taken. They would organize their own school district and build their own school house! It was an undertaking not justified by the existing conditions. A number of neighbors in surrounding territories ridiculed the idea. 'They scoffed at the thought,' one of the pioneers told me. 'It is folly,' they said,'to build a school house in an area where only coyotes and ground squirrels will thrive.' But true to the pioneer spirit, they went ahead with the plan, undaunted and unafraid.

"March 27, 1900, is a memorable date in the history of the school district. I quote from the minutes of the board meeting held on that date: 'The object of the meeting was to decide on the location and purchasing of a school site; consider the matter of bonding or levying a special school tax; talk about building and furnishing a school house; determining size thereof and cost of same.

"The size of the school house was deemed to be 24 x 40, 12' studdings, roof ½ pitch—total cost not to exceed $900. The minutes of this meeting are signed S.T. Woodard, Clerk of the Board. It appears that Mr. Woodard is still residing in Millwood, and as active and alert as ever, was the guiding force in district school matters from the very beginning, continuing as such for many years.

"Apparently, the directors were not satisfied with the specifications given above; they thought they were rather incomplete, so the clerk was instructed to draw the plans and to specify more in detail what was needed.

"The clerk must have done a good job in the preparation of the plans for the school house. He must, also, have had an eye on the board's stipulation that the structure must not exceed $900 in cost. When the bids were opened, it was found that the cost of construction would be less than $600. A levy of 10 mills provided the funds to proceed with the erection of the building.

"The school opened in September, 1900, with an enrollment of 28 children, 16 boys and 12 girls. The average daily attendance, however, was only 14 for the first year. There were no children enrolled in the 5th and 7th grades.

"The matter of securing a teacher was apparently a difficult problem. The first teacher selected, it seems, broke her contract immediately, the second served until December, and the last to be employed carried on the work until the end the year and was subsequently re-elected. It appears that discipline constituted a major difficulty, and the working conditions were by no means conducive to contentment. The janitorial work was done by the teacher, such as keeping the fires going, sweeping the room, dusting, providing the drinking water, etc. Certainly, the environment was not very pleasant, but it was the best that could be provided under the circumstances. The salary was $50 per month for 8½ months, or $412.50 for the school year."

On page 238 of his history, Mr. Ness discussed his ideas of an adequate school program:

"…adequate buildings, equipment, and instructional materials are, of course, extremely important to the educative process. They are invaluable adjuncts in the attainment of the great educational ideal—the guidance and direction of the youth of America in such a manner that they may become worthy citizens of the great country. It involves the harmonious development of a child's physical, mental, and spiritual potentialities. The last mentioned—the spiritual—is by no means least important, since in its broadest sense, it determines an individual's moral and ethical conduct in his relations with his fellow man."

A Battle for Schools

[By Seth Woodard on the occasion of the celebration of the Tercentenary of Secondary Education in 1935, and included in the *History of West Valley High School,* written by students, six teachers, and Mr. Arthur Ness. Seth was a member of the first school board of the Orchard Park District. The elementary school at 7501 E. Mission Road in the Valley was named for him.]

My first connection with what is now School District No. 143 dates back to the formation of the district in 1900. I was one of the original petitioners.

The district was formed by taking some territory from three large districts: Carnhope, Trent, and Chester. Believe me, we had to put up a hard fight to get a district!

There were only a few settlers in all the districts. Trent objected because they did not want to lose any territory. Chester was neutral: we only asked for a small part of their territory. Carnhope, to the southwest, was our worst antagonist, putting up the argument that we lived "over there on the barren plains where nothing could thrive but coyotes and ground squirrels; and we had no children to speak of, and couldn't support a school if we had one."

The district originally was outlined as follows: Beginning on the south bank of the river one-half mile west of the city water works, thence south to Broadway, east on Broadway to Hardesty Road, south to the Appleway, east to Orchard Avenue Road, south one mile, thence east one and one-half miles, north to the river, westerly along the river to the place of beginning.

Believe it or not, in all that expanse of territory, there was not to exceed thirty houses.

In order to get a school district, we had to show that there were a sufficient number of children between the ages of five and twenty-one. By counting several young married women and a few young men who were working on dairy ranches, I found twenty-seven.

Compare that with our present enrollment of over one thousand in our united schools and see how the community has developed.

The district was finally allowed and a school board duly elected. This first board consisted of H.J. Pendleton, N.C. Hair, and Andrew Larsen, directors; and S.T. Woodard, clerk.

We found ourselves the owners, as it were, of a school district with no school house, and not a single dollar with which to build one. However, we had plenty of pep and an abundant supply of faith in the future.

On us evolved the burden of getting ourselves organized into a fighting force.

We had to fight every step of the way—formulate a plan for financing, secure a site, build a school house.

The records show that on March 27, 1900, we had a meeting to choose a site. By September 7, 1900, we had finished the building and opened the first school in the district.

By 1904, we had outgrown the one-room school house. We built a four-room building which still stands at Mission and Park. It is now the Grange Hall.

Chester two-room schoolhouse, date of photo unknown.
Photo courtesy Spokane Valley Museum archives.

Chester School and Town Named

[From "Echoes of Yesterday" by J.Howard Stegner, *Spokane Valley Herald*, February 24, May 8, 1958]

Before the community was ever named Chester, the people of that vicinity decided that they should have a school. A meeting was called for this purpose on August 6, 1888.

This meeting convened in Foster and Tolen's office and was called to order by S.A. Carnahan. Amos Lewis and Harvey Cox were elected directors and Carnahan was clerk. They were to hold office until the annual November election.

Lewis offered to donate an acre of land in a nice location near the center of the district. It was decided to accept this and to build an 18 x 24 feet, by 12 feet high schoolhouse there.

The new district was No. 71.

In pioneer days you didn't bond a district to build a schoolhouse and pay a teacher's salary. It was done by subscription or donation in a fashion similar to that by which churches raise money today.

The new district hired Cora A. Bussard to teach school for a three month term. George and Cora Bussard moved to Chester in 1888 before the village had a name. George operated a sawmill and one of the first threshing machines in this part of the country.

Cora's contract called for a salary of $25 a month. This was to begin on October 1, and to be paid for by subscription from families of children attending.

Individual amounts collected ranged from $10 to 25¢ with maybe $3 being about average. A total of $82.50 was raised. This paid Miss Bussard's salary for three months and for a $7.50 stove, leaving a balance of 20¢.

The next teacher at the school, Cora Butler of Moran Prairie, was hired for a term of not less than three months and not more than four months at $25 a month and room and board. So you see, she got a raise.

In territorial days, three months was the average term of school. Two three-month terms would be held each year, one in the fall, one in the spring, with the coldest winter months and the hottest summer months off for vacation.

Chester was named in 1889 when the Oregon Rail and Navigation Company completed the railroad (now Union Pacific) through the area. Officials gave the station the name Chester.

Churches

"It was their privilege (the pioneer missionaries of the Pacific Northwest) to lay deep, strong and broad foundations, upon which their successors have and will erect grand and permanent superstructures. Though dead, they yet speak, and we enter into their labors. A sense of our obligation to them should incite us to know their memories and perpetuate their names."

[A History of Spokane County, Chapter II, p.4, Jonathon Edwards, W.H. Lever, 1900]

The first of several churches built at Sprague and Union. *Courtesy of Patricia Smith Goetter.*

Churches

CHRONOLOGICAL HISTORY

1880s
Traveling missionaries offered services in the homes of pioneers near the Washington-Idaho state line.

1881
Church services were held at **Saltese Lake** under the guidance of **The Reverend M.S. Anderson.**

1885
A congregational church was formed at **Newman Lake.**

1889
Sunday School at **Trent** was held under the leadership of **Deacon S. Esch.** A preacher from **Pilgrim Church** in **Spokane** came out once a month to preach.

1889
The **First Congregational Church of Trent** was organized and services were held in the **East Trent School** until it burned December, 1899, six hours after church one Sunday. The people of the farming community of **Vera** joined with the **Trent** congregation.

1890-92
Benedictine Sisters taught a two-month session.

1891
Father Barnabas Held met with a group of about 30 Catholics in **Dashbach's** log cabin near the Spokane River and organized **St. Joseph's Mission Church** at **Trent** and the cemetery, twelve miles east of the city limits at the present site of **St. Joseph's Church** on **Trent Road.**

1892
St. Joseph's Valley Mission Church built, offering Mass on Sundays and holidays. **Held** became the regular priest until 1897. The church was called "The Little White Church on Trent Road." (See article, "Parish Churches: St Mary's, St Joseph's, St. Paschal's.")

1900
The first **Liberty Lake Sunday School** service was held in the **"Little White Schoolhouse"** at the corner of **Sprague** and **Molter roads.**

1903
"Fine new congregational church" at **Trent** (now Trentwood). Later converted to a home at **N.3420 Pines.**

1905
Greenacres Christian Church was organized and a church built on **Mission** west of **Greenacres Road.**

1906 **Methodist Church** built in **Greenacres. Ladies Aid** under the leadership of **Mrs. Nipple** raised $500 for the building. **J. Green Long** donated the lots for the building that was completed in 1908. It burned before services were held.

1906 An interdenominational group met for Sunday School and worship in the **Opportunity Town Hall.** This was the forerunner of **Opportunity Presbyterian Church.**

1907 **A.C. Rickel** located on a tract in **Opportunity** and built one of the first homes in the **Opportunity-Dishman** area. He organized the first Sunday School at **Orchard Avenue** and was one of the first superintendents of the Union Sunday School in **Opportunity.** He aided in the construction of the first **Baptist Church** in the Valley at the corner of **Apple Way** and **Union** and for years was its minister. The **Jamison** and **McDonald Land Company** awarded the church the land because it was on their platted land.

1908 Dec.15: The second **Greenacres Methodist Church** was built by **Reverend Henry Brown.**

1908 **Spokane Valley Baptist Church** was organized with 29 charter members. The church at **Apple Way** and **Union** was completed approximately a year later.

1908 **German Evangelical Congregation** built a church at **Otis Orchards,** fronting **Trent Road.** It was dedicated in 1910. First church services had been held in 1906 at the home of **Louis Haas.**

1909 Original wooden **Spokane Valley Baptist Church** burned.

1909 The first service was held in the partially completed **Opportunity Christian Church** located where **Peters Hardware** now stands. The seats were planks resting on nail kegs. The first baptisms were conducted in the **Spokane River** near **Irvin,** then called **Trent.**

1910 **Mr. Joseph Jackson** started a Sunday School in the **Carnhope** (now **Alcott**) **School.** It was the start of the **Edgecliff Community Baptist** congregation.

1910 **St. Paschal's Catholic Parish** was formed.

1910 **Dishman Methodist Sunday School** was held. This group later joined with **Opportunity Methodists** in 1939. The original bell is still in use.

1910 May: **Vera Community Church** (later the **United Church of Christ**) was organized and met in **Vera Grade School.** It later became **Vera Congregational Church.**

1911 **Opportunity Methodist Church** was built on the southwest corner of **Sprague** and **Bowdish.** Rev. M.R. Brown was the first pastor. **Oscar Reinemer** hauled the lumber with a team and sled from Hillyard. The church was demolished in 1959.

1911 **Otis Orchards Community Church** was organized.

1912 Spokane University was founded by **B.E. Utz** of the Spokane Christian **Church.** He served as its first president. (See article, "Spokane University.")

1912 **St. Mary's Catholic Church** was built in **Veradale** at **Adams Road.**

1912 Spokane **Presbyterian Church** held services at **Liberty Lake** in the old **MacKenzie Hotel** located at **Wicomica Beach.** Upon completion of the new red brick schoolhouse, services were held there until World War I when it closed until 1925 when revival meetings were held.

1913 **St. Mary's** became the first Parish church with a priest in residence.

1913 **Opportunity Presbyterian Church** organized with 65 members. They met in the **Town Hall. Dr. S.M. Ware** was the founding pastor. In 1915 when **Reverend A. Weld** came, the **Town Hall** was still used for worship. However the congregation soon moved to the school house to accommodate more people.

1913 **Reverend Jonathon Edwards** began his pastorate at **Vera Community Church** (See article "Vera Church of Christ.")

1914 **Dishman Methodist Church** dedicated.

1915 March 28: Sunday School was held in the **Millwood Grade School.** No church until 1923.

1915 **University Place Church** met in **Science Hall** on the campus of **Spokane University.** It was organized by President **I.N. McCash** (See article, "Science Hall.")

1916 July 9: **St. Paschal's** was staffed by Franciscan Monks. Mass was celebrated at the home of **John Stoltz** in the **Del Monte District** on **Eastern Avenue** near **Felts Field.**

1917 Spurred by need of a home, **Opportunity Presbyterian Church** adopted plans for a building, payment to be made in Liberty bonds. Dedication was held November 23, 1919. 300 handbills were printed announcing the opening day.

1920 **Millwood Community Presbyterian Church** was organized with 98 members. It bought land from the **Paper Mill.**

1920 **Bethany Old People's Home** was built on a 9-acre tract in **Pasadena Park,** financed by the **Swedish Church of the Northwest.**

Religious Aspects of Pioneer Life

[An interview with Seth Woodard, Millwood pioneer, by Jerome Peltier, *The Spokane Valley Herald,* July 1, 1993 (Excerpts)]

"I don't know of any organized church in the Valley when we came here (1883)," said Seth. "There were traveling ministers who would hold meetings any place they could get a chance. My father's house was always open to any minister of any denomination of faith coming through who was willing to talk on the spiritual side of the affair. I remember old Father Cataldo, Father Jacques and others in the Catholic ministry going through, would stop at our house or some other house and hold a meeting. All of the neighborhood would come.

"Some Methodist ministers might come through and if they could get a suitable place, they might hold meetings every night for a couple of weeks. After we got schoolhouses, they were used for churches. Not only were there church services, but soon we commenced to organize Sunday Schools which were taken care of in private houses for a long time. When we had room in the schoolhouse, we began to have regular Sunday School services. For instance, the old schoolhouse located on Mission and Park Road was the first organized Sunday School in this immediate area. Mr. Warren, who had retired form the ministry of the Southern Methodist Church, came out and organized the Sunday School and I was appointed the first Sunday School superintendent.

"By that time the Presbyterian Church at Millwood was getting started.

"Religious men did not discriminate when giving aid to neighbors who were in trouble.

"I remember one time during an extra hard winter, my father's family had a siege of typhoid fever. The snow was so deep that no one could get to us, hardly, and one day there was a knock on the door. My mother opened the door and there was a Catholic Father.

"He said, 'I heard there is a family here that is sick and in distress.'

"My mother said, 'Yes, we are sick but we are not Catholic and I see by your garb that you are Catholic and I don't want you to be deceived.'

"I was in bed but I remember hearing him say, 'I am not looking for Catholics. Father Cataldo sent me out here to find someone who was in distress and see what I could do for them.'

"He sized things up for a while and went away and the next day a whole wagon load of provisions came, and folks stopped and everything that was needed came to us. We got on our feet and were able to finance ourselves again. My father went to their church and tried to repay them for their kindness and they wouldn't take it saying, 'No just pass it on and do good for somebody else.'"

Parish Churches:
St. Mary's, St. Joseph's, St. Paschal's

[From histories written by members of these three parishes.]

From the early 1880s until 1891, the family home of William Pringle was used for infrequent religious services provided by Jesuit priests from Mt. St. Michael's and Gonzaga College. People from the entire Valley gathered on these occasions to attend Mass in a 12 x 18-foot room.

In 1891 about twenty Valley pioneers met with Father Barnabas Held, Benedictine chaplain at Sacred Heart Hospital, to plan for their own church at Trent. Father Held was able to communicate with these people (most of German descent who spoke little English) because he also spoke German.

With the help of about thirty of his parishioners from all over the Valley, he organized and oversaw the building of the church on the north side of the Spokane River at Trent. James McLaughlin donated an acre of land for the church and Max Rauscher donated the adjacent plot for a cemetery. Richard Rotchford, a skilled carpenter, designed the building. It was built by volunteers and Jesuit missionaries, under the direction of Father Held.

A white frame chapel measuring 24 x 40 was completed in the spring or 1892 at a total cost of $1650. The sacristy measured 12 x 20 feet. The church was blest August 15, 1892. It was the first church in the Spokane Valley, and lovingly called "The Little White Church on Trent."

A fire left by a careless camper in the grass in back of the church is blamed for burning it down September 1, 1928. It was replaced by a modern brick structure.

In 1892, Father Held started the first summer school in the area, staffed by Benedictine Nuns from Uniontown and Colton. A primitive convent was erected for the sisters. Father Held remained at St. Joseph's parish until 1897.

St. Mary's Parish

From 1908 to 1913 the Catholic population in the Valley grew large enough to sustain two parishes. St. Mary's was established at what is now Fourth and Adams to serve the residents on the south side of the Spokane River. From that time on, St. Joseph's served those on the north side.

The building of St. Mary's has been termed "a labor of love" and a "family affair." Fathers and sons worked together, including the Dhaenens, Shelley, Sullivan and Ralph families.

St. Paschal's Parish

The beginning of Franciscan religious endeavor in the Valley began July 9, 1916, when Bishop Shinner of Spokane founded the Parish of St. Pascal. The new parish embraced the district between the city limits on the west and the parishes of Veradale (St. Mary's) and Trentwood (St. Joseph's) on the east, bounded by the hills on both sides of the Valley.

On July 9, 1916, a church meeting was held in the schoolhouse at Parkwater.

A few days later the Clerk of the Board of Directors of the School District informed the new pastor that schoolhouses of a district in which there was a community church could not be used for religious meetings. This called for immediate action: a place of worship must be found. The Stolzes of Del Monte (a district named for the railway stop) offered their home for the first Mass of the newly organized parish.

On August 1, 1916, the first piece of parish property was purchased from Fred Stolz. It faced Eastern Road and lay between the Trent Highway and the Spokane River. Ground was broken August 12. The diary of Father Capistran (in charge of the construction) shows how hard volunteer labor worked to build the church. Under date of August 22, he wrote:

"We finished excavating the basement. It was a tough job. Harry Zahniser from Yardley, a non-Catholic young man, worked with his team. I held the plow and the slip. The soil was stony throughout. It took us four and one half days of solid work. The team cost $5.40 a day. I am mighty glad it is over. My bones and muscles need a rest."

Three months later on Thanksgiving Day, November 30, 1916, the Bishop dedicated and blessed the new church, solemnizing the occasion by celebrating a Pontifical High Mass.

St. Joseph's Cemetery

Max Rauscher donated the original cemetery parcel. For 50 years, additional parcels of land were donated and purchased until the entire 20 acres adjacent to St. Joseph's was set aside for the cemetery. In 1952 the St. Joseph's Cemetery Group was organized to preserve the cemetery.

Henry Arbes, a retired painter from the Naval Supply Depot (see article, "A Naval Supply Depot for the Spokane Valley," vol. II), had long dreamed of a shrine at St. Joseph's and in 1955 began to work on it. Arbes' parents had assisted in the building of the original church in 1891 and he had participated in the construction of a new church in 1929.

To help him implement his dream of the shrine, Mrs. Ida Donahue, his cousin, organized parties and bazaars to raise funds.

With no training or experience and working with only a bare minimum of hand tools, meager supplies, and no overall plan, Henry began by carving a pathway into the hillside. Altars were built of granite and landscaping was begun. The 900-pound statue of St. Joseph was the first one fitted in the first niche he built. When the second statue, the Virgin Mary, was installed, official dedication ceremonies were held May 30, 1956, by the church. Henry took frequent trips through the West and even as far as Mexico in search of ideas. His next step was the twelve-foot stone cross with steel frame that overlooked the cemetery. Later that cross was replaced with a wood cross.

Along the steep path and up a stone stairway leading to an abrupt cliff, Mr. Arbes built fourteen stations of the Cross depicting stages in Christ's ascent to his crucifixion. A miniature temple with two tall, turreted entrances took form. Inside was a fireplace whose mantel featured carved wooden children and animals. In front stood a garden and small pool with a gracefully cascading waterfall.

One of the most prominent additions to the cemetery is the Altar at the north end, below the walkway to the shrine, dedicated to the memory of the youth of the parish. It is used for Masses in the summer and on special occasions.

Time and vandalism have taken their toll, but Mr. Arbes' work still attracts many visitors. Under the direction of Holy Cross Cemetery, there are plans to restore the shrine.

Veradale, Veradale United Church of Christ, Dr. Jonathan Edwards

[As told by Dorothy Hartung, age 90, Holman Gardens, September 1993, and Bert Porter, also 90, who hid in a corner of the B.H. Davis home when the church was organized, with excerpts from a manuscript history of the church by Estella Hanson, November,1970, Spokane, Washington.]

The story of Veradale and the Veradale United Church of Christ parallels in many ways the story of other Valley communities and churches. Many early churches began as meetings in school houses or in private homes. All had their ups and downs. The fact that the original congregation was nondenominational and that the renowned turn-of-the-century historian, Dr. Jonathan Edwards, pastored the Veradale church sets it apart.

Dorothy Hartung's memories follow:

The Veradale "community" did not exist before 1900.

Immense boulders and gravel dominated the bare prairie of bunch grass and tumbleweeds. Only during the rains of early spring did the prairie blossom like a garden paradise with buttercups, grass widows, Jim Hill mustard and yellow bells.

This changed when the hidden river beneath the prairie was tapped. "My uncle Oliver Clark's prosperous farm of fruit trees and vegetables was a dramatic demonstration of the potential bounty of the land," said Dorothy.

The arrival of irrigation in 1908 (see article:"Vera Water and Power") brought land developers who bought large tracts and marked them off in parcels of five and ten acres. What proved to be an abundant water supply and the healthful climate brought settlers, those hardy souls venturing west, seeking open spaces.

The first recorded religious meeting of Veradale residents took place about 1889 when the few settlers joined with a congregation at the old Trent School for Sunday School. In December after church one Sunday, the school burned down (due to lack of insulation under the stove) and the congregation disbanded for some years.

In April 1910, the Reverends David Reid and D.E. Wilson of the Congregational Sunday School and Publishing Society became concerned because no church services were being conducted in Vera. They met with a group of residents at the B.H. Davis home.

Bert Porter remembers the planning at that first meeting: "That night the lights burned late in the Davis home located on what is now Valleyway. The few neighbors were talking it over. They wanted a church—some kind of a church. There were not enough persons of a single denomination to start one; but if the settlers were able to lay aside denominational differences and band together, the Spokane Congregational Church Extension Society would help. The little group decided to try it.

"There were days and months of discussion about what denomination to become. In the meantime the Congregationalists supplied Bibles and study materials for Sunday School services, and eventually we voted to respect all Bible interpretations of members, but become officially Congregational."

In May 1910, nine adults met after Sunday School and organized the Vera Community Church, a Congregational Church. Only one of the original nine, Mrs. Fred Conklin, is still living (1993). She is now 92 years old and lives in Great Falls, Montana. The other charter members were W.H. Porter, L.W. Shaw, Mrs. George Sherwin, Mrs. Molly Park, Mrs. G.A. Bartholemew, Mrs. Robert Kershaw, Mrs. H.B. Ferris, and Mrs. B. Davis.

Some early day members or their descendants are members of today's congregation.

Sunday School and church both met for a short time in the old South Trent Grade School on the corner of Evergreen and the Apple Way (later Sprague Avenue). Soon after the church was organized, the school children moved into the new brick school on Progress and the Apple Way and the church moved with them. W.H. Porter bought the South Trent School, moved it to the south hill

79

on Evergreeen and remodeled it into a comfortable home. It burned February 1927.

The leading spirits of the Trentwood congregation served at Veradale as well. Reverend Ellis preached at Trentwood in the morning and at Veradale in the afternoon. "Grandfather" Shaw, Santa Claus-like in appearance and a church leader at Trentwood, became Veradale Sunday School superintendent in 1911.

According to the minutes, the annual meeting of 1913 was a "heady success." Fifty people were present in addition to the Reverend Wilson who had been called as minister the year before. (He conducted Sunday morning services twice a month in Vera and at a second church on alternate Sundays.) The treasury had a respectable balance of $22.95 and total receipts for the year had been a whopping $323.05. There were thirty-two members and the Sunday school was doing very well as was the Ladies Aid Society. The meeting was adjourned to the school lunchroom in the basement for a "home-cooked meal of chicken, homemade bread and Mrs. Bates' dill pickles. The little congregation went home that night rejoicing."

Dr. Jonathan Edwards

Veradale had no church building until the advent of The Reverend Jonathan Edwards.

In 1913 the little congregation determined to take a giant step forward by calling Dr. Edwards, a famous pastor who had retired to the Vera community. He began his pastorate at Vera (his last) October 19, 1913. His salary was $500 a year augmented by the Congregational Home Missionary Society. This Society continued to assist with his salary until 1921.

Dr. Edwards was a philosopher and poet. He became known as the "walking pastor," walking miles through all types of weather visiting and ministering where needed. "A proud and grand pastor remembered and revered by the entire community."

Dr. Edwards had retired to the Vera community after many active years, afoot and on horseback, as missionary to Indians and white settlers. He served Grand Coulee, Okanogan, Palouse and Spokane and built or restored a dozen churches including the Westminster and Pilgrim Congregational churches in Spokane. He wrote a history of Spokane (quoted in this volume) and a prize winning biography of Marcus Whitman. He was literally drafted by the Vera congregation for one more pastorate.

"For years," said Dorothy Hartung, "the Veradale School generously permitted the church to hold services in the school building. Dr. Edwards led us to a miracle, a church building with real facilities for worship and an honest-to-gosh kitchen—a lovely, wonderful building!"

On November 19, 1919, a building committee of 37 people was elected with J. Rufus Gillespie, chairman. The committee secured a loan of $2500 and a grant of $3000 from the Congregational Church Building Society. The new church was ready for the dedication service held December 12, 1920. Membership at that time was 103.

"The church at Sprague and Progress from then on was the locale for all community activities—Sunday School, church, literary club, irrigation meetings, whatever."

When Dr. Edwards retired in 1923, this interview appeared in the *Spokesman-Review*:

"Seated in his favorite chair at his home in Vera, Dr. Jonathan Edwards, who has perhaps done more toward the upbuilding of religious work in the Inland Empire than any other one individual, lived again the days when he acted as missionary to the Indians, when he used to ride horseback 50 miles or more to preach, conduct a funeral service or minister to the sick.

"'Ah, those were the days when we enjoyed life most,' he said. 'In spite of the hardships and the dangers that went with them, my family and I were happy. I don't know that I would care to live that again, but I wouldn't take a million dollars for the experiences those days brought.

"'Yes, I told the Indians of the Christ away back in 1886. I succeeded Henry T. Cowley as their missionary. They rather resented it when I took up the work and were glum for a long time. They would answer me only in grunts and groans, but finally we became friends. They were members of the Spokane tribe and Chief Garry was their leader. Chief Garry was a great character. He had a wigwam out northeast of Hillyard at that time and was very active in the tribe.

"'When I first came to Spokane, I preached to as

many Indians as white people.' continued Dr. Edwards. 'They were a fine lot to work with.

"'I have served nearly forty years in church work in the Inland Empire and thirty years of this has been in Spokane and adjacent territory.'"

J. Howard Stegner remembered attending church in the little old schoolhouse. "It was 22 miles for us to drive," he said, "and we would often take our family organ along in our grocery wagon. My mother was the organist.

"The Reverend Jonathan Edwards would preach at Pleasant Prairie in the morning and East Trent in the afternoon. My father gave him a cayuse and cart so he could make the circuit.

"His daughter, Rosine, was the first teacher at the Trent School in 1893."

Spokane University

[Spokane Valley Today, November, 1989]

If there is a hub in the Spokane Valley, according to County Commissioner Steve Hasson, it is the area at and around University and Sprague. The Valley Transit Center, University City Mall, the fire station, and many other valuable services are located in that area.

But there is no university. So why is the street that crosses Sprague at that busy intersection called "University"? Why not "Central" or a name that designates the economic importance of the district?

Long before the businesses came, there was a true university about a half mile south on that street.

In Spokane in 1912 the Reverend B.E. Utz, pastor of Spokane's Central Christian Church, became concerned because, of the eighty churches in the city and the Inland Empire, only half had pastors. He set about to remedy the situation by establishing Spokane Bible College at the corner of Stevens Street and Sixth Avenue in the city. His desire was to train young people to fill the vacant pulpits.

The school proved its worth when, after only one year, it sent out 18 student ministers to preach and conduct Sunday School.

Rev. Utz decided he needed a larger and more permanent location. With the help of O.A. Adams, pastor of Spokane Valley Christian Church, a suitable site was located in the Spokane Valley one-half mile south of the Apple Way and a little more than three miles east of the city limits.

Today University High School is on part of the original 160-acre site. The campus of Rev. Utz's school, which he called the Spokane University, occupied thirty-three acres, although not all immediately developed. In fact, at the time the school closed. there were plans, even then, for future development.

The coming of the University was deemed of great benefit to the Valley. The streets in that area were named for prominent colleges and the street on which Spokane University was located became University Place. The name has endured.

From an account printed by Leo Oestreicher, a local photographer whose shop was across the street from the "U" we learn of the excitement the dedication generated:

"July 1, 1913, a great crowd met under the pines to dedicate the site and to break ground for the first building which consisted of six rooms in which school opened September 15, 1913. The next large gathering was July 15, 1913, when the G.A.R. came with fife and drum to help erect Old Glory in the top of a pine tree at the brow of the hill where it proclaimed to the world that here an institution was to be promoted to help make and keep our beloved country Christian and loyal to the ideals of freedom and equality. At both these gatherings, large vessels of coffee were made under the pines and a feast of good things were served by the Valley people.

"People living adjacent to the university site offered to share their homes with students, but the limited means of the prospective students would not permit them to accept this proposition. Groups erected tents where they slept and studied. A temporary building consisting of cellar, kitchen, dining-room and matron's room was erected. The generous-hearted Valley people filled the cellar with fruit and vegetables."

Along with the tents erected by students as living quarters were tents set up by real estate developers who were busy selling the lots around the University. Among the purchasers were university dignitaries whose homes, built in those early years, still stand today across the streets from the high school.

A 1914 *Spokannual*, yearbook of the University , tells of the formation of the "Stuffed Club," a solution to the boarding problem:

"A clubhouse with long tables was erected by the University. Students elect their officials who conduct the club on a non-profit basis, the students doing most of the work. The meals have been plain but substantial, there being little pastry and meat. By these methods the club has, during the past year, furnished board to each member at a cost of $5 a month. . .The students are a hard-working, sincere, enthusiastic, and spirited bunch. . .full of good clean fun that is continually breaking out in jokes and pranks."

Rev. Utz was named temporary president at the dedication ceremony but died just three weeks later. Dr. Isaac Newton McCash became the first official president.

Again I quote from the 1914 *Spokannual:* "Everyone realized that his (Dr. McCash's) installation as president of Spokane University was a momentous event for Spokane and the surrounding country and, in order that all might have a chance to see the ceremonies, the installation was arranged at Opportunity with a reception in Spokane for City people. For the event at Opportunity (December 11) the Vera-Opportunity Commercial Club and the Ladies Aid Societies of the various churches prepared a sumptuous banquet . . . the entire student body with arm bands and pennants marched the mile and a half from school to the Opportunity Town Hall . . . giving their school yells. Horses ran away at the sight; and startled inhabitants, unused to such scenes, peered cautiously through upper windows."

Although pioneered and influenced by the Christian Church, Spokane University was non-sectarian. Members of the first faculty belonged to four different religious bodies and the students represented ten religions. The departments of Liberal Arts and Fine Arts always exceeded the Bible School in enrollment.

Growth at the University was steady but slow and finances were always a problem. By 1916 Redford Hall, a girls' dormitory had been built. It cared for thirty girls, two in a room, for $2.50 a week. It housed a hospital ward, a large reception room and the University Commons where the students took their meals.

Earlier, a 60 x 80-foot gymnasium (largest in the Columbia Conference) was erected. Also tennis courts and a large athletic field were leveled.

Much more was planned for the campus, but liabilities of $120,000 forced the university to close in 1933. Faculty members fought the closure by accepting whatever salaries were available, but it was of no consequence. University officials and members of the Spokane Valley Chamber of Commerce reopened the buildings as a two-year junior college that moved to Spokane after four years and finally merged with Whitworth College.

Today three buildings remain. Science Hall is now Sunshine Terrace Boarding Home. Redford Hall is Kirbyhaven Nursing Home and the gymnasium building is used for storage on the U-Hi campus.

SCIENCE HALL AND THE CAMPUS CHURCH

I.N.McCash, first president of Spokane U, organized the University Place Campus Church. Regular services were held in Science Hall. Many Spokane University students and faculty members were members of the congregation and served in helping capacities at local churches, especially Opportunity Christian on South Robie. That young church received many pastors from the college.

In 1927, Opportunity Christian Church and the campus church merged and Science Hall became the official location for Sunday services. Only occasional meetings and some evening services were held at the South Robie address. The congregation had a new name: Spokane Valley Christian Church. Students pastored the congregation.

When the doors of Spokane University were sadly closed in 1934, the congregation unbarred the doors of the building on South Robie and started all over again as Opportunity Christian Church.

Students' Memories of Spokane University

FREDERICK L. CODDINGTON, Reno, Nevada:

By the thirties much of the original campus had been sold off and the University occupied about twenty acres. The large gymnasium was on the far side west. The football field, track, and tennis courts were between the gym and education building (Science Hall). Behind the education building was a wooden pump house and water tower. The school furnished domestic water for nearby homes. Behind the water tank was an ancient sand pit being filled in as a garbage and refuse dump.

The University was accredited with the University of Washington for transfer of two years credit.

On a May evening in 1933, the freshman boys decided to paint our numerals on the school water tank. The sophomores learned about it and closed in on us in great numbers. They caught Fred Goin and me and put us in the back seat of a car. They planned to haul us several miles into the country and make us walk home. The boy guarding me got called to help catch another freshman. I escaped and ducked into some bushes and then into a culvert. I stayed in hiding until the cars with prisoners pulled out. I found some red paint and the paintbrush. I climbed the water tower alone and painted the numbers "36" where they would show up best from the school lawn.

Every spring Spokane U held basketball tournaments for rural area schools. I was assigned to locate housing in private homes for the boys' teams. I needed beds for 120 boys for three nights and could offer complimentary tickets to the tournament as an inducement. It seemed like an impossible task. I began knocking on doors. I was amazed at the response. Very few homes did not take at least two boys. At one freshly painted home, my knock was answered by an elderly lady with thick glasses. She carried a cane, magnifying glass, note pad and pencil. "I'm deaf," she stated in a loud monotone. "You'll have to write what you want." I believed I was wasting my time, but I wrote on her pad. She held the magnifying lens in front of her right spectacle lens. She moved the pad back and forth. She looked up at me and shouted, "Yes, I'll take four boys." Before noon I had beds promised for all the boys.

MARTHA BROOKHART AND MARY FENSTERMACHER, Spokane Valley:

Our parents moved to the Spokane Valley from Latah in 1917 so that their four children could grow up in the Christian environment of a Bible College. Our father, Claude Fenstermacher, helped dig the basement of Redford Hall with a two-horse team and a slip held by hand. Neighborhood kids rolled the dirt tennis courts with a filled metal roller.

Our mother, Gladys Fenstermacher, took students as roomers and boarders. There were bachelor quarters for four young men in the basement of our home at the corner of University and Eighth. Two girls had rooms on the main floor. Mother also cooked at Redford Hall.

We remember the lovely receptions, the beautifully landscaped grounds—so many lovely flowers and shrubs—and the paintings in the art room done by now famous artist (then a student), Clifford Still. The whole community functioned around the University, attending games, operettas, debates, and receptions. The annual basketball tournament involved the entire Inland Empire.

Couples from the campus strolled up and down the tree-lined streets holding hands. At Eighth and Felts was a pine tree grown in the shape of a seat known as Lovers Seat. There was a boys' dorm at Ninth and Walnut that burned. It is now part of the underground storage for Leo's Studio. Rev. Utz's house remains on Ninth across from Sunshine Gardens.

ROBERT A. SANDBERG, Lafayette, California:

I attended Spokane U in 1932. . . bleak days; and then transferred to WSC where I earned an MA. I later returned to WSC as the Executive Assistant to President Wilson Compton.

SU was the beginning for many people who were successful in their careers. Outstanding was Clifford Still who became one of America's great artists. He studied with Maude Sutton who had a great moral and philosophical influence upon her students and was a real friend to them. The collection Clifford gave to the San Francisco Museum of Modern Art was worth several million dollars.

We all had to take Bible classes.

One personal story might amuse your readers. SU had a four-man golf team and played in a circuit of schools including Gonzaga.

I had never played golf, but one morning I got a call from one of the golfers saying that they had a meet with Gonzaga that day and one of the four guys was sick. They had to field four players or forfeit. Would I fill in? That I had never played didn't matter. They outfitted me with knickers and clubs and off we went. I had asked to tee off last so I could see how they did it. It was miserable. We lost, of course. But at the year's final chapel I was awarded a sweater in golf. I've not played since.

JACK FINCH, Spokane Valley:

I remember when the houses were numbered, about 1934. Two enterprising University students, Albert Rasmussen and Daniel E. Taylor, went to the Chamber of Commerce asking if they could sell house numbers to house owners. Until that time, the houses were identified by their positions in relation to a given corner. For example, second house west of McDonald on the south side.

The Chamber granted Rasmussen and Taylor permission. The area between Park Road and Havana was not included in the plan because it was a no-man's land. The only buildings there were Federal Match, Ohio Match and Diamond Match.

The east-west streets were numbered to correspond with the names of streets in Spokane. Shelley Way became Fourth; McCanna became Eighth; Campus became Twelfth; and Saltese became Sixteenth.

In 1936 Aslin Finch located across from Federal Match. Our number became E. 5618 Sprague, a continuation of Spokane numbering.

In 1931 the Spokane University football team was the first in the nation to fly an entire team to a game. I played End. We flew to La Grande, OR, to play Eastern Normal School. We lost 2-0. The planes used were a Ford Tri-motor and a Buhl Sedan from Felts Field.

ROBERT NELSON, Spokane Valley:

Our family moved to Dishman from Chester when I was one year old , and then to Opportunity when I was three. The University came shortly after. The whole area was like a park. The roads were little more than wagon trails and the land was covered with trees and flowering shrubs. A road off Dishman-Mica cut straight through the pines to the Saltese.

There was no vagrancy. The Spokane U was left open on week-ends and we kids played in it and on the athletic field and tennis courts. University boys built famous teacher Maude Sutton's house. It still remains at about 608 Felts Road.

I went to the Junior College from 1934-1936 during the Depression. Economy was at low tide and tuition a problem for all students. Summers I worked at Pierce's box factory in Dishman and one winter some other students and I cut logs on Mica Peak every week-end. These 17-foot lengths were skidded out and hauled to the big Cecil Kellogg Sawmill at the end of Eighth and Dishman Road.

We combined work with pleasure — took our sleds along and stopped at lunch-time for a weiner roast. We tried to cut the biggest trees possible because we liked to hear the thunder when they fell. And all we worked with were cross-cut saws and axes, no chain saws.

The University had a barter system, using scrip for cash. We exchanged services for the scrip with which we paid our tuition.

LEO OESTREICHER, Spokane Valley:

It took me ten years, working at odd jobs most of the time, to get through Spokane U. During those years, I started my photo shop across the street. I learned the skills from books and by experimenting. Until I took courses at the U, I had had only a fifth grade education and had to take exams to get it. I easily passed them. The first year I was there, the original small wooden library building burned down. The library was then moved to Science Hall and the gym was built at the old library site.

My photo shop soon had a large mail order clientele and published all the annuals for the Spokane area schools. Lawrence Morgan took over the business after I retired. The original building on the lot was Benjamin Hall, a boys dorm that burned down. I bought the lot and the old basement and dug by hand storage tunnels which still remain under the building.

Transportation and Mail

In the thirties, a former resident of Millwood visited old friends in the Valley. He had been away for 25 years.

"Why," he remarked, "the last time I came across Dishman north, I opened nine gates. Now the road is paved!"

["Valley of the Sun," Story No. 18, *Spokesman-Review,* June 13, 1932.]

How long do you think it took this letter to get from Spokane to Spokane Bridge? Mailman is Roy Brown of Opportunity. The sporty rig was a familiar sight along Sprague during the early 1900s. *Photo courtesy of Patricia Smith Goetter.*

Transportation and Mail

CHRONOLOGICAL HISTORY

1853   **Plante's Ferry** served cattlemen and wagon drivers as a means of crossing the **Spokane River**. During survey expeditions and Indian uprisings, **Governor Stevens** rendezvoused at Plante's home.

1861-62   **Captain Mullan's** men completed the **Fort Benton-Fort Walla Walla military road** at a cost of $230,000. The road was 640 miles long and 25 feet wide and touched the **Valley** at **Plante's Ferry** and **Spokane Bridge**. Originally an old Indian trail, the section from **Plante's Ferry** to a point a short distance east of **Spokane Bridge** later became the **Boundary Commission Trail**, later called **Wild Horse Trail**, and finally the **Mullan Trail**. In the **Valley** there are monuments indicating the route of the road through the area: on the **Palouse Highway** just south of **57th Avenue;** on **East 29th Avenue** just west of **Glenrose Road;** on **East 8th Avenue** and **Coleman Road;** on **East Sprague Avenue** and **Vista Road;** and at **Plante's Ferry Park** on **Upriver Drive**. Etienne LaLiberte (for whom **Liberty Lake** was named) carried mail over the **Mullan Trail**.

1864   The first bridge across the **Spokane River** was built near the Idaho State line by **Joe Herron** and **Timothy Lee**. There is a marker commemorating this event at the weigh station on I-90.

1867   December 19: The post office at **Spokane Bridge, Nez Perce County, Idaho,** became the post office at **Spokane Bridge, Washington Territory**. It preceded a Spokane post office by five years. It was a link in the mail route from **Walla Walla** to **Fort Colville** north and east and to **Fort Benton**. The first postmaster was **Timothy Lee**.

1871   **James Monaghan** took a contract to haul mail from **Spokane Bridge** to Colville (about 90 miles) at $1500 per year.

1880   **Louis Muzzy** and brother-in-law **Barton Mills** came to **Newman Lake**. In 1882 **Louis** had a contract to furnish meat for the **Northern Pacific Railroad** construction crew. He is said to have killed about 700 deer for that purpose. The crew used only the hind quarter.

1881   Tracks of the **Northern Pacific Railroad** were extended through the Valley from the west. There was transcontinental service by 1883. A railway bridge was built at what is now **Trent**. Mail was carried by rail, no longer by stage.

1883 From a crooked trail, the first county road (forerunner of the **Apple Way,** later **Sprague Avenue**) was constructed east to **Spokane Bridge.**

1884 **Hauser Station** on the **Northern Pacific Railroad** was established. Named in 1885 for **Samuel T. Hauser,** governor of Montana.

1888 **J. Wesley Rinear** opened a post office at **Darknell** and **Gibbs Road** near **Mica.**

1888 **Northern Pacific Railroad** established a siding designated **Otis Siding,** adjacent to the main line.

1889 The **Oregon Rail and Navigation Company** completed a railroad (later the **Union Pacific**) through **Chester** and named the area.

1890 The first wooden bridge was built across the **Spokane River** at **Trent** at a cost of $7000 by the San Francisco Bridge Company. The county owned the bridge at this time.

1895 Because apples lined what is now **Sprague Avenue** from **Dishman** to **Corbin Addition** the road became known as the **Apple Way** or **Appleway** (spelling differs).

1897 **Northern Pacific Railroad** moved its shops from **Sprague, Washington,** to the **Valley.**

1900 The **Inland Empire Railroad Company** (also known as the **Spokane and Inland Electric Railroad**) was organized to serve productive areas east and south of Spokane. One line moved east along **Trent** through **Orchard Avenue, Millwood, Pinecroft** and **Otis Orchards** to **Coeur d'Alene.** Another line angled to the southeast from the car barn near the **Trent Avenue Bridge** and came out on **Sprague** at the old **Interstate Fairgrounds,** now **Playfair.** It ran east (mostly on the north side of the **Apple Way** to **Veradale** and **Liberty Lake.** At **Flora Road** there was a turn-around. The **Liberty Lake** line ended at the lake park which the railroad owned. In the '30s, the **Great Northern** purchased much of the right-of-way.

1901 The first **Free Rural Mail Delivery** from Spokane was operational with routes to **White Bluff, Moran,** and **Paradise prairies** and **Saltese Lake.**

1902 **Seth Woodard** and his father gave a 60-foot right of way through their land to the NPRR. **Woodard Station** was built (located in today's **Millwood**).

1903 July 3: Railway Age magazine reported that Spokane Traction Company's recently chartered **Coeur d'Alene Railway** proposed to build a 33-mile line from Coeur d'Alene to Spokane passing through **Post Falls, State Line, Trent** and **Greenacres** in the rural **Spokane Valley.** It would be a combination steam and electric line, using 60-pound rails. Steam would be used to carry lumber and freight, electric for all other operations. The first trip was made October 21.

The first train was borrowed from **Washington Water Power Company,** operators of the Spokane city systems.

1905 **Interurban Inland Transit System** extended east to **Coeur d'Alene** and **Hayden Lake.**

1905 State Law: Autos could be driven eight miles per hour on city streets, twelve miles per hour on suburban streets and twenty-four miles per hour on county roads.

1906 **Northern Pacific Railroad** bought 118 acres of land just east of Spokane for its shops.

1907 Rural Free Delivery (RFD) mail service was established out of **Spokane Bridge.**

1908 What is now known as the **Argonne Road** led from **Dishman** to **Bowie Road.** It was first known as **Woodard Road** south of the river and **Foults Road** north of the river.

1908 First post office at **Otis Orchards** was in a portion of the general store owned by **Joe** and **Terry Grant** at the corner of **Kenney** and **Gilbert. Terry** became the first postmaster. The community officially was named **"Otis."**

1909 First steel bridge was built at **Millwood.** It cost $6576.

1909 A new station for the **Inland Empire Electric Railroad** established at **Greenacres.**

1909 **Chicago, Milwaukee, St. Paul and Pacific Railroad** built through the Valley.

1910 **Spokane County** had only one and a half miles of paved highway.

1911 **Spokane County** took over **Spokane Bridge** from **Mr. Cowley** and replaced the bridge with a steel bridge.

1912 The **NPRR** erected a roundhouse and car shops at **Parkwater** at the west end of **Millwood.** The Hillyard Townsite Company built **Parkwater** to house the railroad employees.

1916 May: The **Appleway** was paved with concrete from the city limits to the railway crossing at **Dishman.** It was continued four miles east the following year.

1918 A wooden subway was constructed under railway at **Dishman.** This destroyed the intersection of **Sands Road** and **Sprague** known as **Dishman Corners. Sands** was moved a block east and became known as **Dishman-Mica.**

1919 June: The **Appleway** was further continued to the intersection with **Liberty Lake Road.**

1919   April 6: Fare on city trolleys was increased from 5¢ to 6¢. In June 1921, the fare was 8¢.

1920   New sidewalk and frame post office built in **Opportunity** block.

1920   The road and bridge in **Millwood** officially was named **Argonne.**

1920   The **Appleway** was paved to the Idaho line. Wooden subway at **Dishman** replaced by concrete.

1921   The **Millwood Bridge** was rebuilt with a concrete substructure at a cost of $68,148.

1922   **Trent Road** was paved from the east city limits to a point 5 miles east, thence north to the **Argonne Bridge.**

First post office and store at East Farms, established 1914. In the photo: Pearl Strong, post mistress, appointed Nov. 1926, and daughter, Dorothy Strong (Shinn). East Farms mail was sent to Newman Lake after June 30, 1957, when this post office was discontinued. *Courtesy of Dorothy Shinn.*

Ox Teams Were Slow

[From "Homestead in the Valley" by Albert F. Chittenden, *Spokane Valley Herald*, April 29, 1954]

An empire was being built with little direction from the state.

Transportation was a major problem when my mother with five children immigrated from New York City during 1885. Country roads were practically non-existent. Excluding the Northern Pacific which a few years earlier had entered the region, transportation was exclusively powered by horses supplemented by a small number of mules and oxen.

Freighting lines with caravans of large wagons pulled by great teams, pioneered the roads of today. Their drivers competed with cowboys as idols of the youth, even of that day. The ranchers generally rode, but the farmer was dependent on his team, pony, and frequently on his two feet.

For the first two years we used horses on our farm, then for several years oxen. We used two oxen on our heavy Studebaker wagon, and one on our light two wheeled cart.

At first we used the regular yoke, but one day, being unable to find our horse, we tried out the gentlest ox on the cart. Of course, with only one ox, we were not able to use the yoke. So by necessity we used a horse collar, the bottom side up. This proved successful and thereafter we used regular harness, bridles and all, on the ox team.

Driving oxen long distances is never easy, especially when the oxen are young and wild. They are so slow that the element of time alone is tiring. The round trip to town and back of 30 full miles required at least 13 hours driving time, frequently more.

We boys were 12, 13, and 15 years of age when we started using oxen. First we had to break them from their range habits, then to the yoke, then to the harness. Also we had to gentle them to new experiences on a streak of dust that constituted the road over the open range. After all, if frightened, they could run faster than we could.

Both had minds of their own, or thought that they had, especially when they first contemplated their youthful new masters. However they gave up these delusions of grandeur when they finally realized that we could sprout three-inch clubs, bull whips, or sharp goads at will. We were young and yearned to excel even the best drivers of the day. Besides, even in the schools we were taught, and the practice was followed, not to "spare the rod and spoil the child." We were not cruel, but our tempers were short.

Our oxen were the result of one of the bad winters of those early days. Spring found the Valley littered with the bodies of horses and cattle that had starved during the extreme cold and snow. Among them lay all but one of our four horses and one of our cows.

My sister, in a letter to me, recalls those oxen. She writes:

"The next year mother bought a yoke of oxen. You boys broke them to use horse collars and bridles in their mouths and drove them with lines when selling our produce. You were the talk of the town. I often went with you as you insisted you wanted me for company.

"You boys gathered the vegetables, killed the chickens, washed, ate your supper and went to bed, for you had to be up at 3 a.m. to go the 15 miles to Spokane. And driving oxen, you went on their time and not on yours.

"Mother, Clara, and I sat up all night dressing the chickens, packing the eggs, molding the butter, and washing and cleaning the vegetables. You boys had already loaded the potatoes, which you had sacked in the field; and so we made our living, just mere children, and a wonderful mother.

"I remember, too, the time the ox team got frightened and ran away in Spokane. But you boys stopped them before any damage was done other than the broken harness, broken wagon tongue, and the spilled vegetables."

Mail Routes and the California Ranch

In the middle of the nineteenth century, mail carriers on horseback rode their routes from headquarters in Walla Walla into Montana as far north and east as Helena and the Bitter Root Valley with only Indian trails to guide them. To cross the Spokane River, Plante's Ferry in the Valley was used.

After the completion in 1862 of the Mullan Trail (which went through Spokane Bridge), the mail carriers immediately used that route, often stopping at "The Bridge" for supplies. The bridge itself afforded a much easier and speedier transit than the more clumsy ferry.

Soon Spokane Bridge became a regular way-station for the mail carriers (known as the Pony Express) and a post office was established at one of the stores at the Bridge. The mail address at the time was Spokane Bridge, Nez Perce County, Idaho Territory.

When the Washington-Idaho boundary was ultimately surveyed in 1867, it was discovered that the bridge actually was one-fourth mile within Washington Territory. The post office was transferred from Idaho to Washington and thereafter, mail for Spokane Bridge was addressed to Washington Territory. A route was to be established between Colville and Spokane Bridge.

Rosebush in his Story No. 5 of the "Valley of the Sun" continues the story of the mail routes as follows:

"The route between Colville and Spokane Bridge proved to be a hard one—a distance of ninety miles with no settlements for sixty of the ninety, making it necessary for the courier to carry food or forage for it.

"The postmaster at Colville was authorized to offer $1500 per year for a courier to carry the mail over that route. If no one would accept the contract, the post office at Spokane Bridge was to be cancelled. Although authorized in '67, the new courier route was not formerly established until 1871 when James Monaghan took the contract for four years.

"The route, from Walla Walla to Missoula via Spokane Bridge, (known as the north route) was the most direct to all the north and east country.

Directness was important, for the growing mining camps in Montana and Idaho caused additional mail service via the Bridge. The route covered a distance of 400 miles. There were 21 stations and 25 riders, each rider making from 40 to 70 miles per day with several relays. Small packages of express were carried in addition to the ordinary letter mail. Some of the envelopes were printed with the heading in black relief, 'Wells Fargo Express Co. Paid.'

"Wesley Wood of the Valley carried mail over this route for five years. Riders rested at his cabin to make a hasty meal of venison or bear meat and beans while saddle and pack were being transferred to the back of a fresh relay.

"The mail carriers of those days usually made good time but the freighters did not find it so easy. As a young man, Harry Dalton of Greenacres, pioneer of '84, freighted with a six or eight horse outfit from Spokane Falls to Fort Spokane at the mouth of the river, and to Fort Coeur d'Alene (name changed to Fort Sherman in 1891). He describes the roads as deep with ruts—muddy or dusty depending on the season, full of rocks, chuck holes, roots and snags. At night his bunk was made up under the wagon wherever the luck of the day left him. Mr. Dalton was of the old firm of Dalton Kenny, after whom Dalkena, Washington, was named.

"The mail route on the south side of the Spokane River was the shortest and easiest one. The problem was that the bridges there were make-shift and frequently washed out. From time long past there had been a broad Indian trail there touching the Indian camping ground at Spokane Bridge, where the Indians forded the river.

"Colonel Wright had followed that trail to some extent in 1858 to the 'Horse Slaughter Camp' and forded the river in the same place. This ford is almost opposite the present (1930s) home of John Murray, pioneer of '84.

"'Uncle' Dan Drumheller (a famous Spokane 'politician') used the same ford in 1864, crossing with his pack train; so there was plenty of knowledge of this shortcut and in low-water periods, it was much used.

"The trail was just as good as the Mullan Road. After Colfax was settled, the main route from Walla Walla to Spokane Bridge was no longer the Mullan Road, but went via Colfax, coming into the Spokane Valley by way of the California Ranch and Saltese. This route was known as the Old Kentuck Trail.

"The California Ranch was the oldest 'real ranch' and seems to have been in operation in the '60s. Very little information is available regarding its early history. The old accounts refer to it as being located between the Falls and Spokane Bridge. However, originally it probably covered a large part of the country between Saltese Lake and the present town of Mica which was included in it.

"Mr. W.E. Donaldson of Mica, a pioneer of '82, says the ranch now consists of 480 acres situated about one mile east of Mica and astride California Creek which took its name from the ranch.

"The ranch was originally settled by some 49ers from California whose history is lost. In 1876 Pete and Mack Mulewine (or Mullwine, Mulowine, or Mouline) bought the place. Two or three years later Mack died. Pete lived on the place for several years and then sold to J.E. Stoner. Later Stoner sold it to Kimball of Spokane who still owns it."

In 1954, J. Howard Stegner wrote in his "Echoes of Yesterday" that "Mrs. E.J. Finch, a small lady, has the post office, small store and locker plant at Spokane Bridge. She has been the postmaster since 1925. Her brother, William F. Galloway, carried mail from that office from 1907 to 1939.

"In 1945 I stopped at the home of Mr. Galloway, who lived on the site of the famous Horse Slaughter Field located about 1.4 miles west of Spokane Bridge," Stegner said. "Noticing the old mail wagon, I asked Galloway about it. He said that he had used it for several years before the gas wagon came into general use. He covered 25 miles a day behind a horse in the old wagon, six days a week along the east side of Liberty Lake, part of Otis Orchards and over toward Moab."

After a post office was officially established at Spokan Falls in 1872, the pony express route from Lewiston to the Falls came via Colfax, Major R.H. Wimpy's homestead, "Alph" on upper Hangman Creek, the California Ranch near Mica, and Spokane Bridge.

Catastrophe

["Echoes of Yesterday", J.Howard Stegner, *Spokane Valley Herald*, August 12, 1954]

It was 1903, the year of the land drawing on the Spokane, Coeur d'Alene and Flathead Indian reservations.

It was also the year of the Alaska Exposition at Seattle, which drew thousands of tourists. While there, they heard of the land drawings. Many decided to register for these.

Meanwhile I was as anxious as anyone to draw a small number on the Coeur d'Alene Reservation. Many quarter sections there had $10,000 worth of timber on them.

In the last week of July, I called Fred Stitz on the phone and asked him if he didn't want to go to Coeur d'Alene to register. Fred agreed to go. He was to come to our house about two o'clock the afternoon of the thirty-first. Then we planned to walk to Pinecroft Station and take the electric train to Coeur d'Alene.

I got all ready and waited for Fred. But he didn't show up.

That evening I hitched one of the old plug horses to the top buggy and drove down to the C.F. Young place. They had bought the old Hans Carsten place on what is now Argonne Road, just south of the Northern Pacific tracks. While I was there, Mr. Young came out of town with an evening paper. The headlines read: "Two Trains Loaded with Land Seekers Crash Head on at Lacross (now Gibbs); 15 Killed, 112 Injured; Accident Opposite the Stack Gibbs Lumber Mill and on a Straight Track."

Now I hope the good Lord will forgive me for all of the strong cuss words that I was thinking about Fred for not keeping that date. We would have been on that light train and it was literally demolished. I believe that every one in the smoker of that light train was either killed or injured.

The Gibbs Lumber Mill was immediately shut down and the crew came with axes, saws, crowbars and jacks. With these implements the victims were pried loose from the wreckage and laid at the side of the track.

Bodies were frightfully mangled. Physicians and nurses from Spokane and Coeur d'Alene were rushed to the scene. Many of the less injured were taken to the homes of relatives and friends in Coeur d'Alene.

A few days after this wreck, my sister Mary and I took the NP steam dinky to Coeur d'Alene and registered. I did draw a number, a real high number.

I didn't use my number as I was at Pullman and would have had to file before school was out the spring of 1910. But I did take up a homestead a few years later in the Colville country.

But if I had been on that disaster train that night of July 31, 1909, the land that I homesteaded might have been a dark, cold, narrow six feet by three.

Greenacres Railway Station. *Photo courtesy of Spokane Valley Museum archives.*

Valley Train Robbery

[From "Echoes of Yesterday" by J. Howard Stegner, *Spokane Valley Herald*, May 13,1954; June 24,1954]

In 1907, '08 and '09, there were several train holdups on the Northern Pacific system, including two attempts and two holdups at Trent and Irvin.

With train robberies as with many things, the third time is often the charm.

But the big hard-faced thug who shoved a gun into NP engineer Fred Whittlesey's face at Rathdrum, Idaho, on the night of April 29, 1909, wasn't charming. Whittlesey, who had been held up on two other occasions the year before had developed a dread of the Rathdrum stop. In the first two robbery attempts there had been much excitement and some shooting, but no one was hurt and little booty was taken. But this was the third time.

"As we were leaving Rathdrum about 10:25 p.m., I had my fireman get on the rear of the tank (as has been my custom since I was held up last summer), while I held my torch out the cab window on my side of the engine," Whittlesey said later. "Before the fireman could get back to the cab, and as I turned around, there stood a big red-haired fellow with a big gun, pointing it in my face."

The man who had come so suddenly out of the dark thrust the gun closer for emphasis.

"Hurry along and be quick about it," he snarled.

He was apparently the same thug who had held up the train the previous fall. And right behind him came his confederate. As the surprised fireman came down into the cab from off the tank, he too faced a gun whose muzzle looked as big as a rain barrel.

Spurred by the thought of a bullet smashing a forever dark tunnel through his brain, Whittlesey yanked upon the throttle. Rathdrum, but not the train crew's troubles, was quickly left behind.

About three miles out of Rathdrum, the red-haired desperado ordered Whittlesey to stop the train. Then the fireman was ordered to cut the train off at the mail car.

Whittlesey, the mail clerk and the fireman were ordered to stay with the disconnected rear section. With the train disconnected, the two gunmen hurried back to the engine. Their eyes, apparently sharpened by tension, noticed a hobo flattened out on the engine tank. He had evidently been there since leaving Sandpoint, but no one had noticed him before.

"You get off too, you blankety blank so and so," one of the robbers said. Five stabbing flames of emphasis from his gun caused the hitchhiker to fall off the tank so fast that the train crew watching thought he had been killed. But he came up to the disconnected passenger section a little later, a badly frightened youth of not more than nineteen or eighteen.

With one of the robbers at the throttle and the other shoveling coal into the firebox, the engine and mail car speeded toward Hauser Junction. The engine did not slow for signals at Hauser. Jones, the telegraph operator there, noted that it was an unusually short train, that the fireman appeared awkward with the coal shovel. In addition, there were no markers on the rear of the train.

He immediately surmised it was another holdup and wired the dispatcher in Spokane. Officials in Spokane and Rathdrum were at once notified and while the registered mail sacks in the mail car were being robbed between Trent and Yardley, posses were formed on either side of the bandits to overtake them.

The abandoned engine and mail car were found at University Road, the same place as the August 1908 holdup. But the birds of prey had flown.

Six registered mail sacks had been cut open. Six sticks of dynamite were lying on a nearby table. Postal inspectors estimated the plunder would run about $2500.

The youthful hitchhiker said that the two men who had committed the robbery came out of the Palace Hotel at Sandpoint.

Spokane and Inland Empire Railroad Company

It is said that history repeats itself. This is true of the recurring interest in Valley light-rail transit as a possible answer to growing traffic problems.

After a four-year debate on whether or not to build a commuter road known as the South Valley Arterial, commissioners approved the proposal by a 2-1 vote on September 6, 1994, adding the interesting possibility of future light-rail in the Valley. The old Milwaukee Railroad right-of-way, which runs parallel to and south of Sprague through much of the Valley, is the proposed route for the four-lane, limited access arterial between the Sprague-Interstate 90 interchange and University Road.

According to the official description of the limited arterial project by County Engineers, "the right-of-way would be about 140 feet wide. Although only four lanes of roadway would be built as part of the project, the county would reserve the remaining right-of-way to construct the other two lanes and *possibly light-rail transit at a future date.*" (Author's italics.)

Light-rail for the valley is not a new idea. In 1903 the Spokane and Inland Empire Railroad Co. built a line on the south side of the Valley. Service began in Spokane and ran through Union Park and Edgecliff to Park Road where it cut to the north side of Sprague and continued on through Dishman and Opportunity to the Liberty Lake Junction and Coeur d'Alene.

The railway was not intended to be located on the south side of the Valley. The original survey was close to the river on the north side of the Valley; but Mr. Benham, an early real estate salesman, interceded and offered the railway company a right-of-way along one of *his* platted streets. This resulted in the first line being built on the south side of the Valley. During its short life the line operated thirteen locomotives and sixty passenger cars and carried large assignments of freight. In Spokane the terminal was a yellow stucco building, conveniently located only one block from the Auditorium Theater and no more than three or four blocks from

stores and restaurants. There was also a terminal in Coeur d'Alene.

The first passenger train on the line was run in December 1903. At the time of that run, much necessary equipment had not arrived from the East. The company borrowed two old-fashioned open summer cars from the Washington Water Power Company and closed the sides with canvas. "It was a chilly ride," said Alfred Kennedy, who was a passenger on that memorable occasion, "but a jolly crowd. One man had a small bottle of Old Crow, just enough so those who wanted it could have a couple of nips (there being no prohibition in those days) and no one suffered from the cold. Regular trains were run with these borrowed cars up to a few days before Christmas 1903, when the new equipment finally arrived." ("Valley of the Sun," *Spokesman Review,* May 1932.)

A spur line, known as the "Flora Spur" also ran on the south side of the Valley, from Dishman to Flora Road. According to Tom Smith (*Spokane Valley Herald,* September 17, 1969), "The original buildings along the south side of Sprague were of wood frame construction. Some had high platforms for convenience in loading wagons. Most of them, however, were low to the ground with hitching rails along the wood sidewalks. Melting snows and heavy rains ran into the town from every direction. When the Flora Spur of the Spokane and Inland Empire Railroad was built in 1909-10 (from Argonne to Flora on the north side of Sprague), crews ditched (from 30 to 50 feet) and elevated the tracks.

"Later Sprague was graded and this left many of the old stores in more or less of a hole. The Opportunity station or waiting room [on the northeast corner of Pines and Sprague] stood partly on legs above the deep ditch and a small bridge crossed to town."

In 1909 the Spokane and Inland owned and operated the park at Liberty Lake. The train stopped at a junction about one-quarter mile north of the highway to Liberty Lake and was met by

Liberty Lake was the Coney Island of the Inland Empire early in the century. The Spokane and Inland Empire Railroad, owned and operated by the park in 1909, brought passengers to a junction north of the highway and what later became the Wayside Station. There they were met by a horse-drawn stage that brought them to the resort. Left: bath houses, Right: Dance Hall over the lake. *Courtesy of Helen Damascus whose husband was once part owner of the resort.*

Emmett Denison who lived at the junction. With his horse-drawn stage, he transported people to Liberty Lake for picnics and Sunday outings.

The story is told in *Memories of Liberty Lake* by Brereton and Foedish that "when the [railway] company owned the Park, they had a naturalist plant many trees and unusual varieties of flowers. They brought a spur railroad in from Liberty Lake Junction, and Roderick MacKenzie donated fifteen acres for a depot and right-of-way. When the spur was first built, the railroad brought in two-car trains which ran every hour. In 1911 they brought in three-car trains, and by 1913 there were five-car trains every half hour on Sundays, holidays and for large weekday picnics." (p. 23)

In 1909, Jay P. Graves, president of the Spokane and Inland Empire, in his third annual report, said: "We have built up at Liberty Lake, a first class summer resort. Being near the city of Spokane and maintaining a low fare—75 cents for the round trip—has made it attractive for pleasure seekers… and [also for residents of] Greenacres where a number of new irrigated products are under way. It will be necessary during the coming year to double track the road from Greenacres to Spokane. This will complete double tracking from Spokane to the Idaho line."

At that time the Road ran twelve or more through-trains each way daily, hauling passengers and freight. The *Electric Railway Journal* for October 10, 1908, reported: "The Spokane and Inland Empire interchanges freight with all steam roads entering Spokane under a joint tariff arrangement exactly similar to those drawn up between two steam roads. The cars of the electric road, however are never allowed to leave its own rails except in cases of emergency. All equipment for foreign shipments is furnished by the connecting steam roads."

The Spokane and Inland Empire Railway made money the first five years. In 1908 it posted a revenue of $1.2 million; but in 1909 when two special trains crowded with passengers headed for Coeur d'Alene to bid on Indian lands collided, killing fifteen and injuring seventy-five, the company could not withstand the damage claims and sold the line to the Great Northern. (See article, "Catastrophe.")

The Great Northern continued to operate the line until 1930, but carried larger and larger quantities of freight and fewer passengers.

Washington Water Power controlled the light-rail business in Spokane almost from its inception. Its most serious competitor was the Spokane Traction Company which merged with WWP in 1922. About 1912 WWP records show that the electric train business (which power-wise was very lucrative) was seriously injured by the advent of jitneys on the streets of Spokane. The final street car ran in Spokane August 31, 1936. Spokane Line bought the system in 1945.

On the north side of the Valley, residents used the Spokane International Railroad for transportation. It came down from Edmonton, Canada, to Spokane and made local stops along the way. In 1943 sparks from the Paper Mill fire burned the Millwood station.

Electric Car Line vs. Spring Wagon

[By Channon P. Price, March, 1970 (manuscript)]

The coming to the valley of the electric car line was a red letter day and was a big factor in developing the valley. They built a depot on the west side of Marguerite and south of their tracks with a waiting room for passengers, an office for the agent and a store room for baggage and express.

They built a similar building in Opportunity, north of Sprague and west of Pines. At other stops there were heated shelters for the comfort of passengers waiting for a car.

They furnished hourly service to and from Spokane. The first car left Spokane at six in the morning and then each hour until eleven at night. The fare from Dishman to Spokane was fifteen cents.

This car service was hailed with delight by the young people of high school age as it enabled them to live at home and attend high school in Spokane.

The electric car was certainly a big improvement over driving to Spokane in a one-horse spring wagon. The spring wagon was a light-constructed wagon with a bee or box about four feet wide and ten feet long mounted on a chassis over leaf springs. It had a built-in seat for the driver up front. Some were decked out with a large sun shade to protect the driver from the elements. They were serviceable but not a joy to ride in as there was more up and down than forward motion.

In those early days most of the produce of the valley was hauled to Spokane in a spring wagon. Many growers started at three in the morning in order to have their load on the early market when the store keepers bought their day's supplies.

They Sorted Mail on Moving Trains

[*Spokane Valley Today*, May, 1991]

It wasn't easy memorizing every post office in at least four states. It wasn't easy putting 49 cards per minute (representing pieces of mail) into slots (representing post offices) with 97% accuracy.

And yet that was the examination given at regular intervals during the '40s, '50s, and '60s to railroad mail clerks; and it is said that very few scores were lower than 99%.

For 113 years RPO (railway post office) clerks sorted and routed mail on moving trains in special cars called railroad post office cars. They were so efficient that mail leaving Spokane at 11:30 p.m. during those years was delivered in Seattle the next morning—and without the help of today's technology.

The RPO was a gigantic operation. In 1945, routes in the U.S. reached a high of 1500 with 30,000 RPO clerks manning more than 4000 cars. In and out of Spokane alone, there were 34 trains equipped with RPO cars. In addition to the main lines of the Great Northern (Williston-Seattle), the Northern Pacific (Miles City-Seattle), and the Milwaukee (Butte-Seattle), the following branch lines served Spokane: Wallace-Spok, Spok-Lewiston, Spok-Pendleton, Spok-Moscow, Northport-Spok, Spok-Coulee City, Eastport-Spok, Coeur d'Alene-Spok, Spok-Portland, Spok-Pasco-Portland, and Metaline Falls-Spok.

When airmail service arrived on the scene, the amount of mail sent by train declined. "By 1961," writes H.J.Quanbeck of the Valley in *Lest We Forget the Men of the Railway Mail Service*, "only 262 RPO routes remained. Ten years later only eight were operating in the U.S. On the last day of June, 1977, the last operating RPO made its last trip between New York and Washington.

"Service in the west ended earlier. The Northern Pacific pulled its last RPO out of Spokane August 17, 1967. Five years later in 1972 the last RPO on the Great Northern ran from Spokane to Seattle."

Early in the history of the country, mail was carried by horseback, stagecoach and steamboat. But the coming of the railroad in 1834 changed all that. By the mid-1850s the mails were carried over 120,000 miles of rails, but sorted and routed at inland-based post offices, frequently the local general store. Trains were often held up while the engineer waited for mail.

In 1862 the postmaster at St. Joseph, Missouri, tried out a method of sorting and distributing mail on a moving train between Hannibal and St. Joseph in an attempt to avoid schedule delays on departures west. It was so successful that an officially sponsored test between Chicago and Clinton, Iowa, in 1864 resulted later that year in the post office appointing a Deputy in Charge of the RPO and Railway Mails. Thus began the railway mail service and a new job classification called railway mail clerk.

The job required muscular and mental energy. The motion of the train made the work tiresome. Washouts, derailments, collisions, and the threat of robbery made the work at times hazardous and at other times exciting. Regardless, the mail had to be loaded, sorted, and exchanged at a high rate of speed to keep to schedule.

Each clerk was equipped with a .38 caliber pistol with which to guard valuable shipments such as silver from mines at Wallace, "shining new money" being shipped to banks along the route, and bags of nickels, dimes and quarters for the then legal slot machines in local clubs.

Bill Malone, a local man born in 1909, entered the RPO service at Spokane from Worley, Idaho, in 1937. In Quanbeck's book he tells of the day he was issued his gun. "I was admonished to handle the gun with extraordinary care and to have it put in the hotel safe. That evening, I approached the hotel desk and said something like this, 'Here, I would like to have you take care of this.' The man at the desk was horrified. His eyes bugged out from the sockets. He thought it was a hold-up."

Earl Flage, a local retired RPO, remembers when his train was 25 hours late "because of the Great Falls, Montana, flood when the train was rerouted to Helena."

Francis Nickell remembers six trains a day out of the Spokane Great Northern Depot that carried mail cars.

The old timers continue to reminisce—events that are history now—the head-on collision near Fortine, Missouri, during WWII in 1942; the 1931 mud slide near Libby, Montana; the canister fire extinguisher that fell from its hangar and broke open a box of bees; the train that rolled gently to a stop along the Snake River in the middle of nowhere because "we had no engine but there was one several hundred yards up the track;" and the "washout in Spencer Canyon that held us up for about six days. The Clerk in Charge and Baggage Man spent their time rabbit hunting and I used one hundred shot that week on ground squirrels."

"And, oh, yes, the funny little New Meadows and Weiser line with its steam engine and wooden cars. It started out with two passenger cars and the mail baggage car. Had to drop all but the baggage car at Cambridge. All the engine could pull."

"The most distinctive RPO," adds Bill Malone, "was the Grangeville-Lewiston run. It had numerous switchbacks, hairpin curves, tunnels, and high bridges on its way to the fertile Camas Prairie. It was equipped with oil lamps. If they were not lighted when the train went through a tunnel, there was total darkness."

Then came the sad time, August 17, 1967—the last train out of the Spokane NP Depot.

"Only time will tell," says Quanbeck in his conclusion, "whether discontinuance of the RPO service was a negative or positive choice. When the service was suspended in 1977, the cost of mailing a letter was eight cents. Now it is 29¢. The loss of the railroads—will it make our country more vulnerable during times of conflict? Even now as the nation grows, the air lanes are suffering from overcrowding. Will we have to replace the dismantled lines?"

Felts Field

[*Spokane Valley Today*, May, 1990]

The Air Age in the Spokane Valley began humbly in 1913 with the launching of a balloon in the West Valley district near the Spokane River. Today [1990] that area is known as Felts Field, one of the busiest general aviation airports in the Northwest with takeoffs and landings exceeding 86,000 in 1989.

The airfield attracts air cargo, corporate aircraft, air charters, private airplanes and flight schools. It also houses the FAA Flight Standards Office, and FAA Control Tower, and functions as prime reliever of capacity problems at Spokane International Airport.

And all without tax support. The operating funds come directly from airport revenues. Capital improvements, however, are 90% funded by the FAA from the Aviation Trust Fund sustained by taxes on flight tickets and fuel.

Felts is a municipal airport owned by the county and city. Since 1962, it has been operated by an airport board independent of the city and county. According to Dennis Locke, airport manager, the rental of the airport land (which is increasing) is regulated primarily by the FAA. Tenants own their own buildings.

Felts is older than Spokane International Airport. It is located in the industrialized area of Spokane's West Valley on 410 acres that lie mostly within city limits. A small portion at the east end is on unincorporated Valley property. The boundaries are the Spokane River on the north, Rutter on the south, Park on the east, and Waterworks on the west. Many Valley streets, such as Felts, Fancher, and Mamer, were named for aviators who pioneered Spokane's aviation industry at Felts Field.

History of Felts Field

After World War I, the city of Spokane agreed to help its ex-servicemen establish a National Guard flying unit in the area by leasing a site for an airfield. Land set aside for the Upriver Municipal Golf Course seemed ideal. It had an area 1000 feet by 1500 feet which was regarded then as big enough for any airplane. Late in 1919 it became the Parkwater Air Field.

In the spring of 1924 when the National Guard Bureau offered to field a National Guard Observation Squadron in Seattle, Tacoma, or Spokane— whichever city raised $10,000 first, Spokane responded by having the money promised before the train on which the government representative rode, left the city limits. By August, the 116th Observation Squadron, 41st Division Air Service, Washington National Guard, was based at the Parkwater Field (now Felts Field) under the command of a thirty-three year old Army veteran named John T. Fancher.

Fancher's first task was to supervise construction of hangars at the Parkwater Airport. Dynamic, ambitious and hard-working, Fancher manually helped build the first hangar in the spring of 1925. The Federal government provided materials and local funds bought concrete; but most of the labor was donated by squadron members.

When in March 1925, three crated airplanes arrived via Northern Pacific Railroad and no funds were provided to transport the planes to Parkwater, enlisted members of the squadron borrowed two heavy planks from a lumber yard and a crowbar from the Northern Pacific and headed for the railroad yard in a pickup. Using the planks as skids, they loaded the crates and hauled them to the airfield one by one. It wasn't long before three Curtis Jennys were sitting on the new flight line. There were no funds to buy oil. Three companies, hopeful of future squadron business, were induced to donate "samples."

By May 1925, Parkwater was the site of the first regular flying schedule out of Spokane. In July, the first full-time personnel were hired. Six men, referred to as caretakers, maintained the field earning $130 per month. In 1927, when only a portion of the money necessary to fund an administration building was received from the legislature, Major Fancher, who constantly pushed the unit forward, used his own money to complete the building.

Renaming Parkwater Airport

A young lieutenant named Buell Felts was a member of the 116th. He was also owner and publisher of the *Spokane Valley Herald.*

On May 29, 1927, Lieutenant Felts approached the Parkwater Airfield after a training flight. At an altitude of 150 feet, he dropped out of the sky and was killed instantly along with his civilian passenger.

His funeral service was held in the Opportunity Presbyterian Church. The *Valley Herald* reported it as follows: "...attended by throngs that exhausted the capacity of the building and spread out over the adjoining ground and public road. The Rev. A.B. Blades reviewed the widespread activities of the fallen leader in business, education, journalism, aviation and civic circles and the cleanliness and purity of his life."

In September, the Parkwater Airport was renamed Felts Field.

Air Races at Spokane

Major Fancher had a dream: to bring the National Air Races to Spokane. In the summer of 1927, he departed for New York in an 0-20, hoping to achieve his dream. As a result of his diplomatic skill, that autumn Spokane was awarded sponsorship of the races. They consisted of two cross-country races: the San Francisco-Spokane Derby and the New York-Spokane Derby. There were local races as well and contests of aerobatics and formation flying.

The races were a great success and for the first time a paying proposition with a surplus. A direct result of the races was an established northern route from Minneapolis to Spokane.

It later became the route used by Northwest Airlines. A second result was a surge of community pride in the squadron at Felts Field.

Fancher Beacon

Major Fancher was a primary motivator of civic pride. He was active in the Chamber of Commerce and the Republican Party. In 1926 he ran for U.S. Congress from the Fifth District, but could not unseat incumbent Sam B. Hill. In April 1926, he accepted an invitation to help dedicate the Wenatchee Airport. As part of the Apple Blossom Festival, the 116th provided a night aerial show. Fancher gave a dazzling demonstration in his illuminated ship tossing aerial bombs over the side. After the show, concerned that some of the unexploded bombs might be on the field, Fancher personally set out to retrieve them. As he reached for one, there was a blinding flash. He fell to the ground in a heap. His clothes had been blown off from waist up. The explosion shot away his left thumb hurling it into his left eye. His right hand was missing altogether. A metal button from his uniform had penetrated his liver. But his concern turned to the accident.

"I don't want the false idea to get out that this accident was of an aeronautical nature," he said on the operating table. "I want flying to go forward as rapidly and safely as possible."

He died on the operating table April 29, 1926, with his wife Evelyn at his side. In 1928 Fancher's Beacon, a rotating beacon on the hill north of Felts Field, was dedicated with a properly inscribed memorial stone at the base. Expressions of sympathy poured into the area from all over the country.

Continued Progress at Felts Field

Two years later Nick Mamer and Art Walker departed Spokane in the "Sun God," completing the first non-stop air-refueled transcontinental flight in both directions.

In 1930 an addition was constructed to the Administration Building for the 116th Photo Section. In 1932 there were additions to house a medical detachment (flight surgeon) and garage.

During the late 1930s, the Federal Government had a special assignment for the 116th out of Felts Field. The squadron was asked to take photos of the Columbia Basin in order to determine a site for the world's largest dam, known later as Grand Coulee Dam. The precision photos aided greatly in the planning and construction of the dam. At the completion of the concrete and steel span crossing the Columbia Gorge, the 116th made the dedication fly over the dam in 1938.

With the approach of World War II, the Guard moved from Felts Field. Varney Airlines (the forerunner of United Airlines) had begun serving Spokane in the '30s and established Felts as a nationally recognized airport.

Farming

"The first settlers took the land along the fringe of hills on both sides of the Valley, where there were springs, some timber, and the land in the draws was better. The Valley was covered with bunch grass and the settlers thought it only valuable for grazing purposes. Several of them went into the raising of beef cattle, but prices were too low and they had to quit. Then a few who had tried their luck along the river found, to the surprise of the hill farmers, that the land was productive and they raised amazing crops although for two years the crickets came in droves to vie for control of the harvest. In 1885 a big hail storm wiped out the crickets and they were no longer a trouble. Being in a new country the settlers had to learn the climate, the soil, the seasons and the market."

["Valley of the Sun," Story No. 7, *Spokesman-Review,* April 4, 1930

Aerial photo of H.J. Shinn Apple Packing Plant at Otis Orchards, Wellesley and Murray roads, in the early part of the century. Apples were trucked to Seattle and went by boat to Germany. Right: boarding house for workers. Foreground: Sweeny and Karas orchards. *Courtesy of Dorothy Shinn.*

Farming

CHRONOLOGICAL HISTORY

1875   Herman Linke and wife Henrietta preempted 320 acres of land on **Saltese Hill** and built a log cabin there. By 1900 they owned what the **Rev. Jonathon Edwards** described as "one of the largest and finest ranches in this country, containing twelve hundred acres in all." Wheat was Linke's main interest and he produced a strain known as **Linke wheat.**

1878   **Daniel Courchaine** purchased 320 acres of **Saltese** land from the **Indians.** He specialized in cattle.

1889   Several hundred head of cattle grazed on the thousand acres of bunch grass known as "no-man's land" east of **Dishman** near **Opportunity.** The land sold for $10 an acre. **Daschbauch** and **Martha Miller** had dairy farms there. The **Pine Creek Dairy** with its stone-walled milk house was on the east side of **University** between **Seventh** and **Eighth.**

1889   **Charles Stokes** operated a dairy at **Broadway** and **Park roads.**

1892   **Peter Morrison** acquired property in the **Saltese** from **Mr. Simms** and determined to drain the lake.

1894   First **Interstate Fair** was held.

1895   Because apple trees lined what is now **Sprague Avenue** from **Dishman** to **Corbin Addition,** the road became known as the **Apple Way.** (See article, "Apples!")

1900   Because of herd laws and the coming of irrigation, stock raising began to give way to farming in the **Valley.**

1901   The **Interstate Fair** was held on the **East Sprague** grounds for the first time with a paid attendance of 20,000. $10,000 in racing prizes were offered. It was decided to acquire permanent grounds there and erect a silo.

1904   **A.A. Kelly** and **A.M. Sommer** organized the **Spokane Valley Farmers Club.**

1904   Mr. Olmstead of Greenacres grew the first commercial crop of tomatoes and cantaloupes—$700 worth of tomatoes per acre. The farm was watered from Liberty Lake.

1905   Most of Greenacres was planted in orchards.

1907   Henry Van Marter, one of the first orchardists, settled at what is now Valleyway and University.

1907   Harry E. Nelson, one of the founders of the *Spokane Valley Herald,* came to the Valley and soon acquired the nick name, "Mr. Spokane Valley." His twenty-acre orchard was in back of Chester School and above Schaefer Mineral Springs. In 1914 he became associated with the Spokane Valley Growers Union.

1907   Fred Myers built a cannery in Greenacres.

1908   Krause Nursery located south of University City. It was owned by the Krause family until 1920.

1909   A carload of East Farms Wagner apples won first prize at the Chicago Land Show.

1910   Frank Walton bought 300 acres between Evergreen and Sullivan, north of Trent Road. There was considerable timber on the hills, so the word "wood" was added to Trent, hence Trentwood. Then with the increasing fruit business in the area, "orchards" was added and the name became Trentwood Orchards. The fruit business dwindled and "orchards" was omitted, leaving the present Trentwood.

1910   Valley Growers Union built a warehouse in Opportunity at Second and Union. Cost: $78,000. They also had a warehouse at Dalton Gardens near Hayden Lake.

1911   John Gillespie, one of the largest fruit and vegetable growers in the Valley, located in Veradale. As a teen-ager, his son Paul delivered cantaloupes and apples to the Davenport Hotel in a Model-T Ford over a gravel road into Spokane.

1911   Apples sold for $2.50 a box at Greenacres.

1911   Dilworth Dairy was on Twenty-Fourth in Opportunity.

1920s   The Stephen Doaks family owned the Valley View Dairy at Twelfth and University. It was later sold to Early Dawn.

1920s

    Otis Orchards Clubhouse hosted the **Spokane Valley Apple Show** during the middle of November. Apple displays were judged and orchard supplies exhibited. There were agricultural lectures and a grand harvest dance on Saturday night.

1921

    November: **Spokane Fruit Growers Hotel** closed.

Pioneer Farming

[From "Echoes of Yesterday" by J. Howard Stegner, *Spokane Valley Herald*, April 5, 1956]

Very little of the Valley could be plowed without clearing it of rocks. Then, it was said, the soil should be broken as deep as it was expected to be plowed, probably about 8 inches.

To get a good seed bed after breaking, stones should again be hauled off before and after harrowing. Before the days of the spring tooth harrow and the disc, most of the farmers went to a blacksmith shop and had long spikes made for a harrow or drag. This sod had to be thoroughly worked so as not to leave any air pockets. Now with the proper seed bed and with moisture enough to start it, you were pretty sure of a crop of most anything you planted.

Wheat and oats seeding in the early days was done by broadcasting. It wasn't everyone that could do an even job of broadcasting and I for one soon found it out. By the turn of the century, drills or seeders came into general use and you could rent the use of one for about 10 or 15 cents an acre. Starting out with new ground after the third or fourth year, you should summer fallow some of this land and give it a rest.

By plowing in the spring before it got too dry, and cultivating many times in the summer to keep down the weeds, it was ready for early fall seeding to wheat.

Most of the farmers raised some corn for their hogs and cattle. After cultivating it all summer, the corn was cut, shocked and then hauled off. This ground was then ready to sow to fall wheat without plowing again. Wheat, when allowed to ripen, was threshed. Some, when matured far enough to be in the milk, was cut for hay for livestock. Some oats were allowed to ripen and threshed but most of it was cut green for livestock. This was before they started to raise alfalfa in the Valley, before 1900.

Most of the farmers would stack the wheat and oats and a threshing machine would pull into the field spotting the separator between stacks. I do recall one incident where it paid off well that grain wasn't stacked.

This happened on the Stitz farm on the east side of the river just south of the Northern Pacific and west of Evergreen Street. This threshing machine came a few days early before the grain was stacked. So the machine was set in the middle of the field and all the farmers came with their teams and hayracks to haul the grain from the shock to the machine. After threshing a few bushels, the separator blew up with a terrific explosion. The straw stack caught fire, so did the separator.

Sam Esch, who owned the machine, always kept a long cable attached to the separator. Sam ran his engine forward enough to hook into the cable and pulled the separator away. This was a steel J.I. Case Separator so the loss was not great. No grain was lost as the farmers carried the sacks away before it got too hot.

With dry land farming, it took about 160 acres to support a family. Most everyone had their own small orchard, some good berry and currant bushes, also rhubarb plants and a vegetable garden.

For horses they generally had a team of Cayuses to go places in a hurry and about three heavier horses to do the farm work. Cows for milk, cream, butter and beef. Later when milk routes were started, most of the farmers kept 10 or 15 milk cows so as to have a cream check. They all had chickens that supplied eggs to trade for groceries and for home use as well as a chicken dinner now and then. Enough pigs were raised to supply their own pork. They did their own butchering and cured a lot of it for summer use, as there wasn't any refrigeration. Then there were thousands of acres of grazing land in the Valley in the really early days.

There was a large family of us so we ran a store and a farm with lots of stock. We kept on expanding until we had more than 700 acres, and at one time had as high as 68 head of milk cows, also lots of young stock. At one time we also had 100 head of hogs. We raised wheat, oats, alfalfa and corn and filled an 80 ton silo.

After bunch grass became a thing of the past and the pasture grass dried up in August, we would throw green corn over the fence to our milk cows so as to keep up the milk flow.

Little did I think when I was plowing that land with four horses making 26 miles a day that it would be selling at this date for $250 per front foot.

Apples

[*Spokane Valley Today,* October, 1987]

Today the apple is not the big-time Valley crop it once was. In the twenties it was pure gold. A horticultural census of 1922 shows 1,164,686 apple trees in the Valley and 2400 cars of apples shipped all over the United States and abroad and 12,000 Valley acres devoted to apples.

Early in the century most of the land between Dishman and Millwood and between Dishman and Opportunity was planted in apple trees. It is said that six miles of apple trees lined the highway from Dishman east into what was then Corbin, hence the old name *Appleway* for the highway we now call Sprague Avenue.

According to Paul Rhodes in his *History of Vera Water and Power,* the chief varieties grown were the Jonathon, Wagner, Rome Beauty, Yellow Newton, Winter Snow, Delicious, Red June, and Winter Banana.

Says Paul, "In the smaller operations, all work was done by the families — the pruning, spraying, thinning, cultivation, making and tending ditches and rills for irrigation, making apple boxes, picking, hauling and marketing. Some growers had packing sheds where sorting, grading, and packing took place. Several custom packing houses came into being and a great deal of work was done by the Farmers Union, a cooperative venture owned and operated by the growers themselves. Most of the completed product was shipped east by rail in box car lots.

"Occasionally the grower himself would accompany a shipment of apples to an eastern point for marketing. The railroad would provide an old coach to accommodate the growers on their trip east. More than one wife was "stowed away" in the coach to get a free trip east, hiding in the rest room when the conductor passed through.

"Freight rates in those days were rather discrim-

Spokane Valley Growers Union Apple Packing Warehouse at Union and Second. Luke Williams' dad painted the letters on the side of the building. Milwaukee Railroad track in background. *Courtesy of Robert Nelson.*

inatory and were the subject of much discussion and protest. It was actually cheaper to send cars of apples to Seattle and thence east of the Rocky Mountains than to ship directly. However this took longer and the growers were anxious to get the apples to market as soon as possible to get the best price for their product.

"The orchards made a very attractive picture, especially during apple blossom time. Early residents recall climbing up to a vantage point and overlooking a sea of apple blossoms accompanied by a delightful fragrance. When the petals fell, the wind piled them up like drifted snow."

At Garrison, Montana, a helper locomotive was added at the rear to help push the train over the continental divide.

Said George Pierce, superintendent in the '20s of the sprawling $78,000 Spokane Valley Growers packing plant on Union Road in Opportunity, "To a viewer on the surrounding hills, the Valley floor presents a lush carpet-like appearance, broken here and there by orchardists' homes and packing plants"

In Spokane apple shows in which Valley growers participated were held in the fall under the viaduct of the Milwaukee Railroad. A special feature of the show was the crowning of the Apple Queen. During the week apple packing contests were held with the participants wrapping each apple in individual papers used for packing in those days. The contestants were not allowed to moisten their fingers to pick up the papers. That would make the fruit unsanitary!

In the spring of 1920, realizing that many sightseers trekked to the Valley to see the spectacle of the apple in bloom, a group of Valley boosters proposed that the area sponsor annually its own Apple Festival. Old timers say the decision to have the festival was a contributing factor to the formation of the Valley Chamber of Commerce. The Valley needed a united organization to put on the pageant.

Once formed the Chamber not only assumed responsibility for future festivals, but also for the Fall Apple Show, horticultural schools, pruning and spraying demonstrations, and one year helped the growers secure enough railroad cars to handle a bumper crop. (See article, "Chamber of Commerce.")

The Segerstrom Ranch

In 1945 the *Valley Herald* reported that the H.N. Segerstrom Ranch at East Farms was the largest grower of Red Delicious apples in the state, with 15,000 trees and 200 acres devoted to that variety.

Betty Segerstrom, with her brother John, operated the enterprise after the death of their parents. As of 1985 she still resided on Wellesley in the Valley and talked to me about the orchard years.

"I was born in 1914," she said, "and grew up at East Farms on the old road to Coeur d'Alene. There was nothing there but orchards, a post office, and a boarding house for orchard workers.

"Father came to the area in 1912 from Rhinelander, Wisconsin, and became bookkeeper for the Colonial Fruit Company at East Farms, owned by Gary Brown. That first summer he lived in a tent along the Spokane International Railroad tracks.

"In Rhinelander he had become acquainted with Alice Hamilton, a school teacher. Shortly after he arrived at East Farms, she too arrived from Wisconsin and they were married.

"Father knew nothing about farming. He learned by doing, from the other orchardists, and from Gary Brown. By 1914 when Gary wished to sell out, Father had saved enough money to buy the 40-acre farm. For a time he used Gary's Martha Washington label, but shortly thereafter he adopted his own Chief Garry label.

"There were many small farms at East Farms. As the orchardists retired, Father bought their holdings. In 1941 he bought 100 acres plus the house and packing houses in Otis Orchards owned by H.J. Shinn.

"However, in those days, orcharding was a gamble and Father was a gambler. In fact, it was only his gambling in the stock market that saw us through some of the lean years in orcharding. There were always the vagaries of the weather and the danger of fire to contend with. And, of course, the Depression. During that time, there were springs when Father borrowed from the Reconstruction Finance Corporation and worried through the summer, hoping and praying for a good fall crop.

"Father added a cold storage building to the old East farms packing house which would house 80,000 boxes of apples.

"In 1946 the family moved into the refurbished Seaton home built along the Spokane River. It is still standing and is a point of interest.

"Shortly thereafter, in 1949, Father died. My brother John and I took over the operation of the business jointly until it was sold in 1969. At that time the Segerstrom Ranch at East Farms had 450 acres of apples under cultivation. It was the largest one-family operation in the Spokane Valley.

"Soon after Father died, a tornado tore the roof off the cold storage plant. The roof was replaced but about 1953 fire damaged the warehouse building and cold storage building. In 1955 the temperature reached 6 below zero and many trees were damaged. So you see, although we had many good years, the apple business is a very fragile one, and there were many heart aches," Betty said.

The Segerstrom business continued until 1969 although the golden years of the apple in the Spokane Valley were 1922, 1923, 1924. After that, the apple began to decline as a cash crop. Truck gardens were in the ascendancy and thousands of acres were being devoted to the famous Hearts of Gold cantaloupe and to berry raising. Even dairying began to surpass apples.

It was the unseasonal cold snap of 1955, according to Betty, that spelled doom for many orchardists.

Pine Creek Dairy

[From "Echoes of Yesterday," by J. Howard Stegner, *Spokane Valley Herald,* March 10, 1955]

At the age of 21, Will Arend of Cincinnati, Ohio, decided to heed Horace Greeley's advice and go west. His brother George had preceded him by one year and was living in the Foothills.

On March 19, 1889, Will landed in Spokane Falls with $10 in his pocket. He got a job that lasted for three days, then decided to make his way to Leonard Dill's place near Foothills north of the Valley. He had known Dill in Ohio.

Arriving at Foothills, he was reunited with his brother George. George had a white mule. The two brothers decided to make a trip to Spokane in relays, one riding the mule while the other walked.

Will got a job working in the basement of the Spokane Hotel. Then he became sick with "mountain fever." His doctor bill came to $13 and he was broke. So he caught a ride on a wagon going back to Foothills.

He got a job working for E.G. Marstens on Pleasant Prairie for two months. Then he hired out to August Tonnett for 3½ years. Next Will and George ran the farm on shares for one year raising tomatoes, potatoes, egg plants, etc. for the city market.

The two brothers then bought 80 acres near the John Harris farm for $600. This place had a cabin and five acres in cultivation. That first year they raised a ton of onions and five tons of carrots — which they sold for $5 a ton — and several tons of potatoes.

The next year the brothers divided the 80 acres, each taking 40. Two years later Will had a fine house and barn, 20 acres cleared, and a family orchard planted.

In 1897 Will married Elizabeth J. Dyer. They had one daughter who graduated from the Spokane University.

Will and his wife lived on the 40 acres for one year, then rented it out and made a trip back to Indiana where his folks were then living.

When they returned in about a year, they went to work for the Pine Creek Dairy located in the Valley just east of Argonne and south of Trent.

Before irrigation, cattle grazed much of the land. Pine Creek Dairy was located at Eighth and University. *Courtesy of Spokane Valley Museum.*

In 1899 Will and his brother George, with John Erickson and Will Sohns, formed a company and bought out the dairy from Hans Carstens and Jim Erickson for $6000. That is, they took a lease on the property and bought the cows and equipment.

They kept about 100 cows at this location besides buying milk from all over the Valley. My folks always had a small dairy with all the way from 10 to 40 head besides young stock. I can remember when the Pine Creek Dairy paid us 11¢ a gallon for milk delivered there. We had an agreement to buy all of their calves when three days old at $2.50 each.

After a while three of the partners bought out George Arend and took an eight year lease on 400 acres south of Sprague on what is now University, for pasture. They farmed all the way up to Dishman on the south side of Sprague. They milked 120 cows and had stable room for 160 head.

Additional hay was bought from out near Liberty Lake at $6 to $8 a ton in the field. At this time sugar beets were being raised near Waverly. The dairy bought beet pulp by the carload.

Four milkers were employed plus one man to take the milk to the cooler. Milkers were paid $1 a day and furnished a milker suit. A good milker was supposed to be able to milk 10 cows an hour. They had to feed the cows and clean the barn too, but could take it easy in the middle of the day. The Pine Creek Dairy was the first one to use the loafing shed and the milking parlor, according to Arend.

In 1910 the Pine Creek Dairy moved to Rock Creek six miles out of Cheney. Milk was hauled to Cheney where it was shipped to Spokane on the old electric railroad. In 1914 Arend retired but still retained his interest in the dairy. Later, from 1918 to 1924, he took charge of the Pine Creek Creamery in Spokane.

In 1929 the Carnation Company bought out the Pine Creek Dairy . The government acquired the dairy at Rock Creek for headquarters for the Turnbull Natural Wildlife Refuge.

Clyde Clark and the Wilson Pickle Company

[*Spokane Valley Today*, March, 1988]

"If you talk to many Valley people over fifty years of age, you will probably find someone who worked in the cucumber fields; and that person will probably be still complaining of a sore back," said Clyde Clark recently. "Picking was a back-breaking job and required many people to harvest They came from town and local areas — young and old, male and female, walking, in cars, by bus and bicycle."

Clyde should know. He started weeding the Wilson Pickle Company cucumber fields in Pasadena Park in the Spokane Valley when he was twelve years old. By the time he graduated from the old West Valley High School in 1930, he was in charge of the thirty-three acre field (with some help from his mother.)

Early Beginnings of the Wilson Pickle Company

W.J. Wilson, a pioneer, arrived in Spokane by stagecoach in the late 1800s. It is said that he owned five acres of property in the vicinity of Howard and Riverside (hub of present-day Spokane) which he sold for $1200. With Dan Drumheller he operated a meat packing plant for many years on Havermale Island specializing in cured meats — bacon and ham. When that partnership disbanded in 1906, W.J. opened a pickle factory on Havermale Island. He soon moved it to N. 612 Denver. There the business remained until Clyde Clark liquidated it in 1966. The building still stands and is used by Layrite, the present owner.

W.J. Wilson had three children, two sons and a daughter. The daughter was well known socially as Mrs. Desert, wife of the owner of the old Desert Hotel that peaked in popularity during World War II. A son, W.F. Wilson, eventually gained control of the Wilson pickle business and during World War II, took two partners who worked with him for several years. One of these was Clyde Clark. In 1955 Clyde inherited the entire business—both pickle factory and fields.

"I had eighteen months to dig up $40,000 in inheritance fees and taxes." Clyde said. "That wasn't easy."

Clyde Clark

Clyde was born on a wheat ranch between Reardon and Espanola. In 1918 the family moved to Herald Road in Pasadena Park. The little three-room house where his mother, father and four children lived is in use today.

"At that time this area was all orchards and farm land," Clyde said. "Now look how it has developed. Houses everywhere. I went to school in the old Pasadena School on Argonne Road, now a private residence. It never closed because of weather even though most of us walked to school. I had one and a half miles to go. There were four grades in one room. Later I went to a big school, Millwood Grade School—four rooms, two up and two down.

Clyde's parents, Minnie and Ed Clark had a ten-acre truck farm. Clyde helped them build their wooden barn which was later used to house seven head of milk cows when Ed went into the wholesale dairy business.

Sometime about 1920, to control the quality of the cucs, the Wilson Pickle Company acquired the 26-acre field next to the Clark's. Cucumber farming then was done by horses and, according to Clyde, meant long hours of work in the fields and tending horses.

"From 1930 until 1950 when Mother died, she bossed the pickling crews," said Clyde. "Often there were 40 people in the fields. After Mother died, my wife Dorothy (Burger) took over.

"The Wilson Pickle Company paid a few more cents per hour than the other three major pickle makers, so we never had trouble getting pickers. We never paid less than 25¢ and Mother let the pickers rest for fifteen minutes at the end of each row. It paid off. By 1946 the 33 acres of cucumbers were going into 2500 barrels of pickles at the Wilson Pickle Factory in Spokane. The pickles were shipped to Washington, Idaho, Montana, and Oregon, carrying the Spokane label far and near."

In the early years the pickles were sold almost exclusively to local grocery stores. In the '50s the company began to cater to institutional trade—hamburger stands, schools, hospitals, hotels. Finally almost all the trade was of that type.

It was lack of irrigation water that brought about the sale of the company in 1965.

Clyde decided to sell rather than move to new acreage when Pasadena Irrigation District decided not to go along with the new Bureau of Reclamation sprinkling system for that area.

"One year in the mid-20s," Clyde reminisced, "the Wilson Pickle Company leased a 100-acre field north of the road that leads off Pines to the Walk-in-the-Wild Zoo. Many of those pickers rode to the fields from Spokane in a 1918 Republic two-ton truck with hard rubber tires. It took two teams and two cultivators to farm the field. It was watered by the old gravity-irrigation system in District 10.

"There was lots of hard work in those cucumber fields. During the Depression I grew one crop gratis to keep the factory going. W.F. Wilson never forgot that."

After retirement, Clyde became custodian of the Millwood Presbyterian Church from 1967-1981. "Best job I ever had," he said. "Yes, I still make pickles for my own use. With the same secret blend of spices."

Quarries, Mills, Business

"The coming of these two industries (Cement Plant and Paper Mill) has been of untold value to the Valley, in that they furnish employment to so many men, especially the paper mill, which has run almost without interruption since it started over 20 years ago. The first unit of the mill was a very small affair, fitted up with some old second-hand machinery shipped in from Montana. Now they are housed in a magnificent building and equipped with the most modern up-to-date machinery."

[Seth Woodard, " Valley of the Sun," Story No. 18, *Spokesman-Review*, May 13, 1932]

Installing a new sign at the Otis Mercantile Company. Early 1900s. *Photo courtesy Valley Museum Archives.*

Quarries, Mills, Business

CHRONOLOGICAL HISTORY

1880   The first sawmill at **Newman Lake,** operated by **Davis** and **Pierce,** supplied enormous amounts of timber to the **NPRR.**

1880   **J. Wesley Rinear** opened a store at **Darknell** and **Gibbs Road** to serve workers from the **Mica Brickworks.**

1883   **Louis Lee House** was built at **Spokane Bridge** to accommodate miners on their way to the mines of the Coeur d'Alenes. Later it became the **Morton Hotel** run by **J.F. Morton.**

1884   Northern **Coeur d'Alene** area became one of the richest silver-lead mining regions in the world. Traffic through the Valley to the mines increased tremendously.

1887   **Cowley** sold his general store at **Spokane Bridge** to **R.L. Rotchford.**

1888   **Noble C. Hair Lumber Mill** at **Chester** gave impetus to the start of the town. The large plant there kept 30 teams busy hauling away the output.

1889   Spokane suffered great fire losses. **A.T. Dishman** traded his half interest in a Spokane livery stable for a work team and wagon, bought land south of what is now **Dishman,** and began hauling granite from the cliffs to Spokane for reconstruction of the burned town. Later Gonzaga University, the Great Northern Depot, and Lewis and Clark High School were among buildings built by Dishman granite. As many as fifteen teams at one time hauled granite to Spokane.

1889   **Washington Water Power Company** formed.

1890   **John A. Narup** built a blacksmith and wagon shop at **Trent (Irvin).**

1890   The first general store opened about where **Edgecliff Road** joins **Sprague Avenue** (according to **Seth Woodard**).

1891   **J.A. Stegner** purchased land in **Trent (Irvin)** and started the only store between **Spokane Falls** and **Spokane Bridge.** A year later a post office was established in the store. The store closed in 1907 when the family went into real estate.

1892

The four-story **Spokane Distillery** was built by **Henry Theirman** on **Cement Street.** Later the property was sold to the cement plant. **Theirman** had three stores, two stills and a 30 x 50 warehouse. He used 250 bushels of Valley wheat a day.

1893

A major Depression.

1893

Charles P. Oudin and **Martin L. Bergman** organized **Oudin and Bergman Fire Clay Manufacturing Company** on opposite side of Highway 27 from where **Mica Brick Works** is today. It was dissolved in 1910. (See article, "Brick-works at Mica.")

1893

Plots in the **Saltese Cemetery,** one of Spokane's oldest, sold for $5. An **Indian** burial ground on a small knoll near **Thirty-Second** in **Greenacres** was donated to the **Saltese Cemetery.**

1893

Will W. Swartz purchased the general merchandise business at **Mica.**

1895

A.T. Dishman erected a two-story building, 26 x 40 just west and south of the subway on **East Sprague** at what is now **Dishman. W.B. Dishman** opened a general store in the building. He sold general merchandise to travelers from and to Spokane and Coeur d'Alene and to residents of the **Saltese** and **Opportunity-Dishman** area. (See article, "Dishman and the Dishman Brothers.") Within two years, a saloon and blacksmith shop appeared nearby.

1900

Charles Traeger built a roadhouse-saloon and dancing pavilion out over **Liberty Lake.** It became known as **Zephyr Lodge.**

1901

June 10: **O'Brien Store** opened at **Moab. George Wendler** made the first purchase — a sack of flour.

1902

There was a meat market and post office at **Millwood.**

1902

Harry Adams opened a store at **Greenacres.**

1905

A.T. Dishman began making brick and lime at **Bayview, Idaho.**

1905

E.L. Allen of **Vera** and **Gus Janosky** of **Opportunity** operated a store near the southwest corner of **Sprague** and **Pines** in **Opportunity.** A lumber yard was near the northwest corner and a blacksmith shop was not far from the **Allen-Janosky Store.**

1906

July: Suburban telephone lines solicited by **Woodard** were extended to the Valley by **Pacific Telephone,** later the **Home Telephone Company.** By 1909 there was a Walnut and an Orchard Exchange. One office was in the old **Felton Building** and the other in the second house north on **Pines.**

1906

The first **Otis** general store was built for **John A. Halloran** and wife **Annie** on **Kenney Road** about 200 feet south of **Trent.** They had the first telephone in the area. The store was later owned by **Joe** and **Terry Grant.**

1907 Located at **Newman Lake** were **O'Brien's Store, Fox Butcher Shop,** 3 saloons, large cook shack for the sawmill, four hotels including **Day's Hotel, Taylor Hotel, Gillette Park,** and the **Newman Lake Hotel** operated by **Fred Struntz.** The sawmill was torn down in 1923.

1907 **W.B. Dishman** built a lumber mill and box factory with **Mr. McClintock** on property later owned (1931) by **Brownson Motor Company.** (See article, "Dishman and the Dishman Brothers.")

1908 **Grant Brothers General Merchandise Store** at **Kenney** and **Gilbert roads.**

1909 **Perry Myers,** an employee of **The Dishman Trading Company** and his father-in-law, **Eli Farr,** purchased the **General Store** at **Sprague** and **Pines** from **Allen** and **Janosky.** His warehouse was diagonally across the street. (See article, "A Turn-of- the-Century Big Businessman.")

1910 **H.E. Hand** operated a store on **Trent** just west of **Cement Street** at intersection of **Pines Road** until 1924 when he remodeled the building into apartment houses. For a time it housed the **Trent Post Office.**

The H.E. Hand General Merchandise Store near the corner of what is now Trent and Pines. It was built in the early 1900s and purchased by Mr. Hand in 1910. It was remodeled into apartments in 1924 and torn down in the early 1960s. *Photo courtesy of Spokane Valley Museum archives.*

1910   **Greenacres** had 3 stores, a lumber mill and cannery.

1910   Brickyards and potteries were springing up at **Dishman, Chester, Mica, Freeman, Valleyford, Rockford** after clay was discovered in the 1880s by workmen building the **Northern Pacific.**

1911   **Martin L. Bergman** was manufacturing clay tile used for sewer and water systems at **Chester.** There was a clay pit in the vicinity of **Thirty-Second** and the Highway.

1911   **Inland Empire Paper Company** located at **Millwood.**

1911   **Oscar Reinemer** owned the **Dishman General Store.**

1912   **Trent** changed to **Irvin,** named for the principal stockholder of the **International Portland Cement Company** being built in the area.

1912   **Velox** was named by **Arthur S. Glendenning** for his father's prize race horse, Harry Velox.

1912   **Halloran** built a larger store, the **Otis Mercantile,** at the corner of **Trent** and **Pringle.** Destroyed by fire in 1921.

1914   **R.M. Schaeffer,** cigar maker, operated a cigar factory just south of **Vera Power and Water** until 1922.

1916   **Channon Price** started **Price Lumber and Box** in **Dishman.**

1917   A garage and service station was located at **Trent** and **Pines Road** and operated by **George Pringle.** He began a business attached to living quarters a few years earlier at the corner of **Trent** and **Pringle.** He built it by hand using a team of horses to put up the roof trusses. It was a Ford dealership. He sold Model Ts and Red Crown Gas.

1917   **O.D.** and **E.C. Reinemer** operated **Appleway Mercantile Company** on the corner of **Appleway (Sprague)** and **Argonne.**

1920   **Greenacres** had grown to include a post office, school, two churches, electric, telephone, and water.

1920   **A.H. Byram** and **E.D. Sampson** bought **Millwood Mercantile** from **W.E. Hinklie.**

1920
Channon Price and **J.F. Brod** built a brick building on the north side of the **Appleway** and rented it to the **Lynn Tyners** for a grocery store and post office. **Nellie Tyner** became the first postmaster in **Dishman.**

1921
Brief proposal to drill for oil in **South Veradale.**

A Turn-of-the-Century Big Businessman

[*Spokane Valley Today*, November, 1990]

Stand on a corner of busy Sprague and Pines and try to imagine two dusty wagon trails intercepting there. Near the southwest corner is a wooden building proudly displaying a sign that reads GENERAL STORE. The store is the forerunner of today's one-stop mall. There is nothing farmers of the area need that cannot be purchased there. The proprietor W.P. (Perry) Myers stocks meat, groceries, shoes, clothing, hardware, and operates a gas pump that stands in front of the store. Perry and his father, Eli Farr, purchased the business in 1909 from the first proprietors, Allen and Janosky.

The Myers' warehouse, a big barnish-looking building, is located diagonally across the street on the northeast corner of Sprague and Pines. On the northwest corner is the depot and restaurant for the Interurban Railroad that runs parallel to and just north of Sprague. On the southeast corner is the Washington Water Power substation.

The vehicles that approach the intersection spasmodically are mostly horse drawn wagons and shays and Model T Fords.

There is much foot traffic in the area. This is the center of the Opportunity Business District and the center of activity for the big businessman of his day, Perry Myers.

Perry lived near his business in a large white house at Sprague and First. The site is a parking lot once used by what was the Valley Clinic.

The Myers house was grand with an upstairs and downstairs porch. It was the gathering place for the businessmen of Opportunity. Behind the house was a chicken house and run that would seem like Grand Hotel to twentieth century assembly-line chickens. It was lighted and ventilated with floor-to-ceiling windows. There was even a concrete floor (although that luxury proved unhealthy for the brood too cold in winter). Mae, Perry's wife, could be seen during any day gathering eggs and working in the garden and yard.

Perry was easily recognized by his limp and cane. As a young man, while working at the W.B. Dishman General Store, a team he was driving ran away and the ensuing accident dislocated his hip. Perry was troubled with it for the rest of his life.

He participated in community affairs, especially the Odd Fellows Lodge and the school board. At the time, the only schools in the district were the Opportunity Grade School on the southeast corner of Sprague and Bowdish and the Central Valley High School at the bend of the Appleway.

The Odd Fellows met in the Town Hall, just a few doors from Myers' store. Dedicated in March, 1911, the Town Hall remains an Opportunity landmark today.

It is said that between customers, Perry hid out in the basement of his store memorizing the Odd Fellows ritual. He was proud of his Odd Fellows membership and never missed a meeting. When he retired, his brothers honored him by naming him caretaker of the lodge for the rest of his life.

Business was brisk at the General Store and soon Perry felt a need to enlarge. In 1928 he tore down the original building and built on the same corner one of the most modern stores of the time. It was of double-faced brick with a glass-enclosed office for the owner. Many Valley residents remember it later as Kortte's IGA. Ray Kortte bought the store in 1944 when Myers retired.

Each Christmas Perry thanked his customers for their patronage by handing out free candy and a calendar advertising the store. Vi McDonald, Perry's niece and a Valley resident, keeps one of the calendars among her souvenirs. Irene Fowler, Perry's daughter, still resides in the Valley. Perry's son, Warren, lives in Phoenix, AZ.

Dishman and the Dishman Brothers

In 1953, A.T. (Addison) Dishman celebrated his 88th birthday and 67 years of Valley residency. The Tuesday before his birthday, a reporter for the *Valley Herald* found him listening to the inauguration of President Eisenhower.

"I was born in Virginia," he told the reporter, "but I never got to Washington, D.C., to watch an inauguration."

It was a day of reminiscing for the man known as "The Daddy" or "Father of Dishman." His health was still good. He went out for a short drive, pointing out where a new section of Dishman was about to receive its final plat from the county commissioners. The plat included plans to bring the Dishman-Mica Road across the railroad tracks on a grade-crossing a short distance south of the depot to relieve the bottleneck in Dishman west of the viaduct.

Mention of the viaduct (or subway) brought to Dishmnan's mind how much disfavor there was toward it in 1918 when it was being constructed. Many people feared it would mean the end of Dishman business.

Passing the quarry of the Empire Granite Company, A.T. told about "blowing the hill off" from Minnehaha Park to the present quarry to get building stone to rebuild Spokane after the big fire of 1889. At the time of the fire, he had a half interest in a livery stable in Spokane. He traded that for work teams and wagons and hauled granite to Spokane from the cliffs of some land he bought south of Dishman. The route was along a windy road that corresponded to today's Sprague Avenue.

"I had as many as 25 teams working at one time," A.T. said. "Of course men worked for 25¢ an hour and if a team made three or four dollars a day, that was good money."

According to Frank Twohy in "The Valley of the Sun," Story No. 15 (*Spokesman-Review*, April 22, 1932) "when A.T. started his operations, the Valley was all bunch grass and sunflowers with a dusty trail leading to Spokane. There were only three or four farms between Dishman and Spokane; and between Dishman and Spokane Bridge, only six or seven. The road between Dishman and Spokane Bridge corresponded with the old Mullan Trail.

"Two miles east of Dishman, near Opportunity, were the Daschbaugh and Martha Miller homesteads. These contained the largest dairy farms in the Spokane country, having several hundred head of dairy cattle grazing on their thousand acres of bunch grass. There were about half a dozen farms in the Saltese District, which could be seen far across the flat prairie by their windmills or pop-gun pumps. There were two bands of wild horses in the Valley and in the spring large numbers of geese came to feed among the tules which surrounded the numerous small lakes in the area."

The town took the Dishman name when A.T. built his first building in 1895—a store for his brother W.B. (Wilton) Dishman. Wilton was a surveyor for the railroad whose work brought him to Sandpoint and Rathdrum. While there, he visited Spokane, decided it had potential and moved his family to the Valley. At first they camped in a tent at Sprague and Mullan where the Dishman Trading Post was later established. In 1903 the Wilton Dishmans built a landmark home at N. 315 Willow Road. Their fourth child was born while they lived there and was purported to be the first white child born in the area. Their 1908 Oldsmobile was also a first—the first automobile in the Valley.

The store A.T. built for Wilton was a general merchandise store, a two-story structure 26 x 40 feet just west of the subway, facing what was then called East Sprague Avenue. The name was changed to the Appleway when, after irrigation, apple trees lined the road for six miles.

By 1897 a saloon and blacksmith shop were built near the store. In 1905 A.T. operated a gravel pit in Dishman from which gravel, local cement was made; and by 1907 W.B. had invested in and built a lumber yard and box factory with Mr. McClintock.

The rest of the Dishman story I shall tell as it was told to Frank Twohy for "The Valley of the Sun," Story No. 15:

"In 1909 they sold the box factory to Pattison and Severne, who in turn sold to J.F. Brod and Channon Price in 1916. The factory was torn down in 1931 to make room for the expansion of the Brownson Motor Company.

"Considerable gains in property values along with a large increase in population came to Dishman in 1909 when the electric line to Vera and Flora was constructed. These two latter names were given to stations on the railway, Flora being the junction point with the main line from Spokane to Coeur d'Alene. These stations were named after Vera, the daughter of D.K. McDonald, and Flora, the sister of Orla C. Bacon.

"The Coeur d'Alene and Spokane Railway Company bought part of the right-of-way for this line from Mr. Hutchinson and this enterprising gentlemen managed to write into the contract a proviso that the town of Dishman should have its name changed to Hutchinson. This aroused the ire of Mr. Dishman to such an extent that he entered into an agreement with certain of his nephews that he would give them $5 for every time they would tear down the Hutchinson sign from the railroad station and substitute a Dishman sign for it. A state of war prevailed for a time, but in the end, Mr. Dishman's supply of five dollar bills and his nephew's supply of energy overcame all obstacles and so the town still rejoices in the name of its founder.

"In place of Mr. Dishman's original one store, there are now [1930] 20 business establishments in Dishman. Modern, up-to-date brick buildings have in many cases replaced the smaller frame buildings in which business started. These as well as a number of stands which deal exclusively in the sale of Spokane Valley fruits, vegetables, poultry and other local products. Thousands of people from Spokane go to the Valley for their table supplies and Dishman is probably the busiest spot of all during the growing season.

"The Dishman brothers did everything they could to promote the town of Dishman. They are said to have financed many local businesses, and A.T. built many more buildings—the Boyd-Conlee Building, lodge hall, ice plant, gravel plant and Dishman Arena which had a capacity of five thousand. Many of Spokane's major boxing and wrestling bouts were held there."

One of A.T.'s proudest achievements was the little neighborhood theater he built in 1930 and the lines of people who waited for the box office of the family theater to open. It was called the Dishman Theater and when A.T. sold it, the new owner signed an agreement to keep the Dishman name associated with it. A.T. didn't dream that the type of entertainment shown there would change!

In 1910 a four-room school building was erected in Dishman and Dishman was taken into the Orchard Park school district. The school took children through the first five grades after which they transferred to the school in Millwood.

In a story in *Spokane Valley Today* in 1985, Lana Weber quotes Jack Dishman, grandson of W.B. as follows:

"Both men were proud of the family's efforts to help create the town of Dishman. While similar in business attitudes, the men were very different in other ways. Wilton is remembered as gentle and easy going, often tipping his hat and bowing in southern custom while Addison had a somewhat gruff exterior.

"Jack remembers, 'Uncle Add had a big heart. Although he didn't take notes when he loaned money, even so he never got cheated.

"'There was one exception to the no-note policy. A man once spoke with uncle concerning a loan when the men had a chance meeting in the Safeway which was located next to the Dishman theater. Uncle agreed to lend the man money and gave it to him on the spot. The man was uncomfortable not signing a note of some kind, so he tore off the top of a Post Toasties box and wrote out an IOU right there in the store. The man eventually repaid the loan, but Uncle Add got such a kick out of the boxtop IOU that he kept it for years.'"

There is a story pioneers used to tell to their children:

In early pioneer days of Spokane Valley a trip to Spokane by team was an undertaking. The long trip was of necessity broken for watering the horses, and the vicinity of Dishman the logical stopping place.

There were two trading stores opposite each other in Dishman. The owner of the store on the north side of the road built a watering trough and put up a sign stating that its use was for the horses of customers only.

On the south side of the road the owner of the other trading store also built a watering trough, but his sign read, "Free Watering Trough."

The name of the north side owner has long since been forgotten. The name of the south side owner was Dishman, known by all.

Moral: the name of the man who gives service to his community is the one that is remembered.

Brickworks at Mica

[*Spokane Valley Today*, March, 1988]

The town of Mica came into existence because of the nearby brickworks; and today, it is the same brickworks that keeps Mica alive.

In the late nineteenth century it was widely believed that the Spokane area could not manufacture a satisfactory brick product. By the turn of the century, brick manufacture was key to the economic and architectural development of the region. The Spokane fire of 1889 and the fire that burned all wooden buildings in the Opportunity block soon after, taught the practicality of building with brick.

Since that time, for the past one hundred years, the Mica brickworks, about fifteen miles south of the Valley on highway 27, has been a dependable source of brick products not only locally, but all over the Pacific Northwest.

In the late 1880s rich clay deposits were discovered in the area by workmen building the Northern Pacific Railroad. By 1910 brickyards and potteries were springing up at Freeman, Valleyford, Rockford, Dishman, Chester, and Mica.

Most were small temporary operations that produced inexpensive, common brick in seasonal, temporary kilns. That brick was imprecisely made and was used primarily as back-up brick. No one believed that the area could produce satisfactory paving brick or fire brick. Except Charles P. Oudin.

In 1893, hoping to produce fire brick, terra cotta, sewer and chimney pipes and brick paving blocks, he and Martin L. Bergman organized the Oudin and Bergman Fire and Clay Manufacturing Company.

The company was located on the western side of Highway 27 a little north of the present location. It lasted only until 1907, when, according to local stories, the two partners had a falling out. In 1910 Bergman moved to Chester and started another pottery plant there.

In the meantime, Oudin and three other men, Lucien Oudin, James Kilbreth, and Frank Watson, started the American Firebrick Company and located their plant just east of the original brick-

yard. The year was 1902.

Oudin was determined to make the operation efficient and highly productive. It is said that he visited structures in Greece and Rome, and even the pyramids of Egypt, to see how they were put together. He studied and experimented and bought machinery of the latest design. His kilns were permanent structures.

With the turn-of-the-century blossoming of Spokane and the Valley, Oudin's plant prospered.

A *Spokesman-Review* report of April 1, 1917, indicated that interlocking brick from the Mica plant had been ordered for the construction of the Chronicle building, the Symonds building, St. Ignatius Hospital at Colfax, a grocery warehouse at Witherow, Washington, hospital buildings at Fort Benton and Deer Lodge, Montana, for the Bunker Hill and Sullivan mines for smelters at Kellogg, and for the Great Northern Railroad fire box linings of more than 1800 oil-burning locomotives.

And so, although he had been told many times that brick could not be manufactured in the area, Oudin's operation gradually gained credibility. It received a firm vote of confidence that had far reaching effects when then-Spokane city engineer Macartney approved the purchase of Mica brick for use on West Broadway and Hamilton streets.

By 1903 Spokane newspapers predicted that the county brick industry would rival that of Akron, Ohio.

A labor force became necessary and was recruited from nearby farms. Seeing the growth, one of the earliest homesteaders in the area, Max Mulouine, platted a portion of his land near the brickyard for the township of Mica. The store on Belmont Road was built in 1906 and still remains. It has been remodeled in recent years and is now a modern store-cafe.

Soon the post office was moved from a store at Darknell and Gibbs Road to the new community, nearer the brickworks.

Anxious to attract unsettled and single men into its work force, the company built a "hotel" for male workers a few doors east of the store. That hotel was a two story wooden building which lasted only a few years. A second hotel, built of Dennison interlocking blocks made at the plant, was erected in 1929 and still stands next to the cafe.

A short time before the stock market crash of 1929, when Oudin decided to retire, Gladding McBean of California bought the American Firebrick Company. During the Depression there was a decreased demand for brick, but Gladding McBean held on. By the mid-1930s, production began to increase and in the 40s, World War II brought a new demand for products fired in the Mica kilns.

Today Interpace Corporation continues to operate the brick plant. Many of the original structures remain on the site including kilns, stacks, burner shed, test kiln and a brick horse barn built in 1911. The original brick plant was replaced in 1957 by the present plant. The main office building, facing Highway 27, was built in 1955. The plant superintendent's home, built in 1927, is located on the hill east of the brick plant.

Modern technology has been introduced to make faster and more efficient the process of brick making, but the fundamentals conceived by Charles Oudin at the turn of the century remain unchanged.

"The brick kilns at Mica," stated a report made in 1980 when the brickyard was nominated for the historic register, "provide a rare link to our industrial and technological heritage, not only in Spokane county, but for the Pacific Northwest."

Inland Empire Paper Company

[Spokane Valley Today May, 1989]

On a busy day in 1989, Bill Morse, sales manager at Inland Empire Paper Company, opened the door from the offices into the plant. On the loading platform were giant rolls of paper. Train tracks ran right through the building. The busy forklift lifted 2000-pound rolls of paper as though they were feathers.

We passed into the rooms where the wood chips are actually made into paper. We hurried past winders, calendar stacks, dryers and presses that dwarfed the workmen and operated with thunderous speed. Out onto an observation platform, Bill pointed out the piles of wood chips and the fact that the property extends from Argonne almost to the Idaho border.

"This is a large operation for the Spokane area," he said when I commented on its immensity, "but it is small as paper mills go. The mill projected for Usk, Washington, will be three times the size of this—a three hundred million dollar plant."

"Will you be hurt by the competition?" I asked.

"I don't think so," Bill answered, "We have been here for seventy-seven years, have a sound customer base, and manufacture a high quality product at a competitive price."

We walked across a weathered connecting ramp. "These look like the original floor boards," I said.

"We constantly modernize, expand, and improve the operation," Bill said, "but some of the original structures are still in use. All our technology is the latest. There is much more to the operation than you see here. In 1952 the company commenced a land acquisition program for the purpose of insuring a supply of pulpwood in the mill for all time. We acquired the Brickel Creek Tree Farm on the east slope of Mt. Spokane and the St. Joe Tree Farm near St. Maries, Idaho. There we maintain tree planting projects, road construction, fire control, preventive disease and insect control, and logging operations. This is our 'forever' concept which envisions trees on the land forever."

"If you want history," Bill said, "Dean Banta is the one to talk to. His father was one of the earliest plant workers and Dean started working here in 1928. He was general manager from 1955 until he retired due to ill health in 1970.

The Banta story is the history of the mill past and

present. Four generations of Bantas have worked at the Inland Empire Paper Company—Horace, his son Dean, his son Bob, and now his son Brad is working at the mill while attending Eastern Washington College.

The Bantas, Father and Son, and the Paper Mill

Early in the century real estate developers interested a group of Wisconsin paper employees in property along the Spokane River from what is now Argonne Road east to Williams Road. The selling point was the easy access to the Inland Empire's vast timber resources. Led by the first general manager, W.A. Brazeau, the investors dug three wells, built a horse barn and the first unit of the Inland Empire Paper Mill, the first major factory in the Spokane Valley.

By October, 1911, two machines manufactured rag bond and citrus wrap for the large Valley fruit industry. In 1913 the first machine was bought to roll out newsprint. As an incentive for the employees, the company constructed a wading pool for family use and a band stand in which musically inclined paper mill workers performed regularly.

In Michigan in 1910 a relative told a young paper mill worker named Horace C. Banta about a proposed paper mill in the Spokane Valley. He soon arrived in Spokane, spent his first night at the St. Regis Hotel, applied for a job at the paper mill and

When the Inland Empire Paper Mill began production in 1911 it became the hub of Millwood. It provided a bandstand (above) for employees, a wading pool for their children, and the amenities of a company town. *Photo courtesy of the Inland Empire Paper Company.*

was hired. With his wife, Mary, he moved into a house halfway between Park Road and Argonne Road on Empire. Here the couple lived until the company built its first of two batches of company homes.

In 1915 when Inland Empire Paper built its sulphite plant at the Argonne Road site, Horace became woodchip cook. He rose to the position of sulphite superintendent and was recognized as an authority in his field. In the late '20s he sold Spokane on the idea of using the spent sulphite liquor from the paper mill to settle the dust on its streets. It is said that four or five truckloads a day of the liquor was sprinkled on the streets.

The couple had four children, two girls and two boys. The oldest was Dean Banta, born in 1911 and presently of the Valley. He was destined to walk in his father's shoes and learn the paper mill business from start to finish.

Dean attended the old Millwood Grade School and especially remembers his class being marched with the school band to new quarters in the West Valley High School when it was built in 1924.

By 1925 the mill had diversified and was producing poster paper, butcher's wrap and grocery paper.

Meanwhile, Dean, a high school sophomore, enrolled in the Citizens Military Training Camp program held at Fort George Wright. Young men in the program lived on the base for one month each summer until graduating from high school. They were disciplined as though in the regular Army, took rifle training, calisthenics, target practice and marching, much like ROTC of today. The Inland Empire Paper Company rewarded these ambitious young men by providing jobs for them in the paper mill for the remainder of the summer.

Thus began Dean's career: first as a worker constructing the company railroad, then as stock boy, and finally rising through purchasing agent to general manager and vice president.

Dean recalls that the original employees named the streets of Millwood for Wisconsin streets and that the bridge over the river on Argonne Road was an iron bridge with a superstructure, and that Argonne Road was named for local boys who fell in the battle of Argonne Woods in World War I. Also that there was a depot at Argonne and Empire called Woodard Station, named for Seth Woodard,

a Millwood pioneer. Boxcars came to the station marked for the "Mill at Woodard." That address became too lengthy, so the railroad combined the two names and routed their cars to Mill-Wood; hence the town name.

When the Depression of '29 hit, newspapers changed the size of their pages to save money. There was so much paper of the old size stocked in warehouses in Spokane that the mill almost was bankrupt. Recycling, so much a part of today's thinking, saved the day. The mill brought in all its stock, beat it, reran it and recycled it. That was probably the first successful reclaiming project of any size in the area.

Following the Depression, in 1933 Dean married Vera Johnson. They had three children, two girls and the boy Bob who worked his way through college at the mill.

Longtime Valley residents remember the paper mill fire of 1957. Logs piled up along the river towards the cement plant sent into the air clouds of black smoke that could be seen for miles around. During the twelve-hour blaze, the fire burned 8,464,000 board feet, about one-fourth of the logs on hand.

Although the process of making paper today is much the same as it was in 1910, technology has changed many of the individual processes. At first the mill bought logs and produced its own chips for pulp. In 1948 it installed debarkers to remove the bark from the logs with pressurized streams of 1300 pounds of well water forced against the turning logs. Inland Empire was the first mill in the world to manufacture 100% of its ground wood pulp from refiners to newsprint.

Visitors from as for away as Japan came to watch the refiner process and later used the same process in their plants.

When the Inland Empire Paper Company began buying its chips from saw mills in Washington and Idaho, those processes were no longer necessary; and so the sulphite mill and digestor plants were torn down in 1970.

The plant now employs about 125 workers and turns out 215 tons of newsprint a day. Clyde B. Anderson is president and general manager today. He is a Spokane native and a graduate of the University of Washington.

Water, Power

"During the past three years, such abundance of crops were put into the Spokane and tributary markets from this little tract of GREENACRES, watered from LIBERTY LAKE, that not only was Spokane surprised, but GREENACRES' fame went from the Pacific to the Atlantic. People from all over the United States are now awake to the possibilities of irrigation in the Valley.

["Valley of the Sun," Story No. 15, *Spokesman-Review,* April 22, 1932]

"Laura Baum remembers very well when the first irrigation water came through. She was working for the Wells family, helping take care of the children. Everyone was very much excited. The youngsters ran down to the ditch and waded in the first Spokane Valley irrigation water."

["Valley of the Sun," Series II, Story No. 5, *Spokesman-Review,* April 7, 1930.]

Harry J. Neally (right) and Fred Lamott (left) admire the marvel called irrigation, 1908. *Courtesy of Patricia Smith Goetter.*

Water, Power

CHRONOLOGICAL HISTORY

1889   **Washington Water Power Company** formed.

1890   March 19: **Santa Rosa Park** of **Orchard Avenue** platted. Plats were sold without water rights and had no irrigation.

1895   First attempt to irrigate the Valley by **Washington and Idaho Irrigation Company** formed to bring water from **Hayden** and **Newman lakes.** An experimental flume ran from **Newman Lake** to the **Orchard Avenue** area.

1899   July: **W.L. Benham, D.C. Corbin** and **Austin Corbin** formed the **Spokane Valley Irrigation Company** with the right to bring water from **Hayden, Newman, Liberty, Saltese, Fish (Twin)** and **Mud (Hauser) lakes.** The company was incorporated in 1901.

1900   **Albert A. Kelly** bought twenty acres of dry land south and west of what is now **Sprague** and **Havana.** He dug a well and installed a centrifugal pump for irrigation — the first ever used in the area.

1900   Although the Valley is largely undeveloped, the coming of irrigation will change all that.

1901   April 2: **Spokane Valley Land and Water Company** incorporated and a meandering ditch was dug from **Liberty Lake** to a point near **Barker Road** and the electric rail line. The **Wells Ranch** in **Greenacres** was experimentally irrigated.

1902   March: **John Hatch** moved onto the original irrigated tract at **Greenacres.** He had plenty of water but had difficulty getting it around to various tracts due to the unevenness of the land and the loss of water due to seepage out of the dirt ditches. **Mrs. Hatch** boarded workmen for 15¢ a meal.

1903   **James C. Cunningham** organized **Valley Improvement Company** and introduced practical irrigation via the **Corbin Ditch.**

1903   June 8: **Mark F. Mendenhall** and **Laughlan McLean** (first president of the company) formed the **Spokane Canal Company** to bring water from **Newman**

Lake to **Otis Orchard.** The canal used had been dug by property owners to drain the meadow and for floating logs out of the hills to the **Day Sawmill** located near **Moab.**

1904

October 12: **Washington Water Power** was authorized by agreement to withdraw water from in back of the **Post Falls Dam.**

1905

D.C. Corbin took over the **Spokane Valley Land and Water Company** to develop a network of canals that included the **Spokane River Canal System** known as the **Corbin Ditch.**

1905

Modern Electric Water Company formed in **Opportunity District** by **R.A. Hutchinson** and **A.C. Jamison.** Large wells were dug. A tank for domestic water was built and piped to acreage to be sold. First big well was on **Pines Road** just north of **Broadway.** Residents became share holders. (See article, "Modern Electric Water Company.")

1906

Washington Water Power's Post Falls plant went into service.

1906

Surveying work was done on the first unit of the **River Canal. East Farms** received the first water from the ditch in 1907, **Otis Orchards** in 1908, and **Trentwood** and **Palisades Park** in 1910.

1908

April 20: **Vera Electric Water and Power Company** was organized to pump water for irrigation. **A.C. Jamison, D.K. McDonald, Andrew Wood** were organizers. (See article, "Vera Water and Power.")

1908

Domestic water to **Fairacres** and **Grandview Acres** in **Otis Orchards** was supplied by the **Inland Empire Paper Company** and **Portland Cement.** An irrigation district was not formed until 1929.

1909

Well completed at **Orchard Avenue.**

1910

Frank Dalton dug wells and formed the **Trentwood Irrigation Company.**

1918

Spokane Valley Irrigation District #10 supplied irrigation water to **Spokane Land and Water Company** and immediately **Grandview Acres, Fairview,** and **Santa Rosa** bloomed.

1920

Large wells were put down in **Greenacres** on a high point opposite the **Wells Ranch** to supplement the lake supply of water for irrigation.

Water

[From "Echoes of Yesterday" by J. Howard Stegner, *Spokane Valley Herald*, April 29, 1954]

When my father bought lots in the Palisades (Irvin) Addition in 1890, he was fully aware that we had something more to do for water than to tap a water main.

Father had a fine team of horses that he used in traveling for the Singer Sewing Machine Company. He used this team to haul groceries from Spokane Falls. The grocery wagon became a water wagon.

Father would drive down the old Mullan Road that led to the Plante Ferry site, then on out into the low water ford of the river. This would give the horses a chance to drink and father a good chance to fill the water barrels. One day the river was up a little and the current almost swept him away. He lost one of his barrels and was quite fortunate that he did not drown.

It was a mile to the river and we had no idea how deep it was underground to water. In 1891 or '92 we dug for a well. We hired a man named Jim Davis to do the digging and my father turned the windlass. At 93 feet we struck the underground flow of the Valley and discovered a current flowing from the southeast to the northwest.

Buckets and a rope were used to draw the water for about two years. We replaced the bucket with a hand pump, with a windmill soon to follow. Our store was on the south side of the Northern Pacific Railroad, so we built a large watering trough so that passers-by could water their horses. In doing this they would leave the Trent Road and stop at our store.

In 1889, when we bought the Dart store on the Trent Road, it also had a windmill and an elevated tank. When the wind failed to blow, the elevated wood tank would dry out and leak, and in the winter it would freeze up.

By 1903 or '04, we had about 500 acres with the river across one end and along the north side for 22 miles. We wanted to irrigate some of this fine land. My stepfather, Mr. Narup, was a mechanical genius and thought of harnessing the river to pump water. We did a lot of experimenting and finally perfected an undershot river-driven wheel that pumped 150 gallons a minute, 150 feet high.

McGoldrick Lumber Company made a tie drive down the river and the ties piled up against our water wheel and wrecked it.

In 1907, we decided to go out of the store business and we built a 13-room mansion on the site of our first store about one block west of the Trent School. We used our first well and put in a pump house. Then for the first time we had modern plumbing and water for a lawn and garden.

Next we built a 40-foot tower with a 50,000-gallon tank, then piped our first addition, which was Grandview Acres.

In 1922, we helped to promote the south branch of the Corbin Canal and bought water rights for our five additions. I will say that there were times that we were land poor. We sold land along the Trent paving for $500 an acre; I'm told that it would sell for at least $1500 now.

After taking Corbin water, we had to sell as the water was $8 to $10 per acre per year. People have said to us, "If you only had that land now... But the water taxes would have bankrupted us.

A Word About Valley Power

When there is a power outage in the Valley, some residents question why nearby lights are on while theirs are off. Some also do not understand why the rates their friends pay for power are not the rates they pay.

The answer to both dilemmas is that there are in 1991 four power companies serving the area we know as the Valley: Modern Electric Water Company, Vera Water and Power, Inland Power and Light and Washington Water Power.

To add to the confusion, Bonneville Power Administration, a power marketing agency that does not serve retail customers, has direct service lines to Kaiser; and Washington Water Power which generates its own power, in some instances "wheels" its power over Bonneville lines.

The four companies do not all use the same power source. Modern Electric buys from Washington Water Power; Vera and Inland buy from Bonneville.

Each is organized differently and each originated at different periods during Valley history. Modern, Vera, and Washington Water Power came into existence before 1920. Inland Power and Light came into being during the Roosevelt Administration in the '30s when the Rural Electrification Act (REA) was passed. We will discuss at length only Modern and Vera, the two that have their roots in the Valley.

Modern Electric Water Company buildings, 1908. Left to right: No. 1 pumphouse and shop, water tank, No. 5 pumphouse (background) and original office building (still there). Pines Road. *Courtesy of Patricia Smith Goetter.*

Modern Electric Water Company

[From a pamphlet for Modern Electric Landowners, published by Modern Electric Water Company, written by John Vlahovich, editor of the *Valley Herald* for forty-four years.]

If you came to the Spokane Valley in winter, you may find it hard to believe , but this is an arid country. Rainfall averages only about l7 inches annually, and very little of that falls during the growing season. For that reason the rather vast plain which constitutes the Spokane Valley lay practically uninhabited until the turn of the century. Water in large quantities was needed to make the barren plain fruited.

Although a few hardy homesteaders and others had settled at the edges of the Valley adjacent to natural springs or other water supplies and were managing to raise gardens or grow unimportant quantities of small grains, most of the Spokane Valley was an empty cheat-grass plain.

There is a vast underground river of clear, cold water flowing under the Valley, but no one was aware of this wonderful asset until Albert A. Kelly, who was a prominent florist and produce grower, decided to try digging a well.

Ignoring scoffers, of whom there were plenty, he bought twenty acres immediately south and west of what is now Sprague Avenue and Havana Street at the edge of Spokane. In l900 he dug a 50-foot well and installed the first centrifugal pump ever used in the area for irrigation. At his own expense, Kelly erected a mile of poles and strung the lines to carry electric service to his pump motor.

Kelly was able to grow quantities of all types of produce on his plot and his success intrigued three men who took more than a passing interest in Kelly's success. They were D.K. McDonald, R.A. Hutchinson, and A.C. Jamison.

They had visions of selling Valley land to an influx of land-seekers from the East. The three bought up approximately 3,000 acres of rough-looking land at considerable distance from the Spokane city limits and formed Modern Irrigation & Land Company.

Since land here without water was practically worthless, the entrepreneurs also formed the Modern Electric Water Company, whose prime function was to furnish irrigation water to these 3,000 acres.

Distribution of electricity as a large-scale business was not envisioned by these men, and a unique contract between Modern Electric Water Company and the Modern Irrigation & Land Company obligated the former to bring sufficient irrigation water to the high point of each 40 acres of land, along with sufficient electricity to light one 40-watt light.

For all practical purposes the land company owned the water company with stock passing to buyers with each acre of land they purchased from the land company. At the same time, land-owners assumed an obligation to keep the Modern Electric Water Company functioning through an assessment charge which was determined annually by the five-man board of directors elected by the stockholders.

Thus, over a period of time, the 3,000 acres of land originally owned by the three developers was sold to hundreds who planned to make their living raising garden and orchard crops. Along with title to the land, the purchasers also became the owners of Modern Electric Water Company, and assumed the obligation to pay enough in assessments each year to keep the company functioning.

This is the reason deeds for land in the MEW service area carry the lien provision that binds the land to support the financial needs of the company. The contract providing for these assessments, after one amendment, was recorded in the Spokane County Auditor's office on November 6, 1905.

The contract is still in force, the chief difference being that title to the original 3,000 acres of farmland developed by the Modern Irrigation & Land Company has long since passed to thousands of suburban residents. With the transfer of the title to the land also passed title to Modern Electric Water Company, so that Modern Electric is now owned by the owners of the property to which it serves domestic and irrigation water and electricity.

The unique legal document binding the Modern

Electric Water Company to the land it serves was made to run in perpetuity with the land and is part of the title of every tract of land covered by the contract.

With the change in the area's economy, from agricultural to residential-commercial, the annual assessment procedure was discontinued years ago. Instead of operating with income derived chiefly from irrigation assessments levied upon acreage, Modern Electric Water Company now is a prosperous operating entity whose income comes from sale of residential and commercial electricity and water billed monthly.

Soon after creating the corporation, McDonald and his associates had a well dug (the present MEW No. 1) and installed a centrifugal pump powered with a gasoline engine. They set up a 10-acre test plot just east of what is now Pines Road and north of Broadway. This plot was planted in almost everything imaginable, including peanuts and cotton. From these tests it was decided that apple trees would prove the most profitable venture, with berries and other quickly maturing crops to be planted between rows to provide income until the trees came into bearing. Most of the land sold after that had some apple trees on it.

Thus the Spokane Valley developed into one of the leading apple growing areas of the nation. Huge packing and cold storage plants dotted the Valley near railroads.

Vera Electric Water Company built this pumphouse of native stone in 1908. It still stands at 601 N. Evergreen. *Courtesy of Vera Power and Light.*

Vera Water and Power

[From "The History of Vera Water and Power" by Paul Rhodes, a retired electrical superintendent at the plant who researched the history of the company in the 1980s.]

On the 20th day of April, 1908, the articles of incorporation of the Vera Electric Water Company were signed and the company came into being. The stated purpose of the corporation was to construct, maintain, and operate wells, pumping stations, and irrigation plants for the purpose of supplying water and power to 1,000 acres then owned by the Vera Land Company and not to exceed an additional 1,500 acres to be purchased by the Vera Land Company. The additional land was to be adjacent or contiguous to the original 1,000 acres.

Organizers of this corporation were Donald K. McDonald, A.C. Jamison, and Andrew Good, all of Spokane. Mr. Jamison and Mr. McDonald were also the president and secretary of the Vera Land Company. A rather detailed agreement between the Vera Electric Water Company, Mr. McDonald, Mr. Jamison, and Mr. Good, and the Vera Land Company was entered into providing for the Land Company to dig wells and construct an irrigation distribution system. The amount of water to be furnished was not to exceed 14.04 inches of water annually. This water for irrigation pumping was to be brought by facilities provided by the Land Company to each ten acre tract.

The Land Company also agreed to construct a domestic water distribution system to each forty-acre tract, with the Electric Water Company to operate and maintain this system. Provisions were made in this agreement for any unpaid bills for water service to become a lien against the land for which it was furnished. As the land owned by the Land Company developed, it was sold to buyers from all over the United States. Purchase of the land entitled the buyer to one share of stock per acre in the Electric Water Company. Shareholders could vote to elect three trustees who operated the company. And, as wells were constructed, they were deeded to the Electric Water Company. The Land company then became a self-liquidating

entity and as land was sold, control passed away from the original organizers to the buyers, and also the responsibility for the operation and maintenance.

This type of organization and development had worked successfully in the Modern Electric Water Company in Opportunity, the neighboring community to the west. Mr. McDonald had been also involved in developing Modern Electric Company.

Operation of the Vera Electric Water Company in the early years was accomplished in conjunction with Modern Electric Water Company with Modern's supervising personnel overseeing the operation of Vera. Ditchriders were hired for Vera, but the operation of the pumps and electric system was done initially by Modern's personnel. By agreement with the power supplier, Spokane and the Inland Empire Railway, electricity for lighting each home was made available. The assessment for irrigation water, domestic water and lights from 1909 was set at $5 per acre, continuing in 1910, raising to $6.50 in 1911, $7 in 1912, and $8.50 in 1913.

In Vera, large rocks had to be moved before the land could be put to agricultural use, and many property lines were clearly defined by rock piles. Real estate and development companies advertised the use of rock as building material and many houses can still be seen built of native stone. An attractive landmark is the Vera Water and Power District No. 1 pump house located at the District's headquarters at 601 N. Evergreen. This castle-like structure was built shortly after the turn of the century of native stone.

The wells, which provided the water for the District, were all hand dug and are scattered throughout the District. They were cribbed up as they were dug with two-by-fours, usually in an octagon shape. After the main body of water was reached, at from approximately 80 to 130 feet, a four foot diameter perforated steel casing was sunk to provide from 20 to 30 feet of water. The well shaft above the water was then provided with a permanent inner coating of concrete and/or brick, leav-

143

ing a finished diameter of approximately six feet. To provide room for the pumps and electric motors which were located just above the water line, the wall of the well was belled out to around fifteen feet in diameter or short tunnels were dug on each side of the interior.

The depth of the wells constituted a real hazard, and the construction was not without incident. During the digging of No. 3 well, in 1909, and after the desired depth was nearly reached, a worker stepped off of the bucket at the top of the shaft onto a board which broke. He fell to the bottom and was killed instantly.

A building, called a pumphouse, was erected over the top of the well to house the starting equipment for the motors. As previously described, No. 1 pumphouse, built in 1910, was of stone construction. A room was added onto the east side later to provide living quarters for the superintendent. The pumphouse at No. 2 well, located at Sullivan and Valleyway, was also of stone construction, while the remaining well houses were frame. No. 3 pumphouse also included a room for the ditchrider, who slept there during the irrigation season. No. 3 also had a telephone for communication with the growers.

How the Valley Was Irrigated

A large concrete forebay, or division facility with appropriate gates, was erected at each well to provide a means to divide the water to different lines coming out from the wells. The water flowed by gravity through concrete pipes from this location to the customer's delivery point. Normally this point was the highest location on each ten acre tract.

The amount of water delivered per acre was subject to much discussion and controversy, but it was generally accepted that a head of water was commonly measured as the amount flowing over a 6 by 10-inch weir. Normally, a head of water was delivered for two hours for each acre weekly during the irrigation system.

Since the pumps were running continuously, this meant that the water could come at any time of the day or night. A method of staggering the delivery times was desirable in order that a grower

would have an opportunity to receive his water at the most desirable times as well as sharing the undesirable times such as two o'clock in the morning. The ditchrider was responsible for scheduling the water, and this involved firmness, tact, understanding, and many hours of good hard work, especially when lines would break. Rains could cause a different type of problem as some of the users would refuse the water while others would insist on delivery.

Initially, the irrigation pipe lines were hand-made concrete, with possibly a few wood lines. These hand-made concrete lines would not stand much pressure and would "blow out," as it was called, when the lines were filled too rapidly, when someone closed a weir before opening another, when pipe was cracked or damaged by excavations or too heavy loads passing over. In these cases, the line had to be closed down, the damage repaired, the irrigators rescheduled and lines cured before water could be delivered.

Vera Electric and Water Company at one time had a pipe manufacturing plant at No. 3 pump station at 16th and Evergreen. It later moved to No. 4 station at 24th and Adams. The pipe was hand-made at these locations. As the more superior machine-made pipe became available, the hand-made pipe was used less until it finally was discontinued altogether. It is believed that the frugality of the hand-made pipe manufacturing personnel in not using enough cement contributed greatly to the weakness of the hand-made pipe.

Some of the early employees were Roland T. Smith, the father of Tom Smith who later became the Modern Electric Water Co. general manager for many years. Reference is made in the minutes of Smith's employment as a ditchrider in 1913 for $100 a month, the company to furnish a motorcycle and Smith to furnish the gasoline. Another early employee was Bill Tschirley, who was the son of a pioneer of the area. Tschirley started work for the company a few years before World War I, served in the war and came back to work until 1946.

One of Mr. Tschirley's innovations was the development of an elevator to go down into the wells. It was necessary to visit each well during the irrigation season to perform necessary maintenance and since this involved climbing down and up a ladder from 80 feet to 130 feet in length, it is apparent that considerable physical effort was required, especially when the company had five wells in operation during the irrigation season which lasted from the first of May through August, and sometimes September.

Mr. Tschirley's elevator worked by a counterbalance weight and water. To descend, enough water to overcome the weight of the counter balance was run into the tank. Getting on to the platform and releasing the brake gradually, the workman descended smoothly to the bottom of the well where the brake was locked. After the necessary work was performed, the water was drained and upon releasing the brake the counterbalance pulled the elevator and its passenger to the top of the well.

Reference is made many times in the minutes to arrangements made by the Board with growers to accept mortgages on crops, equipment, and livestock in lieu of cash payments in order that the grower might continue to receive water. Water rent rose from $8.50 in 1914 to $9 an acre in 1919 and to $10 in 1920 as the rising costs began to be felt after the war.

Real Estate, Communities, Towns

"With the increase in population along the highways and the railroad, here and there clusters of houses formed about the crossroad store, post office or other natural meeting places. Some clusters grew into communities and some faded away as conditions of traffic or sustenance changed."

["Valley of the Sun," Story No. 6, *Spokesman-Review*, April 9, 1930]

Real Estate, Communities, Towns

CHRONOLOGICAL HISTORY

1881 September: The staff of the *Spokan Times* visited **John W. Arthur** at his ferry near what became **Trent**. A townsite was laid out there to be named **"Cliffton."** Several families had moved in, a store and hotel were being erected.

1881 The area called **Trent** was platted and given **Stegner's wife's** maiden name. At one time **Trent** was an active contender with **Spokane Bridge** and **Spokane Falls** for leadership of the area. **Frederick Post** had considered locating a milling operation there.

1881 **Louisville** was platted at the south side of the right-of-way. The church at **Irvin** was within the boundaries. It was possibly named by a Kentuckian who built a distillery at **Spokane Bridge.**

1881 **Palisades** was platted west of **Louisville,** south of the railroad.

1886 **Newman Lake** residents asked the government to stock the lake with fish. There were no fish in the lake. The following year a car load of carp arrived attached to a passenger train. Settlers carried the fish to the lake in lard pails.

1889 From **Mr. Schrum, Rod MacKensie** bought and developed 1200 acres at **Liberty Lake,** part of which later became known as **Wicomico Beach.** He discovered an Indian cabin over 100 years old on the property below the spring. It was the birthplace of **Quinny Moses (Quinamosa)** an Indian chief. The property had been a Hudson's Bay post for a short period. **MacKensie** built a campground, 20-room hotel and restaurant, made a swimming beach, rented horses and row boats. He had the first boat in the area that was not a dug-out canoe. He stocked the lake with fish and installed a telephone.

1889 **D.C. Corbin** laid out **Corbin Addition** in **Greenacres.**

1890 March 19: **Santa Rosa Park** south of **Orchard Avenue** was platted. Plats were sold without water rights and had no irrigation. It was probably the first addition platted in the Valley. **James Callen** acquired the land from the **Northern Pacific.**

1890 An Indian burial ground was known to be at **Thirty-Second** and **Greenacres Road.** The **Saltese Cemetery Association** was formed.

1891 **Frederick Post** bought 248 acres of land on both sides of the **Spokane River** based on a treaty between **Post** and **Andrew Seltice,** Chief of the Coeur d'Alenes. **Post Falls** incorporated.

1893   Mt. Carleton was renamed **Mount Spokane.**

1900   **Charles Traeger** built a roadhouse known as **Zephyr Inn** with liquor and gambling at **Liberty Lake.** The property was later sold to the **Christian Church** for conference grounds.

1900   Interest in irrigating the Valley became widespread. The interest is reflected in increased real estate activity.

1901   A settlement near **Newman Lake** was called **Moab.**

1902   **Martin Kalez** of Spokane leased **MacKenzie's** buildings and operated them as a resort.

1903   **Mark F. Mendenhall** and **Laughlan McLean** acquired title to 3500 acres, practically all the land in the **Otis Orchards District.**

1904   **George** and **Floy Neyland** settled at **Liberty Lake** and started a resort. **Grant Neyland** a son of **Louisa** and **Daniel,** operated **Wayside Beach** where the first store was located.

1904   **R.A. Hutchinson** paid $25 an acre for 800 acres of land and laid it out in ten-acre tracts, two of which were planted in apples. This was the beginning of **Opportunity.**

1904   Plat for **Greenacres** town was filed.

1904   **Fruitland Addition** was platted.

1904   Townsite of **Mica** (near the brickyard) filed.

1907   **Dreamwood Bay Beach** at **Liberty Lake** was developed by **E.E. Ernst.** It was sold in 1918.

1907   **Dutch Jake,** owner of the Liberty Theater in Spokane, sponsored the "Dutch Jake Club" which met at **Liberty Lake.**

1907   Plat for **Pinecroft Addition** filed (300 acres between **Irvin** and **Opportunity** and **Bowdish** and **Pines**). The land was purchased by **E.C. Blanchard, George Robie,** and **Dr. Kalb.**

1907   **Vera District** platted.

1907   **Orin Bacon** platted **Bacon's Addition** adjoining **Greenacres** on the west. He originally homesteaded the site.

1908   **Fairacres, Grandview Acres** in **Orchard Avenue** were platted.

1908   The town of **Dishman** was platted as part of **Hutchinson Addition** west of the original **Opportunity** tracts.

1908   Pasadena Park was platted by **Beecher** and **Thompson** and later purchased by **D.C. Corbin.** It included the **Hutton Settlement.** It contained the land that became in 1911 West Farms east of Trentwood.

1908   **Frank Dalton** came to **Trentwood,** then called **Steno.** He bought 300 acres from **Mike Blessing** and **Mary Schluch** and named the area.

1908   **Orchard Avenue** platted in acre tracts.

1909   **Kalez** and **MacKenzie** bought property on the east side of **Liberty Lake** and each developed resorts known as **Kalez Park** and **MacKenzie Bay.**

1909   The **Spokane Inland Empire Railroad** owned and operated **Liberty Lake Park.** In 1910 when the railroad was put through from Spokane to Coeur d'Alene, the train stopped at **Liberty Lake Junction** where a horse drawn stage brought people to the lake. After a spur was built, two or three trains every hour on Sundays, holidays, and for week day picnics ran to the lake.

1909   **Trentwood** platted.

1910   **Post Falls District,** comprising **Post's** 3500 acres was platted. Average tract was 10-20 acres settled mostly by families.

1910   **Dan C. Coakley** bought from the railroad the **Liberty Lake Boat Company** and operated four launches, rented out 100 row boats, twelve canoes, and twelve **Evinrudes.** Business was brisk. **Liberty Lake** was in its hey day from 1910 - 1915. The men who gave daily boat service were **D.C. Coakley, E.E. Ernst, Martin Kalez,** and three **Nixon** brothers.

1910   The **Van Marters** had a roller skating rink on the third floor of their home at **University** and **Valleyway.**

1912   **Richard Ashton** promoted **Hutchinson's Addition** north of the **Appleway** and west of **Argonne.**

1912   The **Otis Orchards Men's Commercial Club** and the **Otis Orchard Ladies' Social and Civics Club** sponsored the building of the **Otis Orchards Clubhouse,** the largest clubhouse building built to date at a Valley site. It was located at **E. 22404 Wellesley** and later occupied by the **Otis Orchards Fire Company.** Destroyed by fire in 1927.

1912   **Otis Orchards** was officially named.

1914-23   **Oren** and **Elita Watson** built a resort at what is now **Granite Point.** Later they had the **Watson Boat Works.**

1915   **Spokane Valley Kiwanis Club** organized.

1915   **Harrington Addition** platted by **Cornelius Harrington.**

1916 **Levi W. Hutton,** a railroad engineer who "struck it rich" in a lead and zinc mine in the Wallace, Idaho, area, bought 112 acres northeast of **Millwood** as the site for an orphanage. Founded in 1919, it is known as the **Hutton Settlement** and today covers 364 acres. Levi's wife, **May Arkwright Hutton,** was a leader in the suffragette movement. She was the first woman to attend a national Democratic Convention. Both **Levi** and **May** were orphans with a dream: "a special place to live " for children.

1917 **Kalez Park** at **Liberty Lake** ceased operation. It was sold to the Dominican Order of Monks who stayed only a short time because of extremely bad luck — the accidental deaths of several of their group.

1917 **Orchard Avenue Community Club** was organized.

1917 Food prices rose steadily and sharply after April when World War I was declared. To alleviate the food shortage, hundreds of vacant spaces in the Valley were used to grow vegetables.

1919 Land set aside for the **Upriver Municipal Golf Course** was made into a municipal airfield, later to be known as **Felts Field.**

1920 The **Inland Empire Paper Company** bought 40 acres of land near its factory as a home site for its employees, now called **Millwood.**

Appleway Road at Dishman about 1900. Looking east. *Photo courtesy of Spokane Valley Museum archives.*

Dishman and Kokomo, 1908

[By Channon P. Price, March, 1970 (manuscript)]

This is Dishman in 1908:

The railroad was the Oregon Washington Railroad and Navigation Company and was a big factor in the development of the Valley. Everything west of the tracks belonged to the Dishman Trading Company. On the south side of Sprague was a general merchandise store. The W.B. Dishman family lived on the second floor.

Just west of this was a two-story building. Part of the ground floor was used for a saloon and the rest for a restaurant. Sleeping rooms were upstairs.

South of this was a large barn to care for live stock. On the north side of Sprague was a large warehouse for feed, grain and farm implements. This was served by a car siding for unloading car lots.

At the west end there was a blacksmith shop painted red. This was operated by James Russell.

Crossing the tracks to the east, Marguerite Street intersected Sprague. Traffic moved north on Marguerite to Valley Way and east to Argonne and then north. The hill just south of Valley Way was so steep you could not go up it with a horse and buggy.

Sands Road intersected Sprague at this point and this gave the intersection the name of Dishman corners. This intersection was destroyed when the underpass was built. Sands Road was moved about a block east and is now known as the Dishman-Mica Road.

Argonne had been improved and Marguerite traffic moved to that road. Sands Road carried the traffic south to Rockford and other communities. It was the custom of the people living in the south farming areas to drive to Dishman, stay over night, go to Spokane and back the next day and return home on the third day. This furnished a big share of the Dishman Trading business.

On the southeast corner of Sprague and Sands road, the company operated a wood working plant furnishing material for the new homes that were being built. They also operated a sand pit and a stone quarry. These were hauled to Spokane by wagons and used in the foundations of buildings.

J.F. Brod operated the Opportunity Box Factory in this block. On the northeast corner of Argonne and Sprague, A.R. Moore owned a general store and shortly to the north two buildings. These homes are still in use and are the only buildings left of the original ones.

Now, here is where I entered.

I was working in Colville and came to Spokane for a short vacation and met C.W. Misner whom I had worked with the year before. He suggested that we go for an automobile ride.

Automobile rides were far apart and cost money, so I said I didn't think it was worthwhile.

He said, "Oh, it won't cost anything. There's a real estate firm down the street selling a tract of land called Kokomo out in the valley. They are hauling people out to see it."

Kokomo was on the south of Sixteenth and east of University.

We called the office and made a date to go out the next morning. At the appointed time we arrived and there at the curb was a seven passenger Thomas Flyer painted a fire engine red with a driver dressed in a linen duster, gauntlet gloves, a cap and goggles. He looked like someone from outer space.

We climbed in and were off for Kokomo.

About all there was to see was a patch of tomato plants and a small gas engine pumping water into a vee trough which was made by nailing two six-inch wide boards together. It didn't take long to see all of that and we headed to Spokane.

In Dishman we noticed a sign on the Moore store stating it was for sale. Mr. Misner had some merchandising experience and thought that what looked like a fast growing community would be a good place to own a store.

We came back on the train the next morning and bought Mr. Moore's stock of merchandise. We rented the store building and the home closest to it where we lived.

Homes were few and wide spaces between them and the groceryman had to cover a lot of ground to sell many groceries. It was difficult for the people to get to the store, so each morning the groceryman started out over his route, taking orders and delivering what he had sold the day before.

Hauling a wrinkled prune around the valley on a spring board wagon did not appeal to me and in September, 1909, I sold my interest to Mr. Misner. He immediately started construction of a two-story concrete block building a short way west of Argonne and Sprague.

The first floor was used for a store and living quarters for the family. Upstairs was one large room called Misner's Hall and was for dancing and community affairs.

In 1920 J.F. Brod and I, in partnership built a brick building on the north side of the Appleway and rented it to Mr. and Mrs. Lynn Tyner for a grocery store and post office. Mrs. Nellie Tyner became the first postmaster in Dishman.

A Shooting in Dishman

[By Channon Price, March, 1970 (manuscript)]

In June 1910, three carpenters from Spokane — Mr. Mays, Mr. Mansker, and Mr. Whipple, were building a store building on the west side of Marguerite and north of the car tracks. Hard feelings started among the group and became so bitter that Mr. Mays did not report for work on the morning of the tenth but stayed in Spokane and became highly intoxicated.

About three in the afternoon he came out to Dishman on the street car with a thirty-thirty Winchester rifle under his arm. He got off the car and walked across the tracks to the building where his partners were working and shot both of them.

He walked south along the railroad to a siding where some box cars were stored. He stopped there possibly to decide what he should do next.

Mr. Misner made that decision for him. He had been elected Constable and felt it his duty to uphold law and order. He got out a twenty-two caliber, pearl-handled revolver and went single-handed to capture a crazed man who had just killed two men.

Mays accommodated by shooting him through the heart.

The County Sheriff was called and he came out with a posse. They picked up the trail and followed Mays to what is now Painted Hills. Darkness compelled them to give up the search that evening, but they returned early the next morning. A night's sleep in the open had cleared Mays' head of whiskey and anger.

When the Sheriff appeared, he tied a handkerchief to the barrel of his gun and held it above his hiding place, calling to the Sheriff that if they would not shoot, he would lay down his gun and come out with his arms above his head.

He scolded the Sheriff for so recklessly exposing his men the evening before, telling him that he was a dead shot either from the shoulder or hip and could have killed all of them.

He was taken into custody and taken to jail. He was later tried for the murder of Mr. Misner and sentenced to life imprisonment in the penitentiary at Walla Walla.

The Misner store was sold to Roy Hutchins of Wild Rose Prairie. He had operated the store only a short time when he went to the basement, reached up to turn on a drop light and was electrocuted. It was reported that the Modern Electric Line carrying twenty-two hundred volts had accidentally been shorted in their Number Two well.

The store changed hands a time or two, the last owner being Oscar Reinemer who operated it as the Appleway Mercantile Company.

It was destroyed by a fire which burned the adjacent three story brick building. Both buildings were owned by A.T. Dishman. The walls of the lower floor of the brick building stood for a number of years and was referred to as "The Dishman Ruins."

Jackson and the Pinecroft Development

[From "Echoes of Yesterday" by J. Howard Stegner, *Spokane Valley Herald*, April 14, 1955.]

In 1907 E.C. Blanchard, George Robie, and a Dr. Kalb bought up a half section of cheap, rocky land lying between Trent (now Irvin) and Opportunity, and between Pines and Bowdish. They formed a company and platted this into acre tracts.

They called it Pinecroft Addition. Pine was for the pines on the nearby hill and croft means a small farm or enclosed field.

They hired some professional cameramen to take pictures of bumper crops of apples, small fruit, vegetables and alfalfa grown at Opportunity and Greenacres. Water gushing from large pumps at Opportunity was also shown.

Armed with folders and these pictures of the bountiful crops from irrigated lands, they headed for the East—to Massachusetts, Maryland, New Jersey, and New Hampshire. Their illustrated talks and hand-outs convinced investors that they really had something to offer that would soon make a man independent.

The developers sold most of their land sight unseen for $400-$500 an acre, promising it would be irrigated from a large well, cleared of rocks, and set out to fruit trees.

The price was two or three times what good land in Opportunity was selling for, but the Easterners were impressed.

The company tried to fulfill the promises of its advertising. It hired large gangs of rock pickers and many teams. In 1908 it had a large well dug on what is now Mansfield Avenue about 800 feet west of Pines. Before electricity came, the well was run by a small pump with a 5 H.P. gas engine.

Later a small electric pump for domestic use was installed and a 100 H.P. centrifugal pump for irrigation. A 25,000 gallon water tank was set upon the rock cliff for storage.

By 1909 the developers hired Otto Adams, a horticulturist from WSC [now Washington State University, Pullman] as they intended to set most of this land to fruit trees. Trees planted were Rome Beauties, Jonathons and Wagners, with a filler row in between the apple trees of peaches and pears.

People from the East began to arrive: J.J. Kelly and family, Mr. and Mrs. George Brown, his father and mother, the Henry Shaws, Mr. and Mrs. Herbert Davi and son, Civil War veteran George Allen and wife, the Woodburys, Reeves, Chester Carpenters, Mardens, and Midgleys and son.

Families I remember only slightly were the Tewinkles, Thompsons, the Rev. Christman family, Torreys, Robies, and foreman of the rock-picking gang, Sylvester.

On most of the land the developers were pumping both irrigation and domestic water against a head of 180 feet. This ran the power bill up (and water taxes) and put extra strain on the wooden pipe that served most of the area. Leaks soon appeared and so much water was used on the lower land that people on the hill were out of water. The lack of water on the higher ground caused the wooden water tank to dry out. It soon wouldn't hold water. But water bills continued to climb and taxes to pay for the horticulturist and rock pickers.

There was one purchaser of land named Jackson. He bought sight unseen ten acres north of the Pinecroft Hills, on Pines Road, just across the road and a little north of where Joe Stitz recently built his beautiful stone house. This was a terribly rocky piece of land and the clearing of the land had built up a rock wall 10 feet wide and about 5 feet high on two sides. The purchaser was to pay for irrigation, pruning, and cultivation for two or three years.

At the time of purchase, Jackson was assured there wasn't a rock on the place large enough to throw at a squirrel.

As bills (especially water) increased, Jackson decided to come west and take a look at his land.

He took one look at the water system and the rock wall and as many more rocks sticking out of the ground and said he would no longer pay taxes on the property.

After that, he was known as "Stonewall Jackson."

Shelley Lake (about 1914), named for John Francis Shelley who homesteaded the area in 1881. He owned the lake and the dryland around it including the site of Central Valley High School. Fourth Street used to be called Shelley Way. The lake was the scene of early ice skating picnics and bonfires. Left background: The Vera Congregational Church is next to the Vera Grade School. *Courtesy of Marie Olbright, granddaughter of Mr. Shelley, who still resides on the property.*

Peter Morrison:
He Pioneered the Draining of a Lake

For the most part, those few early settlers who farmed in the Saltese region chose sites on hills surrounding Saltese Lake. Most, but not all. . .

In 1889 a man named Peter Morrison came upon the Saltese district. He was proprietor of a hay, grain and feed business and owned a livery stable at the site of the post office building in Spokane. He was fascinated by thoughts of the development possibilities of the meadow if the lake were drained.

Peter was not the first to entertain such thoughts. The *Spokan Times*, April 22, 1880, made mention of the fact that J.B. Shrum and F.M. Pugh purchased a claim adjoining the lake and secured the right of way through another piece of land with plans to drain the lake when the water was low. There is no evidence that this was ever done; however, in 1892 Peter was able to acquire property that contained part of the lake from a Mr. Simms.

He immediately began operations to drain Saltese Lake. He made a ditch at the north through the natural outlet that led to what later became known as Shelley's Lake, in back of the Rice Meat Packing Company plant. In 1903 he acquired more lake bottom property on the east and tried to form a drainage district with adjoining property owners. No agreement was reached.

Often knee-deep in the rich but mucky peat, Peter persevered and constructed three ditches through the bed of the lake. The work was slow and had to be redone whenever the first ditches filled with water. Horses were a help but a hindrance when they sank into the peat. Peter solved the problem to some extent by building huge wooden shoes for his horses' feet.

About 1910, his work was further hampered when nine men squatted on land in the Saltese Basin, claiming it was subject to Homestead Rights. The majority of the men were on Peter Morrison's property, so he carried the case to court. The case dragged on for twelve years and twice was heard by the United States Supreme Court. Morrison was greatly relieved when the litigation ended and the verdict favored him.

He died shortly thereafter in December 1923, leaving his wife Agnes and four children, Jeanette, Harry, Millar, and Irene and two sons by a previous marriage, Gilbert and Neil.

Gilbert was the father of Jack Morrison, an early president of the Chamber of Commerce and a member of the Central Valley School Board.

The sons carried on the work Peter had begun. Each year the ditches were enlarged until in 1959 there was an outlet ditch ten to fifteen feet deep.

What became known as the Morrison Ranch was by 1959 operated in two units, one by son Millar Morrison and his sons Bud and Pete, and the other by Harry Morrison and his sister Irene. At that time, the brothers had help continuing the reclamation battle. With the assistance of equipment from the Soil Conservation Service, pits 45 feet wide and up to a half mile in length were built to alleviate flooding problems caused by run-off from Mica Peak. Of the 2000-acre property, so valuable for producing hay for the large dairy herds in the Spokane Valley, 800 acres were in the frequently flooded Saltese Basin.

The principle products of the Saltese Meadows during the early years were cattle, grain, and timothy hay that was shipped all over the Northwest. Pete Morrison became the largest distributor of timothy hay in the state.

The Town of Millwood

[*Spokane Valley Today*, November, 1990]

Millwood is the only incorporated city in the Spokane Valley and is unique in that it has no bonded indebtedness.

It grew up as a company town, fathered by the Inland Empire Paper Mill. In the early days the mill built houses, provided electricity, a sewer system, parkways, roads, sidewalks, water from its wells, and even a city dump for its workers. Most important, it provided a secure income for the residents of the town.

Before the turn of the century, the only recorded land owners of what was to be the future site of Millwood were Mrs. Marshall, S.D. Paddock, Benjamin Lewis, M.F. Warren, J.S. Woodard and sons, and Harry Salmons. These settlers dug wells, raised wheat, fruit, truck garden produce and kept dairy and farm stock.

The main thoroughfares were (as they are today) Trent Road, running east and west, and Argonne (then called Woodard Road), running north and south. Both were dusty, two-lane wagon trails.

Important in the development of the area was the coming of the Inland Empire Electric Interurban; and in 1906, the Spokane International Railroad. In 1909 a wooden bridge was built across the Spokane River. It linked Millwood to Pasadena Park and Bowie Road (now Upriver Drive.) This was replaced by a concrete bridge in 1920 and Woodard was changed to Argonne Road. Also, in 1909, William A. Brazeau, associated with the Nekoosa-Edwards Paper Mill in Wisconsin and destined to be the first mayor of Millwood, stopped in Spokane en route to the Alaska-Yukon-Pacific Exposition in Seattle. He noted that, with the advent of the railroad, Spokane was fast becoming a major trading center and that land in the Spokane Valley was cheap. (J.S. Woodard had purchased the NE ¼ section 7-25-44 in the 1890s for $5 an acre.) There was railroad access and an abundant underground water supply. The Spokane River was available for electricity and nearby were rich stands of timber.

Brazeau decided then and there that the Valley was the site he needed for his planned Northwest paper mill. He negotiated for the property where the Inland Empire Paper Mill stands today. He foresaw the plant easily serving a 150-mile radius!

Work on the Paper Mill began in 1910. Soon the little community took on the look of a company town. The railroad stop was called Factoria; but box cars were routed to the Paper Mill at Woodard Crossing. When a spur line was constructed from the SI to the mill, cars destined for the mill were marked to Mill at Woodard, later shortened to Millwood.

On September 1, 1911, the preliminary construction work was finished at the mill and production started. About 100 men and women were employed with a monthly payroll of $8,000. A daily production rate of approximately 18 tons was realized. The initial investment before production was $350,000.

The company land was divided into tracts and the company encouraged their employees to own their own homes by assisting with the building and financing. To enhance the beauty of the area, oaks were planted on the parking strip in the center of Dalton and maples lined the other streets.

The first phase of home building began in 1923 between Liberty and Dalton. Prospective home builders were able to choose a floor plan from plans supplied by the mill or could choose other architectural plans and designs independently. The mill installed temporary railroad tracks in this development so that a crane and bucket could be transported from site to site to excavate basements for the new homes.

The second phase of home construction began about 1927 basically between Dalton and Euclid.

A lumber yard, restaurant, barber shop, general store and hotel were doing a thriving business by 1911 along what was to become the Argonne business district.

But the booming town was not without its setbacks.

Spokane Daily Chronicle, September 28, 1912: "Fired by sparks from the stovepipe, the $16,000 hotel occupied by paper mill employees at Millwood was burned to the ground at 7:30 this morning. The fire equipment which was mustered out in the vicinity proved inadequate to handle the blaze. The hotel was built 18 months ago for R.J. Dwyer, the owner. It had 35 rooms, with a store on the lower level. It was of frame construction and offered no resistance to the flames."

Until 1910 when the Millwood Grade School was built on J.S. Woodard land, most of the children attended the old Carnhope School on the outskirts of Spokane. They reached it over bumpy wagon roads and trails. Subsequently, one block south of the Millwood Grade School, West Valley High School was erected. By 1927, there were 350 students at West Valley High. When high school students vacated Millwood Grade School, there was room in the grade school building for the first public kindergarten in Spokane County.

Sunday School was first held in the Millwood Grade School in 1915. A mission of the First Presbyterian Church of Spokane was established there in 1918 and became independent in 1920. On land bought from paper mill holdings, a new church, Millwood Presbyterian Church, was built and dedicated February 15, 1924.

The development of the area around such a predominant economic company as the paper mill, plus the strong community pride and spirit felt by the people, led naturally to the idea of incorporation.

Spokane Valley Herald, October 21, 1927: "The municipal election held at the Millwood Confectionery store at Millwood Saturday, October 15, showed conclusively that the large majority in that community favored incorporation, 75 voting for and only five against.

"Millwood includes a strip of land 1 1/2 miles long and 1/2 mile wide. It has a natural boundary, the Spokane River on the north, with Trent Highway on the south, Graham Avenue on the west, and Second Street on the east.

"The newly incorporated city has a population of 437. The West Valley High School of District 202 is situated in its midst, also Millwood Grade School, which has 250 pupils. The Inland Empire Paper Mill, which employs between 300 and 400 men, is a big feature that will add to the future growth of the city. The Millwood Community Presbyterian Church, with a membership of several hundred is an outstanding development, and has a drawing influence.

"The new city can boast of a Masonic Temple, a bank, one drug store, two grocery stores, two garages, two lunch counters, a lumber yard, one meat market, two barber shops, one confectionery store, three gas stations, one shoe repair shop and a post office.

"Election of the first officers who will serve a term of two years are: Mayor, W.A. Brazeau; Treasurer, Harry Salmons; Councilmen, A.H. Byram, C.L. Ammerman, J.Y.W. Wilson; F.W. Aucutt, and Seth T. Woodard."

About 300 yards north of Sprague looking south. Left to right on what is now the corner of Sprague and Pines: SE corner, power substation; SW corner, Opportunity Store. *Courtesy of Patricia Smith Goetter and Bea Goffinet.*

Pines Road from site of Opportunity Presbyterian Church at corner of Main and Pines about 1908 looking toward the corner of Sprague and Pines. Extreme left: Opportunity Store. *Photo courtesy of Patricia Smith Goetter.*

A Place Called Opportunity

[*Spokane Valley Today*, February, 1987]

Waiting for the light to change at the corner of Sprague and Pines, with the traffic piled up a block or more, it is hard to believe that not too many years ago Pines was a two-lane road; and at the turn of the century, the place we now call Opportunity was a dry, sparsely settled dust bowl, unable to sustain crops.

Opportunity never was an incorporated town, although Spokane Valley incorporation (including Opportunity) has been on the ballot several times in recent years.

Early in its history, Opportunity, like other Valley communities, was one of several irrigation districts. Later it was a community club, and later still, a township. Now it is identified as a part of Spokane County, governed by three county commissioners.

At the turn of the century, the farms that dotted the area were struggling. Cattle and dairy farming were the most successful. Then Albert A. Kelly installed the first centrifugal pump ever used in this area for irrigation and the possibility of watering the Valley became a reality. (See article, "Modern Electric Water Company.")

With irrigation Opportunity came alive. It was fertile. The rocky quality of the soil held the sun's heat. Orchards thrived. Developers platted the land and called it a name selected by a Miss Kelsey, daughter of a prominent onion raiser. She chose the inspirational name, *Opportunity*. Hers was the winning entry in a naming contest sponsored by an early realty firm.

With the influx of farmers, a business district formed on the south side of Sprague between Pines and Robie. The township hall was built and still stands bearing over the door the erection date: *Opportunity Anno 1912*. Another imprint that can be seen by the sharp-eyed is the name John W. Knight, now partially obscured behind modern signs. John Knight was a carpenter who built a wooden building in the block. The building once housed A.E. Knight's Plumbing and Heating (owned by his son)

and Groves Garage. The same carpenter built the old Opportunity Christian Church. His great granddaughter resides in the area.

Spring flooding was a problem in the early years. Hence the elevated floors and the steps going into the businesses in the block.

The Town Hall housed the first library in Opportunity, later to be known as the Opportunity Branch of the Spokane Public Library. It also served as the early voting place and as a meeting place for Presbyterians before their church was built.

The IOOF Hall

In the early days, neighbors were the only hope of help should a disaster strike. Many of the men of Opportunity organized themselves into the Wilford Chapter of the Independent Order of Odd Fellows. Their main purpose was to lend a helping hand when needed.

The IOOF Hall became part of the business block and was built largely with volunteer labor and financed by members. The deed for the lot was received August 18, 1910. The trustees borrowed $3000 and started work on a building 32 x 60 feet. The excavating, hauling, brick and lumber work and much of the carpentry was donated by the Brothers.

By spring, 1911, the upper hall was completed and the Odd Fellows moved in February 23, 1911. The actual dedication took place March 1911.

The lodge had financial ups and downs but proved valuable to the little community. Like the nearby Town Hall, it was a gathering spot. Men enjoyed playing pool in the basement. Many organizations, such as the Masons, met there.

The lower hall housed the first Opportunity Post Office. Later a new building in the block became the post office. Old timers will remember Mr. Ketterman, postmaster in the early thirties.

In 1926 Mr. Berry of Inland Monument Co., Spokane, furnished and engraved an official cornerstone for a new dining room, an addition to the

IOOF building. The Rebekahs, ladies of the lodge, furnished and equipped it. A loan of $10,000 was necessary.

By 1948 all indebtedness was fully paid and the Brothers again borrowed money. This time $6000 for a heating plant.

Carl Goffinet

Carl Goffinet and Logan Jorgans opened the Frigid Food Bank on the SE corner of Sprague and Pines in 1946. Goffinet spent his childhood in the Opportunity area. He remembers Hart's blacksmith shop on the corner of Sprague and Robie. It was his particular delight to walk from the old Opportunity Grade School at the corner of Sprague and Bowdish (now demolished) to the blacksmith shop, stopping to watch the sparks fly.

Goffinet recalls Groves Garage next to the IOOF Hall and a man named Kincaid who was chief mechanic. He remembers Castle's Grocery, Hart's Dry Goods, Coble's Meats, a drug store and a general store also in the block.

Vivid in Goffinet's memory is the fire in 1921 which burned most of the wooden buildings in the Knight Block.

The fire fighting was done by a bucket brigade that obtained water from an irrigation ditch that ran behind the buildings. The fire attracted all the residents of the area including children. Parents, afraid their children would be burned, removed the candy display cases from the grocery store, moved them across the street and told the children to eat their fill. Thus the fire caused no loss of life although, it is said, many sick stomachs.

At this time across the street on the north side of Sprague was the old electric railroad connecting Spokane and Coeur d'Alene. Goffinet says it ran from Spokane through Union Park to Egdecliff, crossed Sprague at Park Road, paralleled Sprague at the Morrison Seed Company to the Liberty Lake Junction, then to Post Falls and Huetter, ending near the old Templin's Restaurant in Coeur d'Alene. The Opportunity train depot was on the northwest corner of Sprague and Pines and was later remodeled into the Swedish Tavern and demolished in the late 60s.

Kortte's IGA

We are indebted to Mrs. Howard Campbell, the former Mrs. Kortte, for this information about early grocery stores.

The first grocery store in Opportunity was on the SW corner of Sprague and Pines. It was known as the General Store.

In 1909 it was purchased by Mr. Farr and his son-in-law, W.P. Myers. Myers had been a clerk in the A.T. Dishman General Store. (See article, "A Turn of the Century Big Businessman.")

He tore down the old structure and built what was then considered one of the most modern stores of its time. It was of double-faced brick and had a luxury glass-enclosed office for the owner. Shelves of merchandise extended to the ceiling and were accessible by a long pole with a grabber on the end.

Mr. Myers sold shoes, clothing, dry goods items and groceries. He also had a gasoline pump, but no telephone.

Behind the original General Store was a livery barn used by the owner to house the horse and buggy he used to deliver his wares.

Dick Evans, still residing in the Valley, was Mr. Myers' delivery boy when he was twenty years old. On Monday his job was to solicit orders east to Sullivan, west to Apple Center (north University Road), south to Chester and north to Mission. On Tuesday he delivered those orders. He especially remembers handling potatoes in 126-pound bags. He recalls that Ross Dolliver was Perry Myers right hand man.

In 1944 W.P. Myers retired and Ray Kortte bought the General Store on the SW corner of Sprague and Pines. At that time the population of Opportunity was less than 1,000; but Kortte was a far-sighted businessman. He bought Myers' complete stock: groceries, dry goods, shoes, paint and notions.

He had come to the Valley from Montana, having seen Army service overseas during World War I. He studied at the University of Montana at Bozeman with the intention of becoming a veterinarian. Everyone Ray talked to warned him that horses were on the way out as a means of transportation; and so he switched his major and graduated in dairy husbandry.

Ray's first job was at the Fairmont Creamery in Spokane as salesman. He later became sales manager, a position he held until the Creamery moved to the Midwest during the 20s.

Ray then purchased the Orchard Avenue Grocery in 1938. He changed the name to the Park Road IGA and successfully operated that store until locating in Opportunity.

Kortte sensed that the Valley was in a period of growth. He closed the premises for five weeks and with the aid of five men razed the interior from wall to wall. A sidewalk was laid in front of the store. The front was completely remodeled and a modern parking lot was added.

The old dry goods stock was offered to charity. What could not be given away or was of no use to him was dumped in an old basement (probably remaining from the fire of '21) on the west side of the property and covered up.

Some day this site might prove a mecca for an antique collector. Mrs. Campbell remembers among the items buried were many pairs of high button shoes, corsets, and sauerkraut barrels.

The store Kortte built was utilitarian. In contrast to the former grocer's office, his was a loft with a single desk and chair. Along with standard groceries, he had a service butcher shop and bought eggs from local farmers. The Kortte's themselves candled the eggs. They had six employees and a box boy.

In 1957 Kortte leased the building to Archie McGregor and in 1964 sold it to Vern Bromling who operated a drug store next door.

Mrs. Campbell remembers with some sadness that Kortte's IGA met a similar fate as the old Myers General Store. One day the Kortte's went to town. When they returned, the building had been knocked down with a hammer and collapsed into the basement.

Ray died in 1957. He had been a valuable citizen. As president of the Chamber of Commerce, 1947-48, he was anxious to advertise the possibilities of the Valley. He had a sign erected at the State Line that announced the Spokane Valley and its aluminum industry.

Vern Bromling used the former grocery store property for a parking lot. He planted trees and opened the first prescription drive-in window in the Inland Empire.

Dynamic Changes at Post Falls, A Near Neighbor

[*Spokane Valley Today,* May, 1992]

In 1992 Governor Cecil Andrews labeled Post Falls "the fastest growing little town in Idaho." The traveler on I-90 sees visible signs of this growth: Riverbend Commerce Park, Factory Outlets, Jacklin Seed Company, Greyhound Dog Track, the lumber companies, and the signs pointing the way to such attractions as Templin's Resort and Highlands Golf and Country Club.

For years Post Falls was a small lumbering and agricultural town somewhat overshadowed by its larger neighbors, Coeur d'Alene and Spokane. Recent promotion, expansion, and aggressive marketing of the town's many assets by city government, Jobs Plus, and Jacklin Seed have resulted in a booming city.

Post Falls is now a totally diversified community with large and small business and industry gaining a solid footing. Its small town atmosphere and natural beauty attracts tourists and settlers from far and near.

According to Kimberly Brown, manager of the Post Falls Chamber of Commerce and local historian, the development of Post Falls is occurring much as Frederick Post, its founder, envisioned it. He had a positive dream for the town and by starting the timber mill and securing water rights from the Indians, laid the foundation for all that is happening in 1993.

"We're not citified and we're not rural, but we have the advantages of both and we are truly an American city," Post said.

Frederick Post

Frederick Post moved to North Idaho in 1871. He was an immigrant from Herborn Hesse in West Germany via Illinois. At the site of what is now Post Falls, he found an Indian village called Q'emiln (pronounced ka-mee-lin), meaning "throat of the river." If legend is correct, Post immediately struck up a friendly relationship with the Coeur d'Alenes living there.

In Illinois, along with farming, constructing lime kilns and operating a stone quarry, he had developed water power on the Fox River. Because of that experience, he recognized the potential of the Upper Falls of the Spokane River, in Idaho Territory, and obtained water rights from the Indians to harness that power.

In the early 1870s, he began construction of a sawmill at the site of the Upper Falls. It was not finished until 1880; because for a brief period, Post turned his interests to the Lower Falls, in the town of what is now Spokane. He bought forty acres of land at Spokan Falls from James N. Glover in 1876 and there, utilizing the power of the falls, built the area first flour mill. In 1872, he sold his Spokane land and water rights and returned to Post Falls to finish construction of his sawmill there. In Spokane today both Post Street and Post Addition recall Post's early impact on the city's history.

It is interesting to note that in the early days Post Falls provided irrigation to portions of the Spokane Valley and electricity to mining developments in the Silver Valley.

Post's sawmill at Post Falls was located at one of the finest mill sites in Kootenai County. Logs could be brought in booms from Lake Coeur d'Alene down the Spokane River. The mill had a capacity of seventy thousand feet of lumber in twenty-four hours and at full production prior to the turn of the century, employed about 600 men. The town grew up around the mill sites. Soon it boasted a flour mill, shingle mill, box factory, and other light industries.

Post leased the mill for several years and finally sold it in 1894. It was destroyed by fire in 1902. The population of Post Falls immediately shrank to about 300 and remained at that level through the '20s and '30s. The mill site is today the site of the Post Falls Dam completed by Washington Water Power in 1908. That hydroelectric facility has been expanded by the Louisiana Pacific Corporation.

As a living memorial to Frederick Post, the city has an ongoing cultural and community exchange with his birthplace, Herborn, Germany. Students from Post Falls have toured Herborn and the Chamber of Commerce is expanding business and cultural exchanges with the Herborn area. Like Post Falls, Herborn has a lumbering heritage.

Treaty Rock

A local attraction in Post Falls is Treaty Rock, located south of the intersection of Seltice Way and Compton Street. It is a large granite outcropping onto which are carved the words, "June 1, 1871, Frederick Post."

Also on the rock are Coeur d'Alene Indian pictographs done sometime after 1730. According to Kimberly Brown, local legend has fostered the belief that this special rock represents the signing of a treaty between Post and Coeur d'Alene Chief Andrew Seltice

The city celebrated its one hundredth birthday in 1991.

Pleasant View,
The Valley's Ghost Town

[*Spokane Valley Today,* May, 1991]

To get to the Valley's so-called "ghost town," travel east on I-90 ten miles from the Pines Road entrance. Turn off the Freeway at Exit 299 marked "State Line Village." Then will begin a most scenic drive through prairie land and rolling hills dotted now and then with farmhouses.

In the mid-1800s the land at the State Line near the Spokane River was heavily wooded with Ponderosa Pine and was inhabited mainly by the Coeur d'Alene Indians. In 1858 after the Indian battles at Steptoe, Four Lakes, and Spokane Bridge, the Indians agreed to move onto a reservation in North Idaho. In 1891 Congress and the Coeur d'Alenes agreed to a treaty whereby the Indians would move to a smaller reservation near Worley. This opened the area to colonization by white settlers. Some settlers came merely in search of cheap land and adventure. Others prospected for minerals, cut timber, and farmed and ranched.

Among the newcomers was William Frederick Plonske from Germany via Wisconsin. In 1892 he homesteaded land along the Spokane River and built there a one-room log house with attic, still occupied in 1991 by son Fred.

The story is that W.F., as he was known, spoke so often of his "pleasant view" of the Spokane River and nearby mountains that by 1905 the name was widely accepted for the area. The store and blacksmith shop he built became known as the Pleasant View Trading Center. By 1908 Pleasant View officially appeared in commissioner's records.

Today's local maps show Pleasantview Road, Pleasant View School, Pleasant View Church, Pleasant View Bridge, and Pleasant View Cemetery.

The area, as you turn off the freeway, was once the southern extremity of the old town of Spokane Bridge. It is also the site of the Milwaukee Railroad line that went from Spokane to Metaline Falls — up in the morning and back at night every day, carrying passengers and freight.

About two miles on down W. Riverside Road, you will come to the Pleasant View Baptist Church. It was completed in 1910 on donated land with donated labor. It had the best of facilities — privies and a common water dipper. In 1982 a new addition was built. Regular services are still held in the church and as families enter the area, the membership increases.

The little dirt road up the hill just north of the church leads to Pleasant View Cemetery, originally called Mountain View Cemetery. It was used by the residents of Spokane Bridge and Pleasant View. Plots were and are free for those who have lived in the area a designated number of years. That land too was donated land. W.F. Plonske's son, Fred, is caretaker at the cemetery. There are tombstones new and old beyond the modern-looking yellow brick gate. The cemetery is landscaped by nature only — pine cones and pine needles cover the Ponderosa pine-covered acreage. In the far left corner is a tall bluish gray stone marking the grave of Arthur M. Benham, first settler buried in the Pleasant View Cemetery. He died of small pox in 1889.

Farther on down Riverside Drive is the brick and stone Pleasant View School. It too is built on land donated by the Plonskes. It has four rooms and is on the National Register of Historic Places. The school closed in 1937 but is still used as a gathering place by the Pleasant View Community Association.

Turning around and backtracking, we turn at the first road on the right and again at the first dirt road on the left. From the hill we look down upon three buildings along the Spokane River. These made up the Plonske Trading Center, the earliest center of its kind in the area. The building on the right is the old blacksmith shop. On the left with the old pump still standing is the store. In the window can be seen a sign from times past advertising

Tree Tea. Merchandise was hauled from Spokane in W.F. Plonske's Model T Ford truck and included anything the settlers needed — groceries, feed, household supplies and occasionally even a casket.

The Plonskes handled only cured meat. Early settlers tell of a farmer who drove a wagon through the hills selling "on the spot meat." In the bed of the wagon under a canvas (to protect the wares from flies and dust) was a carcass. Approaching a home, he bawled, "You want meat?" To fill an order he pulled back the canvas, cut off a steak, and then (it is said) wiped his bloody hands and knife on his horse's tail.

The buildings that made up the Trading Center are used today as shop and storage by the Plonskes.

The comfortable, friendly-looking home beyond the Trading Center is the home of present generation Fred and Bessie Plonske. The dining-room is the original one-room log home built by W.F. and first located across the road (Plonske Lane) on the bank of the Spokane River. The little house was moved to its present location and enlarged after W.F. married Nancy Giles.

Pleasant View Bridge can be reached by turning off I-90 at the Pleasant View Road Exit. It has quite a history. The first bridge in the Pleasant View area across the Spokane River was built in 1905 about a half mile south of what was known as Signal Point Station. It linked residents south of the river to services north — the highway, the Milwaukee Railroad and the electric train. In 1903 settlers gathered at the bridge to watch Teddy Roosevelt campaign from the back of a slow moving train headed for Spokane Bridge.

In 1920 a second steel and wood bridge was constructed at the present site. In 1952 the 180-foot midsection mysteriously collapsed five days after a Post Falls Highway District heavy 4-wheel truck pulling a bulldozer on a trailer crossed over it. Both the collapsed midspan and the north span were replaced; but after more structural damage appeared, the bridge was declared unsafe for traffic. However people and motorcycles continued to use it. The Highway District, fearing a law suit, burned the wooden south span in the '70s. Today, unused and ghostly in appearance, the middle and north spans still stand.

Medicine and Health Care

"The physician of the Territory accepted the hardships of medical practice on the western frontier. Those who couldn't, soon left. When word came that a woman was in labor at a distant wheat farm or a cowboy had caught a horn in his belly at an outlying ranch, the doctor would pack his saddle bags and answer the call, winter or summer, through blizzards or blinding heat. If surgery was indicated, it was done on a kitchen table, using drip ether for anesthesia. If the labor was hard and long, the doctor stayed with the patient until the child was born."

[From "Doctors on Horseback" by Norman Bolker, MD, *Medical Bulletin*, Volume 62, Number 3, Fall, 1989.]

Medicine and Health Care

CHRONOLOGICAL HISTORY

1850   The **Spokane Valley** was in Washington Territory. Military surgeons attached to forts were the only trained medical personnel in the area. Frontier folk relied on doctor books, home remedies, midwives and the help of neighbors when sickness struck.

1877   The first doctor, **Dr. D.C. Masterson,** arrived in Spokane.

1880   Although small, there was an active medical community in Spokane.

1881   With the arrival of the **Northern Pacific Railroad,** people—and doctors— moved in. **Dr. Waterhouse,** Director of the First National Bank in Spokane, doubled as a proprietor of a pharmacy and as County Coroner.

1885   The **Spokane Medical Association** formed primarily to set up a fee schedule for services. Twenty area doctors were members, coming from as far away as Colville, Rockford, Cheney, and Deep Creek.

1887   January: The three-story brick **Sacred Heart Hospital** opened on **Front** and **Brown** in Spokane with 50 beds and six physicians. **Mother Joseph of the Sacred Heart** drew up the plans and **Sister Joseph of Arimathea,** was the first superior and administrator. Both were nuns of the religious order, **Sisters of Charity of Providence.**

1887   **Cyrus K. Merriam,** a military doctor assigned to the eastern area of Washington Territory, became a part of the medical community and re-organized the Medical Society into a professional group.

1889   **Darius Mason** was an organizer and president of the **Washington State Medical Association.**

1890   **Spokane County Medical Society** was formed although its by-laws were not operative until 1892. **Dr. Fred Essig** participated in the creation of the **Washington State Board of Health** and chartered the **Spokane City Board of Health.**

1890   Eastern State Hospital was established for the "care of the insane. " It was operated by the state and served 176 patients during its first year.

1896

1897

Three deaconesses of the Methodist Church rented some rooms in a home at Third and Howard streets for the care of the homeless and aged. Nine years later, the **Franklin P. O'Neills,** wealthy miners, financed a more suitable one-and-a-half story frame building on **Fourth Avenue** between **Howard** and **Mill** streets. Originally named the **Maria Beard Home and Hospital** after **Mrs. O'Neill's** mother, it was ultimately known as **Deaconess Hospital.**

1898

Spokane's population was approaching 35,000 and more doctors kept arriving. A small group of women associated with the Episcopal Church operated a small two-story church-owned hospital known as the **Spokane Protestant Sanitarium** at **Jefferson** and **Sprague.** In 1910, a group of benefactors provided the building which housed the hospital for many years in the northwest portion of the city on land donated by **John Finch.** It later became **St. Luke's Hospital.**

1902

Fort Wright Hospital became part of the Fort and later acted as a base hospital for **Geiger Field** and **Fairchild Air Force Base. Fort Wright** was built in the 1890s in response to citizens' concern about marauding Indians.

1907

Sacred Heart Hospital occupied its present site at **Eighth** and **Browne.**

1910

A "Pest House" was opened on the **Spokane River** for the care of patients with contagious diseases.

1912

A few physicians had settled in the Valley. Some of the earliest names recalled are **"Doc Walker"** who "lived in the big house on the corner of **Twelfth** and **Pierce"** (the house is still there). His office was in the **Opportunity Block.** Senior residents remember **Doctors Bennett** and **Hopkins** whose offices were in their homes (exact location forgotten), and **Dr. Hinds** the dentist who lived on **Bowdish Road.** The **Segerstroms** remember going to a dentist in **Rathdrum** named **Dr. Hollister** who was part Indian.

1915

The first class of registered nurses graduated from **Sacred Heart School of Nursing.** The Spokane area was referred to as a "mission" by the **Sisters of Providence.**

1916

A hospital was opened on **Park Road** in the **Spokane Valley** for the care of tuberculosis patients. It could accommodate 200 patients, was built with funds from the Tuberculosis League, and was called **Edgecliff Hospital.** The hospital was closed in 1977 and has since been redeveloped into a retirement community.

1918

The arrival in Spokane of **Dr. Charles B. Ward** marked the coming of local radiology. Dr. Ward originally located in the **Mission Avenue** area, using an x-ray machine with a static generator and condenser and developed his x-ray plates in a bathtub.

The **American College of Surgeons** launched the Hospital Standardization Program. Local hospitals quickly fell in line.

Early Medicine

Until 1918 when the then recently formed American College of Surgeons launched its Hospital Standardization Program, medical care, even in hospitals, was more or less hit or miss. Areas such as the Spokane Valley that had no centralized population, sought medical care in the nearest city. For the Valley, the nearest medical center was Spokane.

In the Fall of 1989, the Spokane County Medical Association had its one hundredth birthday. To celebrate, its regular publication, the *Medical Bulletin*, Volume 62, Number 3, Fall, 1989, was titled "One Hundred Years of Medicine in the Inland Empire," and contained articles by physicians about the "old days."

The following excerpts and condensations are from articles in that bulletin. They tell the story of local medical history.

"Washington Territory assumed the present dimensions of Washington State when Idaho Territory was organized in 1863.... Except for the military surgeons attached to the forts, very little trained medical personnel were available (at that time)... Every homemaker had a do-it-yourself doctor book with instructions for self diagnosis and treatment. Women who had observed the birthing process served as midwives. Some who had developed a good reputation for knowledge of home remedies became self-appointed nurse practitioners.

"A good neighbor was expected to enter a home to help the sick even at the risk of contracting the illness. With an entire family immobilized, someone had to bring in the water, cook the gruel and broth and empty the slop bucket. If a neighbor had a potion that cured someone with similar symptoms, the patient could expect to receive it...

"As the population grew, physicians with varying degrees of training moved into the populated areas...

"Spokan Falls had no doctor until 1877. At the time, it was a cluster of log houses, a ferry, a dam and a saw mill. That year, Dr. D.C. Masterson came with his family. Soon after, two druggists, George Davis and C.W. Cornelius, arrived. Dr. Campbell arrived a short time later

"Washington Territory had no licensing board. No examinations were required, and anyone could confer on himself the title Doctor of Medicine. In 1882, the Territorial Legislature passed an act requiring each practicing physician to display his diploma to the County Auditor as well as in his office or be subject to penalty. The diploma could be issued by any legally chartered medical college, and, since there were no standards for such institutions, the legislation, though well intended, was meaningless. The language of the act makes it clear that the legislators did not want to eliminate medical care of any quality, and all practitioners who had established their practice prior to the act were not affected.

"Usually, physicians had received, at the least, an apprenticeship with a practicing physician, during which they read medical texts. Medical schools ranged from valid educational institutions affiliated with colleges and hospitals, to proprietary schools that were no more than diploma mills. For a brief time, Spokane had its own medical school but it existed only as a concept. Spokane College, also known as Jenkins University, was a liberal arts college located on College Avenue between Monroe and Adams Streets. The school offered courses in the biological sciences, and spurred by Dr. G.W. Libby, agreed to provide medical training leading to a degree. The college functioned from 1883 to 1892, when it closed its doors without ever having had a medical student...

The frontier physician had to carry supplies in

his bag adequate to cover any emergency. He had scissors, scalpel, bistouries for lancing boils, delivery forceps, hemostats, probes, ligatures and metal catheters. Bed sheets could be torn to make bandages. He carried along a supply of herbal extracts, tinctures, powders, surface irritants such as mustard for poultices and narcotics.

"If a pharmacy was available, the doctor would write a prescription, usually for combinations of herbal extracts."

[From "Doctors on Horseback" by Norman Bolker, M.D., p.20, 21.]

"The records of Spokane County Health District of June 1887 reveal that the major health problems of the citizens of the Spokane Falls, Washington Territory, were generally one associated with gross lack of sanitation. The City Health Officer in these pre-statehood years was Dr. A.S. Campbell, and his primary duties appeared to be associated with surveying the community for environmental problems, providing and giving vaccinations for smallpox and issuing orders for abatement of public health problems. If the order of the Health Officer was not followed, the Chief of Police, who was also known as the "sanitary policeman," would enforce the Health Officer's order.

"Many early public health activities were associated with the river and drinking water protection.

"From the start, Spokane inhabitants (and those of the Valley) filled their water buckets from the river.

"Health officials had always been aware of the risk of using the river as a source of drinking water, but could offer no practical alternative. Their concerns were relieved by a happy accident in 1907 when excavations for a hydraulic pumping station in the Spokane Valley tapped into an abundant supply of potable and bacteria free water—the Spokane aquifer. Since then, this has been our water source."

[From "Guarding the Public Health" by F. Lee Mellish, Dr.. P.H., Administrator Spokane County Health District, p.69, 70, 71.]

"The first hospitals were informal affairs. A physician could readily convert a large house into a series of bedrooms and, by providing a nursing staff, create a hospital. Nursing schools were nonexistent in this area, and training for the nursing staff was informal and limited to serving meals, giving sponge baths, making beds and carrying bedpans.

"The quality of hospitals improved after the Sisters of Providence responded to a call from Father Cataldo and came to Spokane Falls. In 1887, Sister Joseph and Sister Arimathea opened the first Sacred Heart Hospital on Front Street, now Spokane Falls Boulevard, between Brown and Bernard streets. A frame building two stories high and faced with brick, it not only had indoor plumbing but hot and cold running water."

[From "Doctors on Horseback" by Norman Bolker, M.D., p.23. 24]

"In 1899, the State of Washington was ten years old…aspirin was discovered…and Deaconess Hospital School of Nursing opened its doors for the first class. The six students admitted to the program that year were first in a family that grew to more than 2,000 members. For eight decades, the school educated and prepared nurses for service in health care and became an integral part of the medical community in the region.

"Only two of the original six students remained that first year for the summer, the elder acting as head nurse. The hospital was a three-story frame building with a bed capacity of 30."

[From "Their Caps Came with Caring," by Anna Mae Ericksen, R.N. and a committee of Deaconess School of Nursing Graduates, p.43]

"In 1907, a "Pest House" was opened on the Spokane River for the care of patients with contagious diseases. It is now a nursing home. In this day of antibiotics and chemotherapeutic agents, it is difficult to realize the prevalence of infectious ailments in the early days of this community. The great killer was tuberculosis and, in 1915, a special hospital was opened to care for victims of this disease. Located in the Spokane Valley, it occupied land contributed by the county and was built with funds from the Tuberculosis League. It was called Edgecliff Sanitarium and could accommodate 200 patients."

[From "Spokane, A Community of Hospitals" by Carl P. Schlicke, M.D., p. 32]

"At the turn of the century, the town was growing vigorously, numbering 36,000 people. Sacred Heart, Deaconess and St. Luke's hospitals were all established, functioning and physician-controlled. All were involved in nursing education, a function largely carried on by physicians. A policy of 'open staff' was in effect at all hospitals. With few exceptions, all physicians had their offices in the central downtown area."

[From "A Very Brief History of the Spokane County Medical Society" by Lawrence Pence, M.D., p.9]

"The arrival in Spokane of Dr. Charles B. Ward in 1916 marked the origination of local radiology. Dr. Ward, a native of Canada and originally a gynecologist, was a virtually self-taught practitioner of both diagnostic and therapeutic procedures, using x-ray machines and radium capsules for these purposes.

"He originally located in the Mission Avenue area, using an x-ray machine with a static generator and condenser and developed his x-ray plates in a bathtub. At that time, there were no formal training courses in radiology, so he was obliged to obtain his knowledge of the specialty by visiting various cities all over the country, as well as reading the few articles published in the few medical publications available.

"In 1917, or thereabouts, the national hospital accreditation organization decided to require hospitals to have formally staffed radiology departments, and Dr. Ward was asked to establish these departments in both Deaconess and St. Luke's hospitals sometime thereafter. Dr. Joseph Aspray, another self-taught radiologist, arrived in Spokane shortly after Dr. Ward and organized the Department of Radiology in Sacred Heart Hospital in 1916."

[From "Imaging Enters the Picture" by Richard A. Betts, M.D., p.60]

"The flu epidemic of 1918 accounted for 1,045 deaths in Spokane alone. So severe was the situation that public congregations were prohibited, department stores were prohibited from having sales attracting crowds, schools were closed and a special influenza hospital was set up at the Lion Hotel at South 112½ Lincoln. The flu hospital was open for a period of 89 days and cared for 617 patients of which 68 succumbed to influenza.

"Flu masks were worn by most people in public and the police declared that spitting in the streets would be cause for arrest. Dr. John B. Anderson, health officer, told the public 'that bonfires, spices, salt and vinegar on flames and burning sulfur would not protect citizens of Spokane from flu.' It was recommended by Dr. Anderson to stay away from crowds, drink large quantities of water and avoid fatigue. Gauze masks were also recommended. By mid-January 1919, the epidemic was over for Spokane (and the Valley), but a reported 16, 985 people fell victim to the disease."

[From "Guarding the Public Health" by F. Lee Mellish, Dr. P.H. Administrator Spokane County Health District.]

"In ancient files of Drs. Ward and Betts (local originators of radiology, see above) was found Form 1065 of the U.S. Internal Revenue for the calendar year of 1921. This showed the gross income of the partnership to be $23,251.01. After all expenses of $9,020 were paid, the net was divided by the partners as income before personal taxes. With this princely sum, the early partners could live fairly comfortably, considering that one could get a bungalow for about $1,200 and a new Model-T Ford for about $400. There were few money-wasters, just a few frivolities like movies, if one liked *Birth of a Nation* or *Perils of Pauline*—no television, radio, booze (banned by Prohibition), sports cars or stereos."

[From "Imaging Enters the Picture" by Richard A. Betts, M.D., p. 60]

Science Hall and Doctor Aldrich

[*Spokane Valley Today,* November, 1989]

In 1942 James and Lela Aldrich bought Science Hall with a 25-acre parcel of the University property. [See article, "Spokane University."] They converted Science Hall into a nursing home called the Community Nursing Home, Inc. Bonnie Hudson, a Valley nurse, is a daughter of the Aldrich's. She told me their story, the story of Science Hall:

Lela Aldrich, Bonnie's mother, sought financing for the purchase of the Science Building property from the old Dishman Branch of the Seattle First Bank and was among its earliest customers.

"Father was a colorful figure," said Bonnie. "His story contains the stuff of which western legend is made. And who knows, perhaps some of it is legend. There is documentation that Father was born in Chicago in 1874 and that he was a licensed medical doctor. But his name was Avery.

"Mother claimed he lost his license by treating an unreported gunshot wound, came West, and changed his name."

Bonnie laughed. "I'll probably never know if that is true, but it makes a good story.

"This is fact: Father set up a naturopathic practice on East Frederick near what my sister and I called the Old Minnehaha Dam on the Spokane River. He treated patients by teaching them about good nutrition and is said to have cured many small skin cancers with an X-ray machine he said he built.

"Father was respected and his practice grew. Mother was his nurse for seven years before they were married. She was a skilled and experienced mid-wife. In those days, medical services were scarce and soon Mother and Father needed larger quarters.

"Science Hall was perfect for their needs. It contained offices, laboratories, classrooms, a library, and an auditorium which became Father's lecture hall. It was beautifully located in the pines. Father converted the lower two floors into rooms for patient care. On the third floor were our living quarters (until Father built us a house next door) and the lecture hall where people gathered regularly to hear Father talk about nutrition and diet therapy.

"Father lived only five years after he purchased Science Hall. While he was in charge, it became a delivery home for many unwed mothers. After Father's death, Mother discontinued delivering babies (local doctors also worked there) and the building was used strictly as a nursing home. Hester Kirby, former owner of Kirbyhaven, was one of Mother's employees."

Bonnie continued: "My most vivid memory of those days (except for the crowds that attended Father's lectures) is of a thunderous noise that occurred one morning. We ran outside. An old water tower just southeast of the building had collapsed. Water poured down the hill and into our basement. The roar was deafening. The tower was replaced by a 'modern' pumping station.

"Mother was as remarkable as Father was colorful. She took over immediately on Father's death even though she did not have a high school diploma and had no formal medical training. The state awarded her a license because of her experience as Father's assistant. When she was 58 years old, she earned her high school diploma by correspondence. Her high school education had been interrupted by a case of small pox. She was taken out of high school and sent to what we called the 'Pest House,' a home for those with communicable diseases somewhere east along the Spokane River.

"In 1965 Mother sold the property to Mrs. Margaret Dykes who operated it as Sunshine Gardens, E. 10410 Ninth.

"Mother and Father personified the creativity and motivation that characterized early Valley settlers," Bonnie said with admiration. "I'm carrying on their tradition of health care, but within the boundaries of and with the advantages of the formal education available today. I graduated from West Valley High School, attended Whitworth College, and received my professional training at Deaconess School of Nursing in Spokane. But my interest in people and my love of them I learned from Mother and Father as I worked holidays and vacations with them in the converted old Science Hall."

Edgecliff Sanitarium

For eleven years Valley residents hoped (and some literally prayed) that the majestic Edgecliff Sanitarium building at S. 511 Park Road, owned by the county, would not be demolished.

There were many rumors of impending sales that never materialized. It seemed inevitable: because of mounting bills for the county, that the old building would have to be torn down.

In 1991 just in the nick of time a nonprofit corporation known as Inland Empire Residential Resources bought the property and announced plans to renovate the old hospital and revitalize the potentially beautiful grounds into a 117-unit senior apartment complex.

The plans fell into place. On a sunny autumn day, October 17, 1992, the Spokane County Tuberculosis Hospital at Edgecliff reopened its doors as Park Place Community Retirement Center. Honorable Thomas S. Foley, Speaker of the United States House of Representatives, took part in the ribbon cutting ceremony.

History of Edgecliff Hospital

With the opening in 1915 of Edgecliff Tuberculosis Hospital in the Valley, tuberculosis changed in the area from a highly fatal disease to a disease that became almost completely curable.

At the turn of the century, it was called "the White Plague" and was the number one killer in the nation. Critically ill patients lived with their families causing the disease to spread rapidly. In 1910 the State Supreme Court ruled that tuberculosis hospitals were a nuisance not to be located in residential areas. No one knew how to help afflicted persons.

From 1910 to 1914 with no available treatment center, the incidence of the disease in Spokane as elsewhere increased dramatically. People who were at greatest risk often lived in downtown lodging houses where conditions were just the opposite from what they should be for a tuberculosis cure.

Patients could apply for admission to hospitals, but the hospitals didn't want them.

Social workers, women's groups, and physicians, aware of the tragic plight of such patients, took on the cause. A Spokane Associated Charities nurse went so far as to help patients set up housekeeping in tents in a park at Twelfth Street. In 1907 Spokane County built "a house for consumptives" on the grounds of the County Poor Farm near Spangle.

All of this changed when Spokane County opened Edgecliff in 1915. Six miles outside the city limits on fifty-two acres of pine-covered land and rocky hillside, an Administrative Building and Cottages for tubercular men and women were constructed. It is rumored that people sat on stumps waiting to be admitted.

The spacious grounds, wide lawns, shade trees, vegetable garden, and hog farm contributed to a homelike atmosphere, necessary for the "successful" treatment of the day—good food, fresh air, bed rest, and hospitalization—sometimes for as long as fifteen years.

In 1917 a Children's Building was erected and in 1919 the old hospital was built with a separate powerhouse. In 1949 came a new hospital with an enlarged kitchen, a boiler plant and a surgical wing.

The revolution in treatment came in the mid-1940s with the discovery of antibiotics. From a long period of absolutely no medication, a new era of successful drug treatment was a wonderful change for the doctors in charge at Edgecliff.

As the patient load decreased, funding became a problem. In 1971 the State transferred funding responsibilities to nineteen Washington counties, but in 1975 rescinded that measure. Edgecliff was doomed.

In the final years of operating, part of the complex was used as a detoxification center. It was empty after 1981 until Park Place Retirement Community came into being.

When the hospital closed in 1977, some employees wrote their recollections in *Bedposts,* the official house publication. Some of these are quoted below:

GAYLE CROCKER, director of the nursing when the facility closed: "When Edgecliff opened, there were two large wards with screened-in areas much like porches. In winter they were very cold. Patients woke up with snow on their beds and ice in their water glasses. The beds were poor. The mattresses were thin as were the blankets. Nightwear would be pajamas, mittens and cap and so many blankets that one could not move. Imagine a little 9-month old baby sleeping in an open screened-in ward during cold winter nights. A special sleeping outfit was made to cover hands and most of the body. Hot rocks and hot copper containers, called "pigs," were placed at the foot of the bed to provide heat. There was a teacher for both school-age children and adults."

HELEN CARLSON, office manager: "Eventually the hog farm had to be dispensed with. The ground became so infested with contaminated food scraps from the hospital's patient trays that the hogs were found to have contracted human TB. Raising a garden was also stopped. The employment situation was bad when I started working there after World War II. I took the head housekeeper in my car and drove up and down the roads close to the hospital. Anyone we saw who looked able-bodied, we would stop and inquire if they could come to work!"

DR. GEORGE RODKEY, medical director from 1957-1977: "Over the years Edgecliff served the people of eastern Washington, Idaho, and some of Montana. Nearly 10,000 were hospitalized. Multiple thousands more were seen on an outpatient basis. In the early years before medications, the length of stay was long. As medications became available and collapse and surgical procedures were perfected, the hospital stay was shortened and fewer patients succumbed to the disease. The patients and staff grew to respect and appreciate the surgical skill of Dr. Gilbert Schneider, who performed most of the chest surgery. Dr. Frank S. Miller was the beloved previous medical director who served the hospital for nearly forty years. Not to be forgotten is Dr. Wiliam Hazelton, a mild, mannered perfect gentleman."

In those final pages of Bedposts, many paid tribute to Honey Zorn, activities director whose vibrant personality contributed so much to the excellent morale at the hospital. Also remembered fondly were the many who were employed in nursing, surgery, pharmacy, laboratory, x-ray, social services, occupational therapy, education, housekeeping, dietary maintenance, linen and supply.

When Harry Green, executive director of Inland Empire Residential Resources, undertook and saw to completion in 1992 the immense project of constructing Park Place Retirement Community from the remnants of the abandoned Edgecliff Hospital, he performed a memorable service for the community and the county.

"It has been gratifying," he said, "to return to the community I grew up in and develop two landmark properties (Park Place and the Academy) that have affected the quality of care and housing for our seniors."

Banks, Newspapers

"Faith in the future of this Valley, confidence in her people, and an imperative need as well as a common medium for interchange of ideas on the industrial, social, educational and moral problems of the Valley—this is why we believe no other newspaper ever had a more auspicious beginning or promising future than the *Spokane Valley Herald*.

"This is your newspaper, folks. Use it without stint. Its columns are open to all news fit to be printed and to the championing of every interest that vitally concerns the people of the Spokane Valley."

[From one of the first editorials published in the *Valley Herald* and written by E.W. Mason, editor, May 7, 1920]

The Opportunity State Bank was the first bank in the Valley. It opened for business May 31, 1919. *Photo courtesy of Spokane Valley Museum archives.*

Banks, Newspapers

CHRONOLOGICAL HISTORY

1879   Valley people read the *Spokan Times,* the first newspaper in Spokane.

1919   May 31: **Opportunity State Bank** opened with **Sidney E. Smith,** "Father of Spokane Valley," as cashier. The bank assets were $200,000.

1920   March 24: First number of *Valley Herald* issued by founders **Harry E. Nelson** and **Karl Frolander.** It was "free" and an eight page tabloid. The new **Opportunity Bank** helped finance the paper.

1920   May 7: First full-size, six-column *Herald* published through the Western Newspaper Union, a weekly service. Offices were at 320 Rookery Building, Spokane.

1920   State bank at **Dishman** was chartered and a bank was chartered at **Millwood.**

1920   **H.N. Fogle** became president of the state bank at **Greenacres.**

1924   April: **Buell Felts** and **Wilbur King** became publishers of the *Herald* and for the first time offices were in the **Valley** at the **Opportunity Bank Building.**

Banks, Newspapers

In 1879, the approximately 40 residents of the Spokane Valley read the *Spokan Times.*

By 1900, 1051 people lived in the Valley on scattered parcels. The 96,000 acres of immediate Valley averaged only one person to every 91 acres.

By 1910, 3503 people lived in the Valley. They still read Spokane papers and banked in Spokane.

A 1920 census showed a county population of 6541.

With the arrival on the Valley scene, May 31, 1919, of a bank, the Opportunity State Bank, and in the '20s, of banks at Dishman, Millwood, and Greenacres, and on March 24, 1920, of a newspaper, *The Spokane Valley Herald,* the Valley seemed to come of age.

This aging pointed up the common needs and interests of Valley folk and their interest in forming some sort of union to solve common problems.

In 1921, union happened in the form of the Chamber of Commerce. With the formation of the Chamber, this history book ends; for with union, the Valley took on a new look.

The new era, from the formation of the Chamber until World War II, is the subject of Volume II of this work.

Sidney E. Smith, Opportunity Pioneer and Businessman

Sidney Smith came to Opportunity in 1919, a year when business people in the Valley were beginning to realize that their area of farms and apple orchards held promise of a very different future. There was talk of uniting the communities of the Valley. Sydney jumped right into the action and helped organize the Chamber of Commerce which came into being just two years later, in 1921.

The Valley had no bank when he arrived.

Sidney had banking experience. He had started as a messenger and worked his way up through the old Exchange Bank in Spokane. He also had worked for two years in banking at Wallace, Idaho. Thus he was prepared for the exciting role, soon after he came, of organizing the first bank in the Valley — the Opportunity State Bank.

As the Valley grew, Sidney saw the need for a shopping center. This project he entered into with his son Tom and it became the Opportunity Shopping Center at Sprague and Pines. Tom was the developer, but Sidney worked on the project and leased the property for the business venture.

His home on Perrine Road overlooked the Center. He was proud of it: to him, it symbolized the growth he foresaw for the Valley. The property had been an apple orchard when he arrived; after development, it was commercial.

Sidney also developed an idea of his daughter, Jean's —the Spokane Valley Savings and Loan at E. 12005 Sprague. He not only developed it, he was its first president. Later it became Pacific First Federal Savings and Loan, and in 1993, Washington Mutual Bank.

The Smith family were true pioneers. Sidney's grandparents came to the Willamette Valley in 1853 by covered wagon from Pennsylvania. His father was a policeman, judge and the first postmaster of Palouse (then Washington Territory) where Sidney was born in 1897.

Because of his father's health, the family moved to Grants Pass, Oregon, and lived there for ten years before moving to Spokane in 1901.

In an article by David Petticord in the 1983 Progress Edition of *Spokane Valley Today,* Sidney recalled "riding my bicycle from town to Liberty Lake out what is now Sprague Avenue when it was all stone, rocks, and mud .

"My father was in the undertaking business at that time in Spokane," Sidney said, "and in his business he used to make a circuit into the Valley driving on the south side, then across Spokane Bridge returning on the north side. On the north side before you got to the bridge there was a big field where the bleached bones of hundreds of dead horses were scattered. This was the old horse slaughter camp where Colonel Wright had the Indian horses killed."

Sidney could see Mica Peak and Signal Peak from his front window. He and his young son, Tom, often hiked into those hills.

In the article mentioned above he told about those expeditions:

"We went Upriver to Spokane Bridge then turned south, then up canyon to Signal Peak. We drove part way, then walked up the mountain. The Indians used to use this peak as a signal and lookout point. It was later used for a revolving aircraft beacon."

Sidney lived to be 101 years of age and 72 years of that long life were spent in the Valley, working for the Valley, with Valley growth and progress always foremost in his thoughts. As he grew older, more and more of his enterprises were entered into at the advice of his son, Tom, and his daughter, Jean.

In 1916 Sidney married Isabelle Taylor, who was from Bristol, England, by way of Toronto, Canada. She survived her husband.

Harry E. Nelson— "Mr. Spokane Valley"

[From Harry E. Nelson's obituary, *Spokane Valley Herald,* January 7, 1959.]

Funeral services for Harry E. Nelson, 82 years old, managing secretary of the Spokane Valley Chamber of Commerce, and one of the founders of the *Spokane Valley Herald,* who died Friday, January 9, were held at 1:30 o'clock Monday afternoon at the Opportunity Presbyterian Church.

Many referred to Mr. Nelson as "Mr. Spokane Valley." Generally he was recognized as one of the dedicated residents of the area.

Mr. Nelson worked until late on the afternoon of Friday, January 2, at the Chamber of Commerce office, and according to his office secretary, Mrs. Muriel Little, was in fine spirit. Late that evening while chatting with his daughter, Miss Helen Nelson, at their home, E. 10201 Fourth Ave., Mr. Nelson suffered a cerebral hemorrhage. He passed away at Sacred Heart Hospital.

The Rev. Odin Baugh, in the funeral sermon, found scriptural parallel in the Old Testament when on the death of Moses, his followers were exhorted to carry the challenge of their leader.

Mr. Nelson, who came to the Spokane area in 1905 and to the Valley in 1907, was Iowa born. As a young man he learned carpentry and the printing trade, then followed the silver boom to Colorado, where he published newspapers at Cripple Creek and Snyder at the turn of the century.

He returned to Iowa, married, published more small papers, then headed for the Pacific Northwest to seek his fortune in the apple industry. The family's first orchard was a 20-acre plot in back of Chester and above the Schafer Mineral Springs. The trees, planted about 1889 by Adam Schafer, still produce, although not managed. Photographs of the fine apples taken from the orchard graced Mr. Nelson's office at the Chamber, and he delighted in telling how boxes of fruit prepared for exhibition took prizes. While some of the large growers spent sums for display at the apple shows, Mr. Nelson and his wife, Josie, fashioned a display with pine boughs and other greenery to take the sweepstakes.

Spokane Valley Herald

Vol. I   Opportunity, Washington   March 24, 1920   No. 1

UNION MAKES RETURNS TO THE GROWERS

This week the Spokane Valley Growers' Union made final returns to the growers on the apple crop of the past season, and the results show another very successful season.

The union handled last season 193,-374 boxes of apples and 880 boxes of pears at an expense of 40 cents per box. With the trucks, the union hauled 222,846 field boxes of apples to the packing house at a cost of 2 cents per box.

There were 26,510 boxes of culls that were sold to the drying plant as peelers, and 329,258 pounds of culls that were sent to the cider factory.

The gross price to the union of all varieties and grades, including the small jumble, was $1.93 per box.

Following are the prices received for the leading varieties handled by the union:

	Extra Fancy 163 and larger	175 and smaller	Fancy 163 and larger	175 and smaller	C. Grade 163 and larger	175 and smaller	Com. Ex. & Fcy. 163 and larger	175 and smaller	Or. Run 163 and larger	175 and smaller	Jumble
Ark. Black..	$2.52	$2.22	$2.22	$1.97	$1.87	$1.67	......	......	......	......	$1.3?
Baldwin ..	2.15	1.90	1.88	1.60	1.70	1.45	$2.00	$1.70	$1.85	$1.55	1.20
Black Ben	2.05	1.82	1.82	1.57	1.57	1.32					1.22
Black Twig	2.17	......	1.92	......	1.72						1.32
Champion	2.04	1.79	1.78	1.50	1.60	1.35					1.10
Delicious	3.39	2.99	2.89	2.64	2.69	2.44					......
Grimes Golden	2.45	2.20	2.20	1.95	1.85	1.60					1.34
Jonathan	2.20	1.93	1.94	1.68	1.69	1.43					1.34
King David	2.17	1.77	1.92	1.57	1.67	1.42					1.45
Spitzenburg	2.32	2.02	2.07	1.82	1.87	1.62					1.37
Stayman Winesap	2.25	2.05	2.00	1.80	1.75	1.55					1.30
Rome Beauty	2.10	1.80	1.85	1.60-	1.65	1.40			1.80	1.55	1.20
Wagener....	1.97	1.77	......	......	1.55	1.27	1.87	1.62	1.72	1.52	1.22
Winesap....	2.55	2.25	2.30	2.00	2.05	1.75					1.58
Winter Banana....	3.02	2.67	2.52	2.27	2.22	1.92					......
Yel. Newtown	2.25	2.00	2.00	1.75	1.75	1.50					1.25

1920 RATES FOR IRRIGATION CUT

Statements are being issued for the 1920 water rent by the Modern Electric Water Co. The rates for this season will be $9 an acre for the irrigation water, $15 per year for light, $15 for water, and a $3 assessment for the domestic pipe fund. These payments are due April 1st and a penalty of 12 per cent per annum will be added to all delinquent water and light rent after May 1st.

The statements from the Vera Electric Water Co. will also be cut this month and will be $10 per acre for the irrigation and domestic water and $9 per year for the lights. These rents are also due April 1st and carry a penalty if not paid.

TOWNSHIP ELECTION

The annual meeting of the electors of Opportunity township was held on the first Tuesday of March at the town hall, there being only a dozen people interested enough in the affairs of the township to attend and listen to the reports of the officers. The township supervisor recommended a levy of $4,500 for maintenance of roads for the coming year. The following officers were elected:

Supervisor, E. B. Crawford; clerk, Lelia Wright; treasurer, M. M. Kelly; assessor, Seth Woodard; justice of peace, E. W. Bennett; constable, P. P. Lilly.

The sports at the Spokane University are at their changing lines. The basket ball season was brought to a successful close. The baseball and track teams are now in training and it is expected that they will prove themselves worthy.

Our high-collared, broad-brimmed artist, Clyde Walton, may be brave and all that, but he positively refuses to go out into the chicken coop after dark. And the reason for his extreme timidity is that he knows that the "hens are laying" for him.

The old postoffice location is now renovated and opened up as the Orchard Fountain and Lunch Room, where a stranger and traveler can go and get a nice meal. As an attraction for those romantically inclined, you will find private booths where shy little maidens and beaux can go and whisper love's sweet melodies while the refreshments are gliding down their epiglottis.

UNION HIGH SCHOOL

Would Spokane Valley benefit by a Union High School? Do we have enough children of high school age to warrant our interest in a local high school? Such questions as these have been asked over and over again in the past few months by valley people.

Over one hundred children have left the eighth grade in the Opportunity school alone in the past four years, and thirty will finish this year. If these children are to receive a high school education they must look elsewhere for it. They must either go to Spokane or to one of the neighboring high schools. The city high schools are excellent schools; well equipped, and with competent instructors. But do they fill the valley needs? If the children are sent to the city schools the parents are faced with the problem of increased cost of transportation, and of having their children in town all day.

If they send them to a neighboring high school they are again confronted with the problem of transportation, and these schools, good as far as they go, are of necessity small, poorly equipped and offering a rather narrow course of study.

Would it not be much better if we all joined in one large unit and built one large modern central high school, which could be well equipped in every way? One that would fill the needs of the community at large, and one which could offer such courses as horticulture, agriculture, mechanics and home economics in a practical and vital manner under ideal conditions. A school which first and last would be a Valley High School for Valley children.

Bob Felts, ex-sailor and true son of Neptune, is planning to go to the land of Chinks and noodles, where rumor says that he has a Chinese maiden waiting for him with a patience that would have put Job in second class. It will be a case of a new setting for Kipling's famous poem, "On the Road to Mandalay." Our friend Bob paid a visit to China during the war, and it seems that he got very popular with the slant-eyed girl in Hong Kong, and that is why he is longing to go back.

Apples

In 1912 the Nelsons moved from the hills above Chester into the Valley to farm. In 1914 Mr. Nelson became associated with the Spokane Valley Growers Union, a cooperative apple house. He held the position of secretary-treasurer in his organization, saw the apple business flourish, then suffer devastating blows through killing freezes.

It was while secretary of the Growers Union that Mr. Nelson and Karl Frolander noted the need for a Spokane Valley newspaper.

Spokane Valley Herald

The first copy of the *Herald* appeared March 24, 1920. On May 7, 1920, Mr. Nelson outlined the philosophy of the *Herald*, as well as expressing his faith in the Valley community.

"Spokane Valley—an empire within an empire," he wrote. "Those with keen insight into the future know that the day is near at hand in which Spokane Valley will be so productive of wealth, and so filled with homes that it will be one of the richest districts in the entire Northwest.

"I've never had a lot of money," commented Mr. Nelson, "I sold the *Herald* because more capital was required for development than I had available."

For a short time in the early '30's Mr. Nelson resided in the Wenatchee area, operating the Apple Shop in the Cascadian Hotel. His venture in the gift box business was believed to have been one of the earliest featuring choice boxes of fruit from the Northwest.

Employed by the State

Sixteen years of services with the Washington State Horticultural Department as an inspector was the next phase of Nelson's career. Then came retirement. For two or three years, Mr. Nelson looked after his garden and devoted energies to the Spokane Valley Kiwanis Club, the Opportunity Presbyterian Church, and the Valley Chamber of Commerce.

About 10 years ago the Chamber persuaded Mr. Nelson, an ex-president of the organization, to take the job of managing secretary.

Home for Chamber

The conservative practices of Mr. Nelson's personal life soon were reflected in the Chamber management. The organization, although operating on a budget of only $10,000, soon began to accumulate a bank account, as well as property. Brochures describing the advantages of the Valley soon began to flow from the Chamber. In 1954 when the Chamber budget faced a deficit, Nelson declined salary.

In 1956, principally through the efforts of Mr. Nelson, the Chamber was able to purchase from the J.W. Balfour estate, three-quarters of an acre at E. 10303 Sprague and the Balfour residence. This has become the home of the Valley Chamber, and it is virtually debt free.

For years Mr. Nelson served as secretary of the Spokane Valley Kiwanis Club. His weekly club bulletin was as punctual as were his visits to the bowling alleys where he participated in league competition. On the occasion of his 82nd birthday last October 29, members of the Chamber of Commerce presented Mr. Nelson with a cake. During the conversation it was revealed that at four score and two years, he had rolled 170 in league play and carried an average which just about matched his weight, 150.

Mr. Nelson was an officer in The Pines Cemetery Association and did much to develop the principle burial grounds in the Spokane Valley.

His burial was in The Pines.

Chamber of Commerce Organized, Raymond P. Kelley

Raymond P. Kelley came to Greenacres in 1912 and purchased land which it is said he developed into an orchard show place. Instrumental in forming the Spokane Valley Chamber of Commerce, he was always vitally interested in the development of both the Valley and the city of Spokane. He became a two-time president of the Chamber.

The story of the organization of the Spokane Valley Chamber of Commerce was interestingly told by Kelley in the March 23, 1945, issue of the *Spokane Valley Herald:*

"In the early summer of 1920 a small group of enthusiastic Spokane Valley "boosters" proposed to stage an "Apple Blossom Festival" for the citizens of the Valley and the people of Spokane. At that time apples were the principal crop of the cultivated sections of the Valley. The blocks of orchards, large and small, that lined the main highways and back roads made a colorful and fragrant spectacle that attracted visitors far and near.

"An old fashioned barbecue was counted upon to draw the crowd and this was staged at Otis Orchards, 18 miles from the city limits, because this was the largest concentrated orchard district. To be sure that the visitors saw more of the Valley than could be seen from the Appleway and Trent Road, the official route, duly marked with direction arrows, crisscrossed the Valley back and forth until it finally landed the visitor at the barbecue pit at Otis Orchards, where Major Gwyder, barbecuist extraordinary, was performing his magic.

"Thousands arrived and partook of the repast. In those days the automobile was in its infancy and paved roads were scarce, so the crisscross trip of as much as 30 miles on dirt roads left its mark on all comers, whose identity was all but obliterated by dust. However a grand time was had by all and the demand that the Apple Blossom Festival be made an annual event was unanimous.

"The proposal made it clear at once that to stage an annual event an organization was necessary."

The organization decided upon was a Valley Chamber of Commerce.

Oscar Reinemer Continues the Story

Oscar D. Reinemer, helped organize the Valley Chamber in 1921 and was Chamber president in 1929. A Valley pioneer, in 1911 he hauled lumber on a horse drawn sled for a little brown Methodist house of worship being built on the corner of Sprague and Bowdish.

In 1918 he went into the general merchandise business in Dishman. On March 3, 1969, he reminisced as follows about the formation of the Valley Chamber of Commerce in a supplement to the *Spokane Valley Herald:*

"Originally the Valley had nine community clubs, namely Dishman, Opportunity, Vera, Greenacres, Otis Orchards, Millwood, Pasadena, Orchard Avenue (Trentwood-Irvin), and Orchard Avenue (University Place). These clubs generally took care of problems that arose in their own area.

"It was felt a better over-all job could be done by forming a Chamber of Commerce. The Spokane Valley Chamber of Commerce was formed in 1921 with nine members from each club as representatives to the Chamber.

"The meetings were held mainly at the *Valley Herald* office and the Opportunity State Bank. Each club paid $10 a year to help defray costs.

"The Valley was all orchards and truck gardens then. We participated in the Interstate Fair and held an annual Hearts of Gold cantaloupe feed.

"To build friendly relations with the people in all the communities, we had community dinners each month with a contest to see which community had the greatest representation. Our crowds ran from 250 to 400 people, depending on the size of the hall where the dinner was held. These dinners started with the September meeting and ended in June. July was taken up with a dance at Liberty Lake to raise funds for the annual All Valley picnic held in August when all the businesses shut up shop for the afternoon of the picnic. Our crowds sometimes numbered 10,000 people. The normal charge for dinners was 60¢. 50¢ went for the dinner and 10¢ went into the Chamber fund. Sounds funny when you can hardly get a good cup of coffee and a hamburger for that now.

"The road and street signs and numbers were started through the Chamber with the help of the Township and the Spokane Valley Women's Club.

"During the Depression time the Chamber helped some of the teachers out by using available funds to cash warrants."

A Final Tribute

THE HAND THAT ROCKED THE CRADLE
WAS THE HAND THAT WON THE WEST
by Seth Woodard

Long years ago the Pioneers
Came west to seek new lands
And often had to fight against
Unbearable demands;
Their wives and daughters, brave and true,
Withstood the rigid test;
The hand that rocked the cradle
Was the hand that won the West.

No braver women ever lived
Their nerves were strong as steel
In times of stress they bravely put
Their shoulders to the wheel,
Without these women, men alone,
Could not have stood the test;
The hand that rocked the cradle
Was the hand that won the West.

All honor to those noble wives
Who bore so large a share
In winning of this western land
That which there's none more fair;
Too much in praise cannot be said
They passed the highest test
The hand that rocked the cradle
Was the hand that won the West.

Seth Woodard was a Valley pioneer of 1882 for whom an elementary school in Millwood District was named. His family owned land on which Millwood now stands. His daughter, Marguerite Bartleson, told me her father frequently recited this poem to his children. It is said that the poem was given to Grandma Moses on her hundredth birthday and she loved it.

In Retrospect

["Homestead in the Valley," Albert F. Chittenden, *Spokane Valley Herald*, August 11, 1955 (Excerpt)]

Today it is hard to properly evaluate pioneer living, to visualize a people without the ease of social contacts and the wider field of knowledge afforded by the radio, television, the movie, the auto and good roads.

Today we are apt to imagine that the pioneer had no values to compensate for the lack of these advantages.

He, however, had the home which now is becoming only a memory—a home where children lived and worked under the close guidance of parents until they matured. Then, too, the pioneer had few distractions. He had time to think and digest as well as to see and hear. He read more carefully and more deeply rather than more abundantly. His knowledge was one of depth rather than one of breadth.

Social and intellectual experiences were not imposed upon him. He had to search them out and develop them himself. His field was very big, his results often poor, but the value he received was immeasurable. He never ceased being an individual.

Moving Forward: A Decade Later

[From "The Valley That Has Everything" by Nina May Westmore, *The Bulletin*, Washington State Federation of Women's Clubs, Vol. XVIII, No. 4, January, 1934]

". . .the population of the Valley grew in the decade from 1920 to 1930 at the rate of 52%.

"Running due east and west, the Valley gives the commuter into Spokane the advantage of a short auto drive over his choice of two paved highways, with the sun at his back both ways. This and the slope of the valley give a desirable northern exposure for many of the tracts and this makes a difference in agricultural pursuits of the Valley. With the abundance of clear days with which Eastern Washington and Northern Idaho are noted, the Spokane Valley is literally, as well as figuratively, the 'Valley of the Sun.'

"Thus far we have been speaking of the Spokane Valley as one community. This is accurate enough—even though it is made up of not one but many towns, beginning with Dishman and Orchard Avenue at the west and extending through Opportunity, Vera, Greenacres, Liberty Lake, Parkwater, Millwood, Pasadena, Trentwood and Otis Orchards.

"The Spokane Valley has made a name for itself and for its agricultural products—particularly apples and small fruits (including the famous Hearts of Gold cantaloupes)—garden truck, forage crops, poultry and dairy. There are three sources of irrigation—the seven lakes that encircle the Valley, the Spokane River which threads its silvery way through the length of the Valley, and wells tapping the subterranean lake clear water which underlies most of the Valley and the City of Spokane. 25,000 of the Valley's 40,000 irrigatable acres are under irrigation. It is notable that this extensive development of irrigation has come about without the investment of a single dollar by the United States government.

"Far-sighted Valleyites have agreed for a number of years that the future of that part of the valley within commuting distance of Spokane lies in the direction of suburban homes. The city of Spokane is so located that as it pushes out beyond its present boundaries its expansion is inevitably to the east in other words out into the valley. Thus we see the railroad yards and shops, the packing plants, cement making, lumbering and paper making jumping the city's eastern boundary and extending farther and farther into the Valley proper.

"Many of Spokane's leading businessmen make their homes in the Valley. This gives the Valley a character of home life that can not be excelled. Its cultural advantages are indicated by fifteen grade schools and fourteen churches, Spokane Valley Junior College and West Valley, Central Valley, and Otis Orchards high schools.

"There are several unique institutions in the Spokane Valley including the Hutton Settlement, a home for orphaned children, and the Bethany Home for old people, both located at Pasadena. The former, founded by L.W. Hutton, cares for eighty children between 6 and 18, in brick cottages. The home has 320 acres of ground which is cultivated to supply the institution with much food. Bethany Home, with a capacity of twenty-five, is caring for sixteen people whose ages range from 70 to 97.

"Another Valley institution is the *Spokane Valley Herald*, edited and published by E.Z. Smith, president of the Washington Press Association. Speaking as the voice of the Valley and bringing each week the intimate neighborhood news in addition to the accounts of world events, this publication supplements the three Spokane daily papers which circulate throughout the Valley. Indeed, close-in Valley dwellers enjoy all city conveniences including domestic water under pressure, electric service, movies, telephone service as a part of the Spokane exchanges, stores and city service to laundries, ice companies and department stores.

"Being a natural gateway to the Spokane country from the east, the Valley enjoys the best transportation. Its concrete roads which run the length of the Valley are links in the national highways. In addition there are four transcontinental railroads, bus lines and transcontinental airways which land passengers at the magnificent airport at the west end of the Valley.

"Within the memory of people still living and active the Spokane Valley has developed into a community of homes in the midst of wheat fields, orchards and diversified farms, presenting an idyllic combination of city and country life that attracts the better type of substantial American citizen."

Bibliography

Anderton, Peg Gott: *800 Indian Horses and a Ghost Town Buried at Washington-Idaho Border*, published by Anderton Genealogy Services, Post Falls, ID., 1985

Barr, William, "Man Against the Corporation," *Pacific Northwesterner*, Vol. 31, No. 4, 1987

Becher, Edmund T: *History, Government and Resources of the Spokane Area*, printed in Spokane Community College Print Department

Becher, Edmund T: *Spokane Corona, Eras and Empires*, C.W. Hill, printers, Spokane, WA., 1974

Berglund, Mary Hanly: *Otis Orchards: the First Fifty Years*, Ye Galleon Press, Fairfield, WA., 1987

Brereton, Mildred, and Evelyn Foedish: *Memories of Liberty Lake*, printed and photographs reproduced by Leo Oestreicher of Leo's Studio, Spokane Valley, WA., 1951

Durham, Nelson W.: *History of the City of Spokane and Spokane County*, 3 volumes, S.J. Clarke Publishing Co., Chicago, 1912

Edwards, Rev. Jonathan: *History of Spokane County, Washington*, W.H. Lever, San Francisco, 1900

Fuller, George W., *The Inland Empire of the Pacific Northwest, A History*, W.G. Linderman, Denver, Spokane, 1928

Goldsmith, Roberta: *Memoirs of Yesterday and Today, Freeman, WA, 1885-1985*, privately printed, March 1, 1986

Lewis, William S: *Reminiscences of Pioneers of the Inland Empire* (a series of articles in the Sunday *Spokesman-Review*), 1925

Mica Peak Woman's Club: *Down Memory Lane with Mica Peak People*, privately duplicated, 1979

Ness, Arthur B: *History of Orchard Park Schools and West Valley High School*, Millwood, WA., about 1950 (on file at the school, duplicated)

Ogle, George A., and Company: *Standard Atlas of Spokane County, Washington*, 1912

Peltier, Jerome: "Pioneer Seth Woodard, a Deep Influence on the Valley," *Spokane Valley Herald*, p. 12, June 24, 1993

Peltier, Jerome: "Antoine Plante," *Mountain Men and the Fur Trade of the Far West*, Vol. 5, A.H. Clark, Glendale, CA., 1968

Pratt, Orville C: *The Spokane Valley*, privately duplicated, 1951

Price, Channon P., "Channon Price Reminisces" (manuscript)

Rosebush, Waldo Emerson: "The Valley of the Sun," a series of articles published in the *Spokesman-Review*, 1930-1934

Roth, Madeline Blessing: "Before and When I Was" (Family Memoirs)

Sager, Mildred. *Treasured Recipes from Old Spokane*, privately printed, 1948

Shideler, John C: *A Century of Caring*, Sacred Heart Medical Center, Spokane, Washington, 1985

Smith, Tom M: *History of the Spokane Valley Chamber of Commerce*, privately printed, October, 1971

Spokane Corral of Westerners: *The Pacific Northwesterner*, Vol. 23, No. 2, Spring, 1979

Spokane County Medical Society: *Medical Bulletin*, Vol. 62, Number 3, 1989

Stegner, J. Howard: "Echoes of Yesterday," a series of articles published in the *Spokane Valley Herald*, 1940-1960

Stratton, David: *Spokane and the Inland Empire*. Washington State University Press, 1991

Yates, Keith L: *A History of Spokane Valley*, privately duplicated, January, 1951

ERRATA

The author and publisher apologize for the following errors which inadvertently appeared in this volume:

Dr. Jonathan Edward's first name is misspelled "Jonathon" in several instances.

Page 34, 52, 53. The names of Joe Ulowetz and John Kories are misspelled.